S 41

ADVANCE PRAISE

"The book gives us the guide we have been waiting for, from how the current anti-Americanism came to be, to the policies needed to reverse it, all of it brilliantly told and superbly documented."

—Simon Bourgin, TIME Bureau Chief in Vienna, Austria

"A clever, well-documented, articulate and—above all—generous book."

—Yves Quéré, former Foreign Secretary, Academy of Science, Paris

"A must-read for all Americans who are concerned about the future, uneasy with the past, and looking for a path forward. The Schweitzers present a compelling and immediate case for change."

—Raphael Perl, Senior Foreign Policy Analyst,
Congressional Research Service, Library of Congress

"America today is a military giant, but a 'soft power' pygmy. This book points to how American hubris, as well as its firepower, has helped make Uncle Sam Public Enemy Number One in many countries around the world."

—Roger Eatwell, Professor of European Politics
Head of Department of European Studies and Modern Languages
University of Bath, United Kingdom

"The authors offer a broad look at the causes of anti-Americanism and the problems US policymakers must therefore contend with, particularly in the Muslim world. . . . The book poses thoughtful, 'outside the box' proposals for tackling these critical challenges."

—Steven Pifer, former US Ambassador to Ukraine

AMERICA ON★NOTICE

STEMMING THE TIDE OF ANTI-AMERICANISM

Glenn E. Schweitzer with Carole D. Schweitzer

Prometheus Books

59 John Glenn Drive
Amherst, New York 14228-2197

69256

Published 2006 by Prometheus Books

Inquiries should be addressed to
Prometheus Books
59 John Glenn Drive
Amherst, New York 14228–2197
VOICE: 716–691–0133, ext. 207
FAX: 716–564–2711
WWW.PROMETHEUSBOOKS.COM

10 09 08 07 06   5 4 3 2 1

Library of Congress Cataloging-in-Publication Data
Schweitzer, Glenn E., 1930–
    America on notice : stemming the tide of anti-Americanism / by Glenn E. Schweitzer ; with Carole D. Schweitzer.
    p. cm.
    Includes bibliographical references and index.
    ISBN 13: 978–1–59102–428–6
    ISBN 10: 1–59102–428–5 (hardcover : alk. paper)
    1. United States—Foreign relations—2001– 2. Anti-Americanism. 3. United States—Foreign public opinion. 4. United States—Foreign relations—Philosophy. 5. Engagement (Philosophy) 6. Mediation, International. I. Schweitzer, Carole Dorsch. II. Title.

E902.S435 2006
327.73009'0511—dc22   2006012116

Printed in the United States on acid-free paper

Contents

5

ACKNOWLEDGMENTS

The fingerprints of hundreds of colleagues can be found throughout the pages of this book. I am a practitioner in promoting international cooperation. I am not a government official, a foreign policy analyst, or a social scientist. These specialists spend many years delving into the factors that drive the behavior of individuals, groups, and governments in distant lands. Thus, I have relied heavily on the insights of longtime experts in these fields—and many more—in understanding how worldwide admiration enjoyed by America and Americans a few short years ago has deteriorated into growing animosity and outbursts of violence aimed at the United States. And I have listened to their prescriptions for reversing the tide of anger washing onto the coasts of America as I formulated my own suggestions to do precisely that.

Among my many mentors, I pay special tribute to the following:

- Colleagues at the National Research Council who are managing international exchange programs, seminars held throughout the world, and policy studies of many dimensions of globalization. For twenty years, I have had the privilege of working with talented staff members of all disciplines and with advisory committees involving leading scholars and managers from both the public and the private sectors in our efforts to unravel some of the knottiest international challenges facing the United States.

- Officials of the Department of State based in Washington, DC, and in our embassies abroad who have never hesitated to share their perspectives with me. They design the types of policies discussed in this book, and they are on the front lines of the US government's efforts to convince the world of the benefits that will flow from these policies.
- Foreign assistance specialists of the US Agency for International Development, who represent our nation's strongest assets in winning hearts and minds, often under the most difficult conditions. From Bangladesh to Armenia to South Africa, they grapple with daily problems to transform poverty and despair into bright futures for tens of millions of people.
- Officials of foreign governments who are concerned over the growing rift between the perceptions of their governments and the views of Washington. These officials—in Finland, in Russia, in Tajikistan, in Pakistan, in Indonesia, and elsewhere—look for the best ways to deal with emerging international crises.
- Leaders of academies of sciences and of medical sciences who believe that their members can make strong contributions to building and repairing bridges of understanding with America. These academicians play significant roles in the evolution of attitudes in the Muslim countries of Iran, Uzbekistan, and Azerbaijan, for example.
- Scholars who are based at Washington institutions—such as the Brookings Institution, the Carnegie Endowment for International Peace, and the Heritage Foundation. They are consistently conducting important research on issues that are causing turmoil throughout the world.
- Officials of international organizations—and particularly the International Science and Technology Center in Moscow, the World Bank, the World Health Organization, and the Food and Agriculture Organization. They have been surprisingly open about difficult issues confronting their member states.

I often cite in the book the views of experts from these organizations, but the observations and recommendations that are presented are my own. While the National Research Council, where I am employed, encouraged me to write the book during my free time, the organization did not review the manuscript nor did it place any limitations on the coverage or the recommendations of the book.

Included in the discussions are many personal experiences I hope will be accepted in the spirit in which I offer them. I am but one of millions of Americans who are vitally concerned about restoring America's reputation throughout the world. I have been fortunate to have had some unique experiences, and this book provides an opportunity to share with a broader audience a number of personal observations that have special relevance to the theme of the book.

I am most appreciative of the support provided by the staff of Prometheus Books in the preparation of the manuscript. In particular, Linda Regan's encouragement to write the book and her numerous contributions in improving the logic and readability of the presentation were invaluable.

Also, Diane Schweitzer provided important ground truth for the manuscript. Widely traveled and well informed on international developments, she helped ensure that the observations reflected real trends abroad and that the recommendations made sense in cultures with different values and various capabilities to move forward.

Finally, and most important, I express my deep appreciation to my wife, Carole, who was my collaborator in writing every sentence of the book. She is an astute observer of today's international scene and a source of logic when it comes to structuring the discussion of complex issues. A skilled writer and editor, she was tireless in her efforts to ensure that the text was fresh, understandable, and useful for our neighbors as well as for specialists in the field.

INTRODUCTION

S ince the turn of the twenty-first century, anti-Americanism has trig-
gered hate-filled headlines throughout the Muslim world. In
Baghdad, "Iraqis Revel in US Deaths." In Amman, "Arabs Praise
Iraqi Insurgents, Condemn US Occupation." In Dhaka, "This Is a War on
Muslims." In Cairo, "US Stood for Liberty; Now Stands for Imperi-
alism." And in Tehran, "We Must Cut Off the Head of the Snake—the
Great Satan of America."

Further documenting this growth of rage are authoritative polls that
have reported record levels of hostility toward the United States in almost
every one of the fifty-five countries with predominantly Muslim populations. For example, in 2004 support for America in fourteen countries of
North Africa, the Middle East, and South Asia dropped to a level repre-
senting not even 5 percent of the total population. Just three years earlier,
40 to 70 percent had looked favorably on the United States. At the same
time, 84 percent of the population of Egypt and 82 percent of Jordan considered the spread of American ideas and customs to be a dangerous
development. Even with regard to the American concept of democracy,
69 percent of the population in Jordan and 60 percent in Pakistan thought
that the United States was advocating a threatening idea.[1]

By mid-2005, favorable images of the United States had slightly
rebounded; for example, in Turkey, 23 percent of the population held a
more positive image; Lebanon, 42 percent; Jordan, 21 percent; Indonesia,

38 percent; and Pakistan, 23 percent. Still, populations of these countries, by strong majorities, considered *Americans* dishonest, immoral, greedy, and violent. Throughout the Muslim world, a broad consensus indicated that the United States had no right to use force in Iraq in 2003 and that the world had become more dangerous as the result of the ouster of Saddam Hussein. According to the polled populations, a combination of the media, the Jews, and the military establishment was driving US policy, and those surveyed held little hope for a turnaround. While a few welcomed the elections in Iraq and the US commitment to the spread of democracy, these opinions did not change the overall ratings significantly.

The single most important action taken by the United States that helped quell Muslim apprehension was the US response to the tsunami disaster in South Asia at the end of 2004, an act that significantly increased favorable ratings, particularly in hard-hit Indonesia.[2]

But America had a long way to go, and attitudes toward the United States remained quite negative. Slowly, hostility toward America eased in some countries, and progress in improving America's image could finally be measured in small increments.[3]

However, as this manuscript went to press, many inflamed Muslims began rioting on the streets in a number of countries, protesting the publication in Denmark of cartoons they felt ridiculed the prophet Muhammad. This outburst of violence initially targeted European embassies and other assets in the Middle East, but the spillover into the cauldron of hatred toward America was quick to follow. Any pro-American trends were suddenly reversed as Washington defended the freedom of the press and condemned violence but did not comment on the inflammatory nature of the cartoons.

At the same time, the extremist Palestinian group Hamas had just won an unexpected victory during the elections for delegates to the Palestinian parliament. Some specialists called the election a referendum on the disastrous internal policies of corruption and mismanagement by the Palestinian Authority. Others viewed the election results as a Palestinian vote of no-confidence in the "spineless" negotiating position of the Palestinian Authority in the peace process. Clearly, the political ascendancy of Hamas immediately increased turmoil throughout the Middle East. To the Arabs, Hamas had a strong record as a political resistance movement fighting for the territory of their brethren. In Israel and the West, Hamas had become synonymous with wanton killings of innocent Israelis by a group that refused to recognize the legitimacy of Israel as a state. As discussed in chapter 9, the widespread impacts of this transformative event will play out over the months and years ahead.

Anger toward America is not new, nor is it confined to Muslim populations. Much of the hostility has been building for many years, but the war initiated by the United States in Iraq dramatically increased strong criticisms due to American "recklessness," even in the capitals of traditional supporters of the United States. For example, in Seoul, violence erupted when students demanded withdrawal of American forces from Korea. And in Singapore, headlines blared, "American Exceptionalism Has Proven to Be Fraudulent."

During this period, mobilization of a "coalition of the willing," directed and largely financed by the United States to intervene in Iraq— irrespective of the views of the United Nations and many important governments—sealed the demise of multilateralism as a way to resolve serious global conflicts. The polls have repeatedly documented that Muslims believe the United States ignores their interests. The perception that the United States conducts a unilateral foreign policy is widely shared across the surveyed countries. Overwhelming percentages of people in Europe and the Middle East believe that the United States does not take their countries' interests into account when making foreign policy.[4] The recoil of countries and populations around the world to this lack of respect for views of others has been swift and sharp. Political rebellion dots the entire Muslim landscape.

The widespread perception of political and military arrogance of the United States is but one of many factors that has increased the hostility of Muslim populations toward America. At the top of the list of grievances is united condemnation of American favoritism toward Israel in its fifty-year dispute with the Palestinians.

Additional complaints of Muslims are manifold. For many years, resentment over the stationing of American troops on the holy soil of Saudi Arabia has been a recurrent rallying point of the followers of Osama bin Laden and many other groups. Arab governments and populations have recoiled in horror to the revelations of sadistic American abuse of Iraqi prisoners in prisons in Baghdad and Kabul. The purported (and later disputed) flushing of portions of the Koran down a toilet at Guantanamo Bay triggered violent protests in Afghanistan and elsewhere. And Muslim officials and scholars alike continue to sharply criticize the seeming deception by the US government in portraying the presence of weapons of mass destruction in Iraq.

In short, a variety of past and recent policies of the United States have contributed greatly to the global hostility toward America. These policies can ignite explosive reactions, particularly when coupled with perceived injustices reflected in the daily excesses of Americans—excesses that are in contrast to the poverty suffered by hundreds of millions of people in many other countries. Further adding to the potency of the reactions is the disgust at an American culture that unabashedly displays tattoos, breast implants, and naked navels, which are repugnant to Muslims accustomed to modesty.

In Washington, many policy officials have assumed that in time other governments and their people would simply "get over" their dissatisfaction with the policy choices of the world's superpower. But they have been wrong. Not only are people turning away from the United States, they are embracing leaderships of other countries, including those of some European governments, as well as of China and Russia.[5]

As the United States becomes a target of an expanding numbers of terrorist recruits, Americans are well aware of the significant impact on their daily lives. Travel has changed from an adventure to be savored to a nail-biting experience. American taxpayers are financing huge investments in never-ending peacekeeping and reconstruction activities in addition to covering the costs of increasingly frequent wars. Ubiquitous security barriers degrade the value of and complicate access to many theaters, museums, and other historical icons of our country. New neighbors are subject to scrutiny while color-coded security alerts do more to confuse than to inform. The overarching "war on terrorism" is at the center of an omnipresent, and very uncomfortable, national paranoia.

It is clear that we must buttress our homeland security to fend off immediate attacks. We must also give comparable priority to the task of transforming the growing hatred of America into global respect. This is no easy assignment.

It means rebuilding broken relationships, constructing intellectual and cultural bridges where few have existed, and helping other countries offer frustrated populations opportunities for better lives. Most important, we must more often share global decision making that affects hundreds of millions of lives in other countries. Only by doing so will Americans begin to feel safe again. Only then will the US government be able to put a cap on the invasive and costly security precautions now being undertaken in every city and neighborhood. Only then will America gain—or regain—truly committed international partners to help solve global problems.[6]

THE PARADOX OF AMERICA

Deep animosities toward America date back almost four hundred years, when the early immigrants in the new land of plenty had the audacity to reject subservience to England and the determination to battle the Native Americans. For several centuries, the settlers concentrated on building a new country, fighting occasional wars with other claimants to the newly occupied territory, and quelling internal violence over the rights of citizens of different lineages. Both foreign governments and pirates viewed with envy the wealth of America, but they were kept at bay by two broad oceans.

Then, during the twentieth century, the United States dramatically expanded its international presence. "Yankee, go home" became a catchphrase in Latin America as Americans became viewed as imperialists. "Overpaid, oversexed, and over here" was the all-too-common reaction to American troops stationed in Europe after World War II. "The Ugly American" characterized, more often than we wanted to acknowledge, some out-of-control travelers to Asia and other regions.

Still, until recently, the enormous contributions of the United States to world peace and justice easily squelched such minor and regional outcries. We had some successes in implanting American values, American-style democracy, and American culture abroad. While suspicions over American motivations were often high, the American way of life had an infectious appeal to both the rich and the poor. Foreign students flooded America's universities, and those students who returned home were usually loyal alumni of the American experience. Many frustrated intellectuals shouted at America one day and sought green cards the next.

All the while, the United States prided itself on taking the moral high ground. It championed the rights of the downtrodden and welcomed disenfranchised immigrants. American-led triumphs in the two world wars quelled temptations of despots to conquer peaceful nations. The United States turned back an attempted takeover of South Korea and did its best to prevent subjugation of the people of South Vietnam. In more recent times, US troops ousted the Iraqi invaders of Kuwait.

America stood firm against dictators and other autocratic leaders when they repressed their own people. US policies played a pivotal role in the transformation of hundreds of millions of lives in the former Soviet Union and Eastern Europe. The United States came to the aid of oppressed Muslim populations in Bosnia and Kosovo. Americans had good reason to believe that they had developed large cadres of friends and admirers almost everywhere.

In the mid-1990s, terrorists attacked the World Trade Center, as well as US embassies in Africa and US military facilities in the Middle East. With hundreds murdered, it was all too clear that hostile groups were seeking the ultimate in retribution for problems they attributed to America.

Even then, as the twentieth century drew to a close, the American homeland seemed distant from the world's trouble spots. US military excursions into Lebanon and Somalia had disastrous endings, but they had little impact on American life—only on the families and friends of the casualties. The wars in Bosnia and Kosovo, although ragged in leadership and execution, stopped ethnic cleansing, and reconstruction became a *European* problem. Fears of catastrophes from the constant nuclear face-off on the Korean Peninsula seemed exaggerated. The US borders were secure from penetrations by missiles, airplanes, and submarines, and we had the aspiring terrorist bombers under control, or so we thought.

Then came the most telling headlines of all. In New York, "Death Toll from World Trade Center Attack Approaches 3,000." In Washington, "Pentagon Smoldering in Wake of Crash."

The world's only superpower had received punishing body blows on its own soil. With little delay, the United States launched a massive and diffuse counterattack against an elusive target. The attack and counterattack changed the course of world history.

A VIGOROUS APPROACH IN RESPONSE TO 9/11

Initially, with global sympathy in its corner, the US government easily elicited support from most of the world's leaders for new efforts to track down terrorists and to foster freedom and democracy in troubled lands. Homeland defenses were strengthened. A global hunt for the perpetrators of 9/11 was launched.

At the same time, both governmental and nongovernmental organizations initiated new dialogues, exchanges, and research efforts to understand the frustrations and aspirations of neglected populations. Our public television stations brought in leaders of the Muslim, Jewish, Protestant, and Catholic faiths for a forum with local residents. The focus was on building bridges with Muslim populations at home and abroad.

However, demands from confident American politicians, determined military leaders, and well-meaning patriots throughout the nation for quick and decisive armed responses to the terrorist acts of 9/11 soon dominated the halls of Washington. The embryonic efforts of the US government to win hearts and minds in distant lands became an afterthought to military expeditions. Hearts and minds could wait while military power ensured that 9/11 was but a one-time scar on America.

Of course, when adversaries resort to terrorism, the United States has no choice but to respond promptly and forcefully—and military forces must be in the forefront. Two and a half years after 9/11, Vice President Richard Cheney succinctly summarized the American policy that had been established in 2001 with the following words: "The terrorist enemy holds no territory, defends no population, is unconstrained by rules of warfare, and respects no law of morality. Such an enemy cannot be deterred, contained, appeased, or negotiated with. It can only be destroyed. And that is the business at hand."[7]

The US government had declared war on terrorism. Tens of thousands of troops went to Afghanistan and many more to Iraq. Army reservists donned their uniforms. Congress appropriated hundreds of billions of dollars to support a war the American public believed the country would win without delay.

But this is not a war, and the enemy is not terrorism. We have embarked on a new phase of a never-ending struggle with global turmoil that can and must be reduced but will never be eliminated. The use of the tactic of terrorism by some disenfranchised groups is a particularly ugly manifestation of global turmoil.

The mischaracterization of the challenge confronting America as a war on terrorism was a huge mistake. It has resulted in a short-term focus on responding to *outbreaks* of violence while giving little attention to reducing the *causes* of violence. In *Patterns of Global Terrorism 2004*, the US Department of State defines *terrorism* as "premeditated, politically motivated violence perpetrated against noncombatant targets by subnational groups or clandestine agents, usually intended to influence an audience." Noncombatant targets include military personnel who at the time of the incident were unarmed and/or not on duty. Our policy emphasizes ending the violence through military power, while neglecting the long-term consequences of such a one-dimensional effort. Indeed, winning the military battles has been the centerpiece of the government's message to the Pentagon, the American people, and the world.

Belated recognition of the need for actions beyond military intervention came in August 2004, when Condoleezza Rice, speaking on behalf of the US government, advocated a greater balance in the American approach. She recalled the conclusion of the 9/11 Commission that long-term success demands the use of all elements of national power: diplomacy, intelligence, covert action, law enforcement, economic policy, foreign aid, public policy, and homeland defense. She identified a number of trade and aid initiatives to improve US relations with the Muslim world, and she called for broader exchange programs. However, the government's overriding priority clearly was taking down the terrorists while improving the international marketing of American policies.[8]

As Rice suggested, the road to victory, however defined, demands a bifocal lens. The path illuminated through the shorter-term lens may lead to success on the battlefield. But it must not unnecessarily complicate the longer-term journey toward reconstruction and reorientation of those societies that spawn extremist leaders who advocate terrorism as their followers' best hope for a better life. The lens with the longer focal length must magnify the importance of reducing incentives for violence aimed at America and its allies. These incentives are closely tied to lack of respect and, indeed, disdain for America's values and policies.

CONFRONTING THE DILEMMA

We know that when all else fails, die-hard opponents of America must be isolated from the mainstream of national and international activities. We are rapidly improving our capabilities to do that. We are working with other governments—and operating undercover when necessary—to eliminate their safe havens, to put crimps in their financial lifelines, and to apprehend them when possible.

The long-term vision for reducing the number and influence of emerging hostile groups bent on destroying America is, unfortunately, less straightforward. What we do know is that we need our friends to join us in the effort. Our leaders must recognize that in trying to engage these critical relationships, shock and awe will alienate more than they will persuade. We must understand not only that policy adjustments are key requirements in building support, they must also be noticeable in impact and clearly explained as to their intent. While building democracy can be a noble concept, it must not be the sole justification by the US government to simply eliminate regimes not to its liking.

The purpose of this book is to suggest ways to repair America's tattered reputation—and to rebuild the bridges critical to an international effort to contain terrorism while promoting better lives for all. The core objective is to encourage current and future leaders in countries that have tolerated the growth of hostility toward America to change course and work in new directions. Then, self-styled antagonists, without the support of these leaders, will have increasing difficulty in their efforts to terrorize the United States and its allies. To this end, we focus special attention on a few policy areas that have huge influence on foreign attitudes. We also concentrate on the effective use of the "soft power" of engagement and conciliation, power that both complements and—whenever possible—replaces military force.

The range of factors influencing the attitudes of foreign governments and their populations toward America is broad. Indeed, visions of America are broad: the world's superpower, a land of economic opportunity, a source of foreign investment, a place to study, the source of Hollywood movies and glamour, a selfish bully, and more. These images will change only slowly. But if the US government develops sound policies that adequately protect US interests and also command strong support abroad, a giant step toward reducing distrust and hatred toward America will have been taken. The United States may then become less dependent on missiles, nuclear weapons, and fat bankrolls in combating the zeal of the proponents of global violence.

Working within such a framework, Washington should also have an easier job in encouraging its allies, who have distanced themselves from some American policies, to assist in repairing the fractures that increasingly split rather than unite the global population. Such global approaches are obviously needed to deal with many problems confronting the world. Population growth, environmental degradation, contaminated drinking water, dwindling energy resources, spreading of infectious diseases, increases in narco-trafficking, and the proliferation of weapons of mass destruction can be addressed only through common efforts.

At the same time, the transition period to a more perfect world will be long regardless of the political and financial commitments of Washington to right the wrongs of the past. During this period, American military capabilities will continue to be an important component of approaches in developing a more stable community of nations. The United States needs to demonstrate to the rest of the world that at the same time it is pressuring others to show military restraint it is also prepared to scale back its own military adventures that are viewed as provocative. To do otherwise, we risk creating a world in which every country feels it has the right to attack any other country that might threaten it in the future.[9] Do we really want such a world?

We are not starting from scratch. Important opinion makers on every continent and in every country deeply respect the American way of life. America's independent judiciary and adherence to due process, for example, are admired in countries where decisions of guilt and innocence are made by single executives. Economic opportunity and social mobility are broadly recognized as strengths of America. And, as already noted, America's system of higher education is admired by even radical foes who are eager to send their children to American universities.

Each year tens of millions of visitors travel to the United States. Most return home with positive impressions from their travels. This admiration of American institutions presents many opportunities for fruitful people-to-people engagement that can help mold favorable attitudes toward the United States.

The end of the Cold War led to new possibilities for people who seek and cherish freedom. For many societies, that long-elusive freedom became a reality. Unfortunately for many others, freedom remains a vague and elusive concept. Their much deeper and more desperate concerns lie in the desires of their individual citizens for economic opportunity and for respect and equality. These aspirations must be recognized and satisfied; only then will the world begin to drain the swamps of despair that breed terrorism. The first steps in this long road are to stop demonizing each other, respect our differences, and pull together in setting the stage for openness and equality to take their places at the tables of all nations.

THE SEARCH FOR GLOBAL HARMONY

Will we ever see the day when global jihad aimed at Washington is replaced by global cooperation and mutual respect?[10] If the United States uses its power more judiciously, shares its prosperity more generously, and becomes a champion for respect for all people, we can create that change. However, there will be no second chance. The alternative will be uncontrollable bloodshed, permanently depressed economies even in the most prosperous countries, and lifetimes of fear for all populations.

We can also move closer to global harmony by joining with Muslim countries in promoting concepts that their religion and our own teachings hold dear. Islam takes strong enlightened positions in opposing drug and alcohol abuse, divorce, violence among teenagers, crime, ethnic and racial prejudice, neglect of the poor and aged, rampant materialism, depletion of natural resources, and ecological degradation.[11] Who could not embrace such positions?

As to use of military power, it must become but one of several elements, and only when absolutely necessary the central element, in America's approach to halting terrorism and helping to bring stability to a world in turmoil. That restraint will not come easily.

In the spring of 2003, I joined my former classmates in the procession of the Long Gray Line across the Plain at West Point. We shared our pride over the many contributions that the US Army made in promoting peace and understanding during the half century since our graduation. We knew intimately the meaning of victory on the battlefield and we were determined to encourage the new classes of officers to uphold the long traditions of courage and service.

One year later, I witnessed two thousand American war veterans on motorcycles roar through Crystal City, Virginia, en route to the Memorial Day parade down Independence Avenue in the District of Columbia. They were unabashed in displaying flags and memorabilia on their Harleys as reminders of how they defended American interests. They, too, were reminding America that military service is a noble profession.

We should indeed honor America's battlefield accomplishments of the past. But even the most ardent defenders of America—whether they be in the Long Gray Line or on Harleys—must embrace the reality that raw military power is no longer an adequate formula for protecting America now or in the future. Those victories were the victories of yesterday. The victories of tomorrow will be entirely different. They will be won in the governing councils, the parliaments, the courtrooms, the universities, the madrassas, and the homes of many countries throughout the Middle East, North Africa, Central and South Asia, and, indeed, the entire world. They will be won at the tables of the United Nations and other forums where all countries have an opportunity to make their views known. In all of these forums, America must be prepared to adjust its objectives and its policies if they are to be accepted as a credible basis for the countries of the world to move forward together and not splinter in counterproductive directions.

Only America has the capability to lead a global effort toward a more prosperous and hospitable world. But *how* America leads is the critical issue. The United States cannot be the captain of every ship. Nor can it dominate the implementation of every policy. Can Washington develop and bring about a concept of shared leadership, or will the United States insist on standing at the top of the mountain with a loud megaphone? Can America set a vision for a new world order that all stakeholders can accept and work toward? And can America help remove barriers on the road that impede common efforts in the quest for a better life for all?

In 1846 French writer and politician Alexis de Tocqueville, after seeing volunteerism in action in many American towns, wrote, "America is great because she is good. If America ceases to be good, America will cease to be great." Now a militarily and economically strong America must use this spirit of volunteerism and offer, but not impose, a helping hand to populations around the globe. There is no other choice if America is to remain great.

CHAPTER 1

A FRACTURED INTERNATIONAL ENVIRONMENT FOSTERS ANGER TOWARD AMERICA

★ ★ ★ ★ ★ ★ *A Clash of Civilizations or a Backlash against US Policies*

A central question confronting America and, indeed, the world is: How do we encourage and support the evolution of Muslim states that seek justice and equality for their people as well as international approval for their policies in the drastically altered conditions of Western modernity? Muslims need space to adopt this modernity in their own ways, and they should not be expected to simply swallow Western approaches. At the same time, a widespread perception of Western contempt for the Islamic world makes it difficult for Muslims to engage in internal criticisms of their own interpretations of Islamic precepts.

In recent years, historians have repeatedly recounted how the first centuries of Islam witnessed rapid expansion of new beliefs across most of the known world. In more recent centuries, however, Muslims have suffered a series of crushing defeats. They have been subjected to a brutal history of political, cultural, and sometimes religious oppression. Western powers established an indelible track record of political and economic colonialism that created artificial states and further divided less-than-cohesive ethnic groups into subnational entities. Thus, Muslims have good reason to be suspicious of the West as they try to come to grips with internal political and cultural issues. Hostile Western attitudes are too often on center screen. In his April 29, 2003, lecture at George Washington University, Washington, DC, historian and professor Bernard

Lewis put it this way: "Western attitudes toward the Middle East can be characterized as ignorance of the past, contempt for the present, and disdain for the future."

Fortunately, during the past several decades, Western scholars have intensified their scrutiny of developments in the Middle East, North Africa, and Central Asia as they attempt to develop intellectual bridges from turbulent times of the past to present realities.

HUNTINGTON AND HIS CRITICS

Few post–Cold War writings on international affairs have stirred as much controversy as Samuel Huntington's essay "The Clash of Civilizations."[1] The paradigm shaping the destiny of the world, he argues, has shifted such that the fundamental source of conflict will not be ideological or economic but cultural. In Huntington's view, "The fault lines between civilizations will be the battle lines of the future." Brisk sales of his expanded book *The Clash of Civilizations and the Remaking of the World Order*[2] demonstrated the eagerness of many intellectuals around the globe to explain the mounting troubles within a number of regions of the world by seizing on what many others considered the well-engrained stereotype of Islam and the West as age-old enemies.

Six tenets support Huntington's hypothesis:

- Differences between civilizations are "basic" and are embedded in culture, for example, variations in history, language, tradition, and, most important, religion.
- Increasing interactions of civilizations in a shrinking world intensify consciousness of those cultural differences.
- Global economic modernization and social change are separating people from their local identities and weakening the state as a wellspring of identity.
- There is a widespread return to cultural roots within non-Western civilizations, perhaps in reaction to the rising power of the West.
- Cultural differences are less easily compromised than political and economic objectives.

- Economic regionalization is increasing and it is strengthening common cultural ties.

Huntington's detractors were not persuaded by his arguments, however. They believed that civilizations do not control states. On the contrary, they believed states control civilizations. In their view, Huntington did not adequately recognize the tenacity of modernity and secularism, and he failed to appreciate the importance of instant information and economic interdependence. Overall, they concluded, he underestimated the worldwide appeal of Western civilizations and particularly the attractiveness of democracy and personal freedom—traits that are linked to capitalism and successful economic development. But they did not venture an alternative view of the world as they rejected Huntington's paradigm.[3]

Huntington's endorsement of a north-south fault line from the Arctic border of Russia and Finland through Eastern Europe to Romania and then to the Adriatic Sea seemed particularly questionable. This border between Western Christianity to the west and Islam and Orthodox Christianity to the east hardly appeared to be a major cultural cleavage in 1993. Countries on both sides of the border were clamoring for membership in the European Union, and the conflicts among the abutting countries were not rooted in cultural heritage as much as in political and economic disagreements.[4]

In Islamic countries, reactions to Huntington's theories were forceful and negative. In Iran, for example, his writings were widely denounced as degrading and provocative. Particularly offensive was his statement that Islam's borders are bloody and so are its innards.[5] Scholars in other Muslim regions quickly pointed out that conflicts between different groups of Muslims were often more intense than conflicts between Muslim and non-Muslim groups in the same geographical areas.

One hotly debated issue has been the extent to which the attitudes of Muslims toward other societies have commonalities throughout the world of Islam. To what extent do local circumstances, including foreign presence, determine behavior? To what extent do religious convictions and other historical and cultural traditions with global appeal outweigh such local determinants of behavior?

In addressing Muslim violence, another particularly contentious point is whether Muslim societies have inherent characteristics that make them more likely than other populations to spawn angry young people. Certainly an unusually high number of acts of terrorism involve young perpetrators from Islamic countries.[6] Alternatively, are followers of Islam who become radical jihadists simply reacting to perceptions of immoral and culturally threatening global trends? Are they banding together to condemn military and economic colonialism by the West as the cause of intractable poverty and joblessness? Or is it simply that al Qaeda and related terrorist groups excel in recruiting large numbers of trainees? And what role do antagonistic US policies play in this regard?

In Huntington's view, "Throughout the Muslim world and particularly among Arabs, there exists a great sense of grievance, resentment, envy, and hostility towards the West, and particularly the United States. This is in part a result of Western imperialism and domination of the Muslim world for much of the twentieth century. It is also in part the result of particular Western policies."[7]

Pakistani scholar Akbar S. Ahmed poses an interesting counterpoint: "Isn't the real clash, the root causes of the turmoil, to be located within Islam. . . . For Muslims, their leadership has failed. This failure is caricaturized by stories of hidden, illegal wealth looted from the people and kept abroad and corruption and cruelty at home. Hence the depth of Muslims' despair, the extent of their anger, and the desperation of their response."[8]

Academics will continue to debate the cultural traditions, economic disparities, and political confrontations that frame the international issues before policy makers in Washington and other capitals. Meanwhile, policies emanating from Washington will surely have major impacts on how different societies continue to share the earth. These policies will determine in large measure whether others view the United States as a self-appointed bully and imperialist, the superpower guardian of the planet, or something in between.

ATTACKS ON AMERICA AND ITS ALLIES

As we wrote in 1998, much of the terrorism of the mid-twentieth century took place in areas remote from mainstream America.[9] Conflicts in the

Middle East, India, Ireland, and other distant lands hardly touched the American consciousness. Then the technological advancements that brought about international air travel also ushered in airline hijacking. Other international incidents that gradually awakened America included never-ending violence in Israel and Palestine, taking of American diplomats as hostages in Tehran, murder of Israeli athletes at the Munich Olympics, and seizure of the *Achille Lauro* cruise ship off the coast of Egypt.

In 1993 the terrorists truly hit home, planting a bomb that exploded in the underground garage of the World Trade Center. They struck again eight years later, with the devastating attacks of 9/11. No longer were quick financial gains, release of political prisoners, or retaliations against Israeli incursions into neighboring territories the direct motivations for violence. The foreign perpetrators were determined to get even with what they perceived as America's political, economic, and cultural assaults on their societies.

In the wake of 9/11, the threats of additional terrorist attacks on US cities from abroad loomed large. The response of the US government has been massive. At the federal level, expanded law enforcement legislation and ballooning budget requests arrived in record time on the president's desk for quick approval. The new Department of Homeland Security mobilized one hundred and seventy-five thousand civil servants with all types of scientific, technical, and legal skills to protect America. Airports, seaports, and road crossings at the borders with Mexico and Canada were equipped with sensitive devices to detect dangerous smuggled materials; and all entry points into the United States adopted new security procedures to identify high-risk visitors. At the local level, hundreds of thousands of firefighters, police officers, and other law enforcement personnel are purportedly ready. Evacuation plans are piled high and many have been rehearsed.

From Saudi Arabia to Kenya and from Pakistan to Colombia, terrorist groups have killed, maimed, and kidnapped hundreds of Americans. They have destroyed US embassies and they have wrecked the facilities of companies with headquarters in the United States. They have vowed to expand their assaults on all continents until, as many contend, America withdraws from their lands.

Regretfully, anti-American hatred is now firmly embedded within the psychological makeups of legions of Islamic militants. In the Middle East, in particular, fanatics are convinced that Americans are "Zionists" and therefore what they consider to be enemies of God. The US government must continue to deal with these twenty-first-century marauders harshly and without reservation. These terrorist groups and their sponsors behave as cold-blooded killers regardless of the religious or other cloaks used to protect them. The international community should pursue legal steps to ensure that terrorists are so labeled in international law. Most important, terrorists should be denied access to safe havens and the associated opportunities for spreading and acting out their anger.

Are Americans destined to spend the rest of their lifetimes preparing for the next attack by a faceless enemy whose agents have infiltrated communities in the United States? Will international travel warnings become so routine that they permanently discourage trips to tourist sites in historic or romantic settings and to hubs of international trade and commerce? Unfortunately, the answers to both of these questions could very well be yes. But a new strategy for American engagement with the world can help spin the wheel of chance toward no.

However, the continuing spread of hostile acts pushes further into the future the likelihood of a turnaround in animosity toward America. Bombings in Turkey and Spain in 2003 and 2004 were dramatic testimony to the danger countries face in aligning themselves with American policies. Both countries had long-standing reservations about seemingly excessive American aggressiveness in pursuing terrorists and in invading Iraq. In Spain, after the bombing in Madrid, one-quarter of the nation's population took to the streets to protest the government's support of the United States. Indeed, the general population promptly voted to dismiss the government that had sent troops to Iraq. And, while the underlying motivations of the London subway and bus suicide bombers of 2005 are not completely clear, these actions have served to further erode support of the British populace for US policies that encourage terrorist attacks in the West.

The threadbare US legal brief of 2002 justifying military intervention in Iraq remains a particularly divisive issue in Europe as well as throughout the Middle East. Equally disturbing are the serious rumblings within governments of traditional US allies about the unwillingness of the

United States to share decision-making authority in the battle against insurgents and terrorists. Journalists have repeatedly commented that Saddam Hussein succeeded in accomplishing a goal that eluded communist leaders in Moscow, Beijing, and other capitals for half a century—dividing America and Europe, at least temporarily.

At the core of the perception problem facing the United States is the universal belief that the United States always presses for immediate *American* security and *American* prosperity. *International* security and *global* prosperity are not genuine concerns of the United States in the eyes of the world, since they have witnessed the refusal of the United States to participate in international agreements concerning global warming, biodiversity, banning of land mines, and establishment of an international court of justice. The US government has strong reasons for declining to commit to these treaty obligations. But US policy is viewed as a threat to the interests of many countries.

Fortunately, most foreign critics of American policies and actions are not seeking confrontations, and huge reservoirs of goodwill toward America remain on every continent. Large clusters of populations are eager to revive their faith in America. They long for ideological and political rapprochement. They are waiting for the United States to take steps that will quell their apprehensions about America's true intentions. Without concrete evidence of a more enlightened American worldview, foreign leaders have hard sells at home in generating support when it comes to reaching out to the United States.

The number of potential anti-American warriors—call them student revolutionaries, organized militants, or simply angry protesters—is on the rise. Some may be worried about future American interventions into their cities and cultures, and some may already be inflamed because of past US actions. Others may simply need an excuse to vent frustrations and, hence, will join demonstrations that are intended to force a change in government leadership. But whatever their grievances, frustrated youth with time on their hands are often easy recruits for extremist groups. A new generation of angry young people is rapidly emerging in turbulent areas from the deserts of Pakistan to the jungles of the Philippines and from the temples of Syria to the slums of Indonesia. Sooner than we realize, they and their generational counterparts will be at the forefront in determining the fates of large areas of the world.

New approaches are needed to win the struggle for hearts and minds around the world. Underlying such changes in direction should be a US foreign policy based on not only immediate challenges but also on "future think." Such an orientation recognizes that the long-term consequences of near-term policies really matter. Future think, which should help blunt the continuing spread of anti-Americanism, is of no less importance than the tightening of current security bastions against today's terrorists.

NEW WEAPONS IN THE HANDS OF TERRORISTS

Even the most modern defensive systems deployed in the United States cannot ensure the protection of the public from devastating attacks launched by determined opponents. On 9/11, the world witnessed how passenger aircraft were turned into suicide missiles. Fortunately, a number of other potentially disastrous schemes have been nipped in the bud since then.[10] These include plots to transform transatlantic airliners and freighters into carriers of infectious biological agents, schemes to derail American trains, and a planned attack on the Los Angeles airport. At the same time, the US government has repeatedly warned that new terrorism scenarios are on the drawing boards of America's adversaries.

Terrorists have many advantages. They know how, where, and when they want to strike. They have collaborators in the United States. They have access to cash. And they are not afraid to sacrifice their lives or the lives of their closest relatives or friends. America's enormous advantage in numbers of military and civilian protectors with advanced technological capabilities is not sufficient to deter or defeat a technically savvy, ruthless, and elusive opponent with "Ground Zero America" etched many times on its maps.

The United States truly has a soft underbelly—a vulnerable physical infrastructure that cannot be fully protected at any price. Crowded subway systems, traffic-laden bridges, sprawling chemical storage facilities, crackling power grids, crammed apartment buildings, packed stadiums, and even busy hospitals are among the many targets that are difficult to protect from determined terrorists.

Of course, the most devastating attack of all would be a nuclear explosion in a metropolitan area. While nuclear weaponry may currently be beyond the reach of rogue groups, in time terrorists will master the challenge of detonating a critical explosion. At present, well-educated terrorist groups are probably capable of constructing a nuclear weapon from items available on the open market, should they acquire the explosive fissile material. At the request of Senator Joseph Biden (D-DE), scientists went to hardware stores and supply houses to demonstrate how all but the highly enriched uranium, which is needed for detonation, could be obtained and easily assembled. Thus, the need for tight control of fissile material is clear.[11]

Hence, the United States must not relax its efforts to prevent weapons of mass destruction from falling into the hands of rogue states or terrorist organizations. There is time to prevent a true technological holocaust, but the clock is ticking.

CONTINUING CONTROVERSY OVER THE INTERVENTION IN IRAQ

Whether characterized as a liberation campaign or as an invasion, America's intervention in Iraq in 2003 ignited repercussions that will challenge the legality and wisdom of US military deployments for many years to come. The intervention was the most inflammatory manifestation of US foreign policy since the war in Vietnam. Outside Washington, few believed that al Qaeda had any roots in Iraq before the war, but many now believe that Iraq has become a dangerous breeding ground for recruits to terrorism. Success in establishing a bastion of democracy in the Middle East, if indeed one takes hold, will be widely acclaimed. But adverse impacts of the Iraqi incursion will also continue to dominate international discussions throughout the world.[12]

On the positive side, influential leaders within and outside Iraq have heralded the intervention as a vigorous demonstration of America's commitment to human rights and democratic principles. They believe that as a result of the overthrow of a despicable dictator, other autocratic regimes will pay greater attention to the demands of their own populations. Such recognition of public aspirations is an essential element of democratization, they add.

Even if the new government turns out to be far from perfect, it will undoubtedly be less repressive, and, with substantial American assistance, Iraq has a chance to slowly become an economically viable state. Fewer Iraqi resources will be devoted to building military capabilities and to sustaining a high lifestyle for the ruling elite. Then, too, we can hope that the general population will receive many more benefits from oil revenues than in recent decades, despite allegations of America's intentions to control the oil resources for its own ends.

At the same time, many Arab leaders attach great importance to strength and determination, with some being quite impressed by the US show of force, an act that demonstrated that the United States means what it says. Rogue regimes will likely think long and hard before seeking advanced weapons systems, lest they, too, be displaced. Perhaps the apparent change in attitude of Libya to abandon efforts to acquire nuclear weaponry was influenced by the devastating military might that the United States exhibited in Iraq.

Many of America's traditional friends—both governments and their national leaders—believe that the United States made a mistake in invading Iraq, however. They argue that we should have been more patient. They believe that the ever-increasing diplomatic and economic pressures for Saddam's compliance with the UN resolutions would have forced him to come clean.

Alternatively, some of America's most bitter critics simply believe that we should have left the problem to the countries in the region. To them, US exaggerations of both the linkage of Saddam Hussein to al Qaeda and the imminence of the threat of Iraq's use of weapons of mass destruction were smokescreens to hide long-standing American intentions simply to eliminate Saddam. Testimony by the former US secretary of treasury, a member of President Bush's cabinet prior to and after 9/11, certainly seems to confirm this view.[13]

At more junior levels of American society, a senior thesis at the University of Illinois turned up twenty-three different rationales of the Bush administration for going to war in Iraq. The student researcher innocently concluded, "If they had to keep coming up with new reasons for going to war, we probably shouldn't have done it. It's almost like the decision came first, then the rationales."[14]

Thus, American unilateralism supported by military power and then justified through new interpretations of international law is a hard sell in foreign capitals. For many critics of US policy, Saddam's repeated violations of UN resolutions were not a good enough rationale for an invasion. Governments often fail to comply with UN resolutions, and such violations had not warranted military attacks in the past. Resolutions are to encourage diplomatic and economic pressures, not to authorize military invasions, contend skeptics who question the basis for the Iraqi invasion.

Beyond Iraq, the military campaign heightened fears of some Arab leaders that the United States might challenge their own personal positions of power in the future. These leaders could be threatened by a democracy that works in Iraq, not one that fails. Thus, it is not surprising that one response in the Arab world to US efforts in Iraq has been the subtle tightening of control within other societies, a move that in time could encourage even more extremism. At the same time, Pakistan, Egypt, and even Saudi Arabia are attempting to install a veneer of democracy via new elections and pronouncements of reform. These responses raise the question: Could such manipulations to achieve the *appearance* of democracy actually create new threats to US interests that outweigh the positive impacts of democracy as an antidote to terrorism?

Other objections to the US-led intervention are also easy to detect. Important rulers of Islamic countries simply resent American armed forces taking charge of Middle Eastern territory. African leaders confronted with rebellions in their own countries decry the American priority for the Middle East while the United States neglects their continent. Asian energy ministers are increasingly nervous about a US presence in the Middle East that exacerbates regional political turmoil with attendant threats to their sources of oil.

All the while, thousands of eloquent testimonies of returning American soldiers and aid workers concerning the gratitude of Iraqis for the American intervention are largely ignored by the media. Many Iraqi citizens were personally touched by the kindness of the troops. Also, new school buildings and modern hospital facilities, attributed to American assistance organizations, have affected the lives of hundreds of thousands. These largely untold stories, when added together, indicate that

America will have many friends in Iraq for the indefinite future, whatever the turn of events in the country.

However, then other depressing reports offset the assertions of instant friendships. For example, one report notes that Iraqis were insulted when US troops offered one dollar for each bag of trash they collected, that they scorned glossy pro-coalition magazines prepared by American psychological warfare units, and that they were appalled by what seemed to be indiscriminate shootings by American forces. They were taken aback to find out that, when offered medical assistance, no medicines or diagnostic equipment were available. In one incident, a farmer simply couldn't understand why American troops would kill his only cow (an unintended casualty of a nervous military unit on patrol).[15]

Most important, American intervention in Iraq has dramatically changed the international ground rules as to the right of one country to invade the sovereignty of another. If America has the right to launch invasions when its security is at stake, should other countries have a similar right? Most Americans don't think so. Many continue to ask, "Was America's security *really* at stake?"

The lack of respect for territorial sovereignty is a life-or-death issue for poor countries that have little else. The United States easily won the military battles in Iraq. Backed by a US military presence, leaders friendly to the United States seem to be winning the short-term struggle for governance of the country.

However, the side effects reverberate around the world. Some groups are more determined than ever to unleash new efforts to take on the United States. Arab officials are torn. They don't want to see the United States succeed easily, lest it conclude that unilateral wars of preemption are the way to go. On the other hand, they fear that a US failure would unleash increasing Islamic militancy.[16]

CORNERSTONES OF AMERICAN POLICIES

From the Washington perspective, US policies are designed to foster peace and international stability—key ingredients for America's prosperity in a global economy. However, policies that seem realistic and compassionate when viewed through an American prism may be perceived abroad as deliberately constructed to aggravate other societies—especially since 9/11 among populations in the Islamic world. In particular, the use of US military power to compensate for inadequate constraints on foreign leaders who commit unconscionable deeds has stimulated a potentially lethal form of global road rage along the major highways and the remote byways of the planet.

At the heart of US policies must be advocacy of American interests and core values. "This should be an easy sell," argue the Washington politicians.[17] But core values are not well defined, and Americans must accept the reality that their core values are not universally shared.

Probably the best descriptor of American core values is the Constitution of the United States. Looking beyond the Constitution, should an honest work ethic be a core value? Should higher education and healthcare be core values that are assured for all Americans? Is community service a core value? In these and other areas of importance, the United States has often failed to live up to the expectations of its own citizens. Without a strong sense of humility in "selling" American values abroad, the United States appears to be simply a determined colonialist, with little regard for local values whatever their origins and their virtues.

At the extreme, American neoconservatives have argued that the foreign policy of the United States must be based on extending an international order friendly to *its* security, *its* prosperity, and *its* principles. They add that in support of a campaign to do just that, America needs increased defense spending. The United States must challenge regimes hostile to US interests. It must export democracy. And America is obliged to promote abroad its own version of economic freedom—a free-market economy.[18] This tack is certainly designed to protect US interests in the short run.

If the goal is a world that is safer for future generations of Americans, a longer-term perspective is essential. As global volatility increases almost everywhere, Washington must give greater heed to the interests of all countries—their differing histories, local values, and popular aspirations concerning self-governance. In the absence of more sensitive and nuanced US policies toward nearly two hundred different countries, the dangers to America and to Americans who are present on all continents will continue to rise.

That said, four cornerstones of US foreign policy deserve brief commentaries: promotion of democracy, protection of human rights, benefiting from economic globalization, and national security—each of which can trump all other considerations.

Promotion of Democracy

In general, Americans believe that democratic governance will help ensure that national leaders respond to the interests of their populations—including minorities—and that all citizens are treated fairly and equitably. Democracies also embrace such concepts as free and fair elections, an independent press, an independent judiciary, and checks on the authority of a nation's leading executive. Democratic nations have often shown that they are good neighbors, even in dangerous neighborhoods. They are often sympathetic toward American policies that oppose despots who try to suppress their own populations.

A key aspect of building a democracy is the rate at which a new system of governance replaces other systems that may have been in place for centuries. Too often the US government presses too hard and too fast for changes. Excessive zeal can disrupt economic and social activities and generate hostilities toward the United States. This can, in turn, set back progress toward meaningful democratization. As we learned in Russia and in other countries undergoing radical political change, realistic transition periods are usually measured in decades, not years. Even successful transitions often involve temporary reversals of democratic trends.

In the words of former State Department assistant secretary Carl W. Ford:

> The rush to embrace democracy, capitalism, and more open markets during the 1990s entailed numerous changes we regarded as positive; but . . . democracy does not guarantee effective or honest government or ensure higher living standards. In parts of East Asia and Latin American, despite steps toward more democracy and market economies, increasing inequities and a growing perception of inequality fed by rapid urbanization and global communications contribute to resentment of "greedy western capitalists." . . . Over the last twenty years all of Latin America save Cuba has been labeled "democratic" but the nations

of the region occupy varied positions on the continuum between democracy and authoritarianism. Relatively free and fair elections and observance of the most basic democratic and constitutional norms are commonplace. But so too are the debilitating levels of crime, corruption and socioeconomic inequities. Fewer than half of Latin Americans surveyed now contend that democracy is always preferable to authoritarianism.[19]

Democracy must evolve from the inside. Preconditions for planting seeds that will quickly grow usually include at least an average level of education, an absence of extremes of wealth and poverty, an absence of ethnic and religious conflict, an understanding of minority rights, the balance of a strong middle class, and widespread acceptance of the rule of law. Thus, we should ask the most fundamental question: Ready or not, can democracy be imposed on nations by outside force? Will the efforts to instill democracies in Afghanistan and Iraq lead to popularly embraced democracies over the long term? At the same time, the likelihood of early establishment of democracy more broadly throughout the Middle East, whatever the external pressures, seems remote.[20]

In the same vein, Henry Kissinger's observation concerning the support of democratic movements in the region seems on target:

> Where societies are divided by faith or ethnicity, our practices [in democracy building] run the risk of ratifying a permanent distribution of power based precisely on these ethnic divisions. . . . Because democracy must be rooted in domestic factors, it will thrive only where it reflects cultural, historical, and institutional backgrounds. This is why the attempt to impose western institutions elsewhere rarely succeeds without protracted western tutelage. . . . When democracy is pushed in a cultural and political vacuum, the outcome is likely to be chaos or regimes inimical to our values.[21]

In May 2005 the administrator of the US Agency for International Development proudly announced that his agency was spending $1.2 billion per year to support democracy around the world with more than four hundred specialists within the agency and many more within contractor organizations assigned to the task.[22] In addition, the Department of State and the National Endowment for Democracy have annual budgets in the tens of millions of dollars to subsidize efforts to establish democracies. Can the

United States really "buy" democracy? Will "purchased democracy" survive if financial support abates? Are the democratic revolutions in Ukraine, Kyrgyzstan, and elsewhere, which have received such notoriety, really true manifestations of the will of the people or are they, in large measure, paybacks to the US government by local beneficiaries of assistance?

Whatever the source and inspiration of democracy, it is unlikely that it will be a major cure for terrorism. The emergence of radical groups targeting America is not only the consequence of autocratic governments. Anger at American policies is of comparable importance. Indeed, some of the most successful efforts to control radical Islamist political groups have been *anti*democratic—repressive campaigns waged in Tunisia, Egypt, and Algeria in the 1990s, for example. Also, the notion that democratic governments in the Middle East would be more effective in fighting extremism is wishful thinking no matter how valuable democratization might be for other reasons.[23]

Protection of Human Rights

International acceptance of the UN Universal Declaration of Human Rights provides an important standard for protecting oppressed people throughout the world. There are eight subsequent UN elaborations of international obligations to protect human rights.[24]

1. Covenant on Civil and Political Rights
2. Optional Protocol to the Covenant on Civil and Political Rights
3. Covenant on Economic, Social, and Cultural Rights
4. Convention against Torture
5. Convention against Genocide
6. The Geneva Conventions
7. Convention on the Rights of the Child
8. Convention on the Elimination of Discriminations against Women

Another important document developed by thirty-five states of Europe and North America known as the Helsinki Accords articulates additional important principles, such as respect for the national sovereignty of states, which intersect directly with the struggle against terrorism. In advocating measures to stop human rights abuses, the US government must be careful in balancing concerns over national security and human rights, taking into account differing interpretations of agreed-upon international texts.

A particularly relevant development is the effort of the United Nations to provide guidance for dealing with terrorists while also protecting their personal rights. There seems to be broad recognition that some rights must be abridged in specific circumstances, particularly during wartime. While there may be agreement that law enforcement organizations should not have unfettered discretion in interpreting their charters and their obligations, debates over the extent of permissible actions will remain on center stage for years to come. The USA PATRIOT Act, for example, has been used to justify holding suspected terrorists for extended periods of time without benefit of legal representation. Can "enemy combatants" be detained indefinitely—or be considered guilty until proven innocent? These questions are not easily answered when the definitions of *war* and *terrorism* are blurred.

On the whole, protesting egregious abuse of the human rights of residents of any country—if supported by the facts—and making every effort to guarantee such rights are increasingly accepted as not only appropriate but also mandatory policy.

Benefiting from Economic Globalization

To many, globalization is synonymous with McDonald's restaurants and Coca-Cola signs punctuating landscapes around the world. To others, globalization means dominance by multinational companies, new trading rules established by the United States, and control of financial markets by Americans and Europeans. As simple examples of the impact of Americans, major orders for inventory by Wal-Mart can affect jobs in many countries, and adjustments in US tariffs are heard around the world. One annual survey of international developments uses a less threatening definition of globalization in ranking the outward reach of countries:

- **Technology**: number of Internet users, Internet hosts, and secure servers

- **Political engagement**: number of memberships in international organizations, UN Security Council missions in which each country participates, and foreign embassies that each country hosts
- **Personal contact**: international travel and tourism, international telephone traffic, and cross-border travelers
- **Economic integration**: trade, foreign direct investment and portfolio capital flows, and income payments and receipts

An early conclusion of these surveys was as follows: "We found that the world's most global countries boast greater income equality than their less global counterparts—a counterpoint to the common argument that developing countries are poor and unequal because of globalization, suggesting instead that history, economic policies, welfare programs, and education policies may play an important role in shaping income distribution."[25]

The United States has been a stalwart supporter of economic globalization, firmly convinced that such activity will benefit its economy. Many other countries, whatever their suspicions of American motives, have had no choice but to participate in globalization as both suppliers and consumers of items that circulate in international markets. At the turn of the twenty-first century, the global economy was suffering from the backwash of terrorism, while some economists predicted a less optimistic path to economic integration than the one so enthusiastically put forth by Thomas Friedman in *The World Is Flat: A Brief History of the Twenty-first Century*.[26] Regardless of these differing scenarios, globalization will not easily disappear. The interconnectedness of the world is growing rapidly, and the reversal of such a trend seems out of the question.

In some ways, globalization compounds the problems for governments of isolated states. Electronic media highlight the successes of others, making local disappointments even more dismal in contrast. A better-informed public thereby becomes impatient and sometimes violent. International exposure certainly contributed to the collapse of the Warsaw Pact. Such exposure can also increase public awareness of widening income gaps, growing corruption, and shameless nepotism.

The states of the Middle East have for decades enjoyed soaring incomes from the global demand for their oil. The inevitable tug-of-war with the foreign companies over the financial benefits to be reaped by each side is causing increasing stress. But the global markets need the oil-rich countries just as the countries need the global markets, and economic pressures from many directions will overcome political boundaries temporarily drawn in the sand.

Promotion of democracy, human rights, and globalization will continue apace. US efforts to gain acceptance for these concepts may continue to create negative impacts. However, progress in all three areas is very important, and the priority should be to have policies that lead to positive outcomes for all stakeholders, including the Islamic nations.

National Security

Turning more directly to national security, in 2002 the Bush administration adopted a National Security Strategy that has been both welcomed and despised. The general objectives set forth in this strategy are certainly laudable, as exemplified by the following statement of President Bush: "America must stand firmly for the non-negotiable demands of human dignity; rule of law; limits on the absolute power of the state; free speech; freedom of worship; equal justice; respect for women; religious and ethnic tolerance; and respect for private property."[27]

In countering critics of the strategy, Secretary of State Colin Powell asserted: "U.S. strategy is widely accused of being unilateralist by design. It isn't. It is often accused of being imbalanced in favor of military methods. It isn't. It is frequently described as being obsessed with terrorism and hence biased toward pre-emptive war on a global scale. It most certainly is not. . . . Partnership is the watchword of U.S. strategy in this Administration. Partnership is not about deferring to others; it is about working with them."[28]

Presumably, Secretary Powell accurately reflected the intent of the strategy. Unfortunately, the strategy raised as many questions as it answered. The objectives were too general, carefully leaving to government departments and agencies many decisions for adjusting policies to fit the political signals of the day. Also, several portions of the strategy are troubling. The Department of Defense, for example, was given broad latitude in carrying out preemptive military actions when determined by the president to be in the interest of the nation. The strategy gave short shrift to the United Nations, despite Powell's contention that the strategy strongly affirmed the vital role of the United Nations along with other international and regional organizations. Even the impressive section on new approaches to foreign aid conveyed an imperialistic spin.

The US government is driven by many forces to protect America's assets now and in the future. But frequent pauses are needed to assess how American policy is playing abroad. Political repression, economic deprivation, and social injustice are widely recognized as incubators of terrorism. The incubation period is hastened by widespread convictions around the world that imperialistic leaders in the wealthy nations and the policies of the sole superpower are largely to blame for the miserable conditions.

One of the reasons for this critical assessment is that the United States is generally perceived as the guarantor of the status quo in other lands, however unsatisfactory that may be to residents of particular countries. The United States is in the driver's seat and doesn't want to take a wrong turn, so goes the logic. Some violent groups believe that they can most easily attack the out-of-date policies of *their own* governments by attacking American assets. By causing the US government to realize the costs of continued support of such unsatisfactory regimes, such groups hope to influence the United States in forcing changes in their governments.[29] Until the United States is prepared to accept other countries as full partners in deciding the future of societies that have differing visions of the future, no real progress can be made in overcoming this source of deep anti-American animosities. The United States need not defer to the views of others, but it should certainly give them a fair hearing *before* decisions are made in Washington.

Engagement, not confrontation, coupled with respect, not disregard, for the views of others is central to international peace and prosperity. Otherwise the world will be operating dangerously close to new fault lines that divide people, that is, people increasingly armed with weapons that can destroy massive population centers with less and less difficulty. Of course, it will be difficult to overcome the views of many Middle Easterners, as illustrated by Pakistani scholar Khurshid Ahmad: "The United States dreams of world domination, resolves to control the resources of other nations, wants to shape the world according to its ideas, and seeks to impose its values and ideology on others by force."[30]

Some experts in Washington have concluded that changing international opinion—and particularly Muslim hatred—against the United States is nearly impossible. A respected consensus statement concluded that "the long-term looks bleak as the United States loses its campaign for the hearts and minds of the Arab world."[31] But the United States must not be pessimistic. The stakes are too large not to explore every avenue and then to pick the streets that are most likely to lead to a safer and more prosperous global commons.

As to the focus on terrorism, former secretary of state Powell made this declaration on behalf of the Bush administration: "We fight terrorism because we must, but we seek a better world because we can—because it is our desire, and our destiny, to do so. . . . Today US motives are impugned in some lands. . . . But we will see the United States vindicated in the eyes of the world in the twenty-first century."[32]

However, the United States must change its fundamental strategy of simply going after the terrorists while not fully recognizing how American policies are feeding the appetites of aspiring extremists. Reducing acts of violence aimed at America and its friends can only be achieved by winning the confidence of the populations that will deny our adversaries sanctuary.[33] To this end, American policymakers must incorporate legitimate priorities of other nations into our agendas, working with them to help build satisfied and responsible societies on terms they fully embrace. Only then will America slowly restore its reputation, reduce the threat of attacks on its cities, and become a force for peaceful change.

TAKING A TRANSFORMATIONAL APPROACH

While the United States shores up home defenses and improves the overseas effectiveness of its intelligence agencies to stave off the next terrorist attack, hatred toward the United States continues to fester. Transforming this anger into respect that encourages other nations to work with us and not against us is crucial. At the core of this transformation must be the development of US policies and programs that resonate well abroad, and particularly in the Muslim world, while still effectively promoting US interests.

To transform anger into respect, we should adopt foreign policy approaches that

- improve the effectiveness of US foreign assistance
- support modernization of education and creation of job opportunities in the Muslim world
- combat the global threat of diseases
- reduce controversies over nuclear weapons
- strengthen the role of the United Nations
- end the Israeli-Palestine cycle of violence
- modify the international reach of the US Department of Defense

If adjustments are made in each of these crucial foreign policy areas, a giant step toward sustained peace and understanding will certainly be achieved. However, even optimistic projections of progress in these areas will not level all the bumps on the long road to reconciliation and mutual respect, nor will they persuade radical zealots bent on destroying the United States to change course. But the United States will be pointed in the right direction. With persistence in these areas, it is reasonable to expect the beginning of a widespread transformation of attitudes toward America within a few years.

Detractors of policy adjustments in these and other areas may claim that any change in US approaches to the grievances of disenfranchised groups is tantamount to giving in to terrorists. Such changes will simply inspire future ugly attacks to obtain further concessions, they may add. But to turn a deaf ear to the views of most of the rest of the world would be folly indeed. When friends as well as foes of the United States are questioning the wisdom of American policies, hiding policy stagnation behind the excuse that change would be letting the terrorists think they've won makes little sense. It's definitely time to change our approach—or we, in fact, *are* letting them win.

Finally, political scientist and statesman Zbigniew Brzezinski argues that while the current focus on terrorism per se is politically captivating, countering terrorism as a long-term strategy lacks staying power, can be internationally divisive, and can breed intolerance of others. It poses the risk that America will be perceived abroad as self-absorbed with its own interests. Anti-American ideologues will then gain international credibility by labeling the United States a self-appointed vigilante.[34]

Brzezinski contends that global turmoil should be recognized as the basic challenge of modern times. Terrorism is only one consequence of the unsettled international environment, which he perceives as follows:

> This turmoil is intensified though not entirely caused by persistent mass poverty and social injustice. In some regions, it involves ethnic oppression; in others, tribal conflicts; elsewhere, religious fundamentalism. It generates hate and envy of the dominant and prosperous; and it is likely to become more sophisticated in its lethality, especially with the proliferation of weapons of mass destruction. Some of the violence is much more indiscriminate than terrorism in its victims with tens of thousands killed every year, hundreds of thousands maimed, and millions affected by primitive combat.[35]

Can the United States assume a leadership role in mobilizing the world community to temper global turmoil? If so, respect for America will certainly climb steadily upward.

Development of a consensus on the economic and social issues of the day will not obviate the need for judicious use of the military power of the United States to maintain a sense of order throughout the world. However, international consensus on when and where that power may be used has become more important than ever before. An important bottom line is that killing more insurgents will not defeat insurgencies.

CHAPTER 2

POLITICAL OVERLAYS ON CROWDED LANDS WITH TOO FEW RESOURCES

★　★　★　★　★ *Where Are the Breeding Grounds of Hatred?*

W hy do poor nations remain poor? Conventional wisdom has long answered, "Location, location, location." Countries with abundant natural resources, fertile soil, or inviting environments have prospered. Resource-poor nations located in miserable climates, disease-infested regions, or areas isolated from prospering nations of the world do not stand much of a chance. At the same time, countries with terrain that provides easily defendable borders have an advantage in repelling pillagers.[1]

What about human factors and, particularly, a bulging population that places ever-increasing demands on limited resources? Can a determined society overcome the vagaries of nature and thrive against all odds? Does opting for democracy rather than autocracy improve the chances for prosperity?[2] How important is political will that invites or resists entanglements with well-financed global extremists?

The international community and, particularly, the United States as the most powerful player on the world scene, can often cut across these concerns. At times we can encourage the international community to throw lifelines to struggling populations. On occasion we can prevent aggressive states from causing trouble for their neighbors. We can provide trade and aid opportunities. We can offer counterincentives to financial offers from terrorists who are seeking sanctuaries. Or we can simply be spectators as crises unfold and hope they are resolved.

Here, we will explore geographical and related considerations that stymie advancement of economically depressed countries. We will also examine opportunities for the United States to play a positive role in addressing difficult barriers to progress. The focus is on Muslim countries, beginning with Uzbekistan. Of course, many problems confronting individual countries—such as food shortages, communicable diseases, refugees, and ethnic turmoil—are rapidly becoming regional and even global challenges.

DISRUPTIONS, UNEMPLOYMENT, AND THE RISE OF MILITANCY IN CENTRAL ASIA

In 1966 I climbed over the crumbled remnants of mud and unreinforced masonry buildings throughout a large section of Tashkent, a city of two and a half million people. The capital of Uzbekistan had just been jolted by its seventh earthquake in a millennium of unrelenting tremors. Twenty years later, I saw a rebuilt city, a city with hope that the next large seismic explosion was at least a hundred years away. Newly reinforced buildings had been erected in the commercial area of the city, but the urban poor continued to live in crowded houses and apartments that would easily again collapse.

Even though future earthquakes are inevitable, the people of Tashkent have become accustomed to periodic rebuilding of homes and shops on top of layers of rubble. There are few geographical choices where cities can support large populations in this arid country of twenty-six million people covering an area slightly larger than California. Beginning in the early days of the Silk Road that stretched through the historic centers of Samarkand, Bukhara, and Khiva, and even during the reign of the Soviet Union, the innermost reaches of Central Asia were a distant journey for the occasional visitors. The isolation eased during the latter half of the twentieth century as Tashkent became an air and vehicle hub for tourists and traders. It was the port of embarkation for exports of cotton ("white gold") from the world's fourth-largest producing country and real gold from the world's largest open-pit mine.

Then in the early 1990s, Tashkent experienced another type of shock.

The Soviet Union splintered into fifteen independent states, and Uzbekistan was suddenly on its own. Many of the economic lifelines from Moscow to Tashkent were abruptly severed. Uzbeks were in charge of their own country.

Uzbekistan had been one of the poorest Soviet republics, but it became even poorer after independence. Factories closed, unemployment increased, school enrollment dropped, and healthcare services deteriorated. By 2002 the annual per capita income had declined to $350 and was still falling. Since then, corruption has risen to new heights. Land mines have been deployed along the border to discourage narco-traffickers, terrorists, and illegal immigrants. They have deterred few smugglers of goods and people, but they have killed and maimed numerous innocent herders and their flocks. Remarkably, as a Soviet legacy that promoted education, literacy has remained at more than 98 percent, and the average life span of the hardy people continues to hover around sixty-four years.

The economic adjustments have been painful. The political and social adjustments have been even more so. Stories of infighting among Islamic groups and between these groups and the Russian minority have chronicled many brutal acts—arbitrary detentions and imprisonments, harassments at home and at work, and, most recently, suicide bombings. While the West has repeatedly promised economic support, delivery on these promises has been limited.

As expected, the US government has been interested in the establishment of a Western-style democracy in the country. Also, Washington wants to ensure that the Russian government keeps its distance from the newly emerging government. Thus, we have promoted dozens of exchange programs for political leaders to convince them of the advantages of democracy and to clarify steps needed in the transition to new approaches.

All the while, the water-sucking cotton crop, which had been an important economic bargaining chip with the mighty Soviet Union, came under attack from environmentalists throughout the world. The slow death of the Aral Sea was belatedly bannered in global headlines as a death attributed to the cotton farmers. As journalists streamed to Central Asia to witness the ecological tragedy, this calamity diverted the attention of Western governments away from critical governance decisions being made in Tashkent.

By the early 1990s, the perimeter of the sea had shrunk to one-third of the original volume of many decades earlier, as the cotton farmers drained more and still more water from its tributaries. The wind picked up salt and pesticides from the newly exposed seabed and systematically deposited these destructive materials on previously productive agricultural land. Fish catches in the sea declined. Production of food crops declined. But the anger of workers who lost their livelihoods increased. In the halls of Tashkent, however, cotton was an indispensable source of national income and foreign exchange.

Many Westerners remain determined to find a solution to the shrinking of the Aral Sea. Indeed, the Uzbeks say that if each American expert visiting the Aral Sea carried a bucket of water and poured it into the sea, the original size would be realized once again. Despite this attention, the cotton crop continues to be Uzbekistan's principal export while the Aral Sea struggles to come back to life.[3]

As the Aral Sea was receiving enormous publicity in the West, the real story shaping the destiny of the new country—the installation of a new governance structure—was unfolding. Despite Western hopes and efforts, the government remains far from achieving an international stamp of approval as a true democracy even though popular elections have repeatedly endorsed the ruling party. This party has shown little tolerance for dissent. Opposition parties barely exist. The press can hardly be described as independent. Perhaps an autocratic approach cloaked in democratic ornaments was necessary at the outset to rid the country of residual influence by the Russian diaspora and to stabilize the country under new leadership. Once in power, however, the new government was not about to let rival groups have influence.

A key issue for the nation and for the entire region is the future role of Islam in a country where 88 percent of the population is Muslim. For some, Islam is a personal religious commitment. For others, Islam is more accurately described as a label of ethnicity with religion taking a back seat to other aspects of life. But Islam also fills a political void as a rallying point for disgruntled Uzbeks since there is no other effective dissent channel in Uzbekistan.

Seventy years of Soviet rule did not crush Islam. However, the Soviets were successful in firmly secularizing society. Nevertheless, when given a chance, large communities of dormant Islamists challenged the legitimacy of the newly established government in their quest for power sharing and their desire for a state more aligned with Islamic beliefs.

At the extreme, a militant group, the Islamic Movement of Uzbekistan (IMU), was organized by inflamed Muslims who had fled in the early 1990s from Uzbekistan and neighboring countries to Afghanistan, where they elicited support from the Taliban, an Islamic extremist group. As the IMU began to mobilize for violent outbreaks, the US and other governments promptly labeled the group an international terrorist organization. The political leadership of Uzbekistan welcomed this action, as it was determined to prevent any type of Islam that was not sanctioned by the state from becoming a rallying point against the government.

More recently another Islamic movement has emerged as a force in Central Asia and particularly in Uzbekistan—the Hizb ut-Tahrir, or HuT. With roots dating back fifty years to Palestinian organizers, the HuT pursues international Islamic solidarity in countries with large Muslim populations. It has not yet resorted to violence on a significant scale. It advocates a unified Islamic grouping of vast proportions—a caliphate encompassing the Middle East and South Asia. The new caliphate would be regulated by Islamic law that can address the ills of society. The faithful contend that modernization and secularization in Muslim-populated states reflect a Western plot against Muslims as a whole. While committed to nonviolence in principle, the government of Uzbekistan will have none of this. However, the highly respected International Crisis Group outlines a number of reasons that may explain why HuT members join the movement, including the following: "There is no single issue that attracts recruits, but there often is a psychological response, related to loss of social status, lack of belief in the future, and a desire to 'do something' about changes in society that deeply affect people's lives."[4]

In an important way, HuT provides a release valve for the frustrations of thousands of young men in Central Asia who might otherwise be languishing on street corners looking for some action. Through their HuT membership, they have acquired a structured purpose in life based on a shared belief in an era of otherwise confusing and difficult change. At the same time, HuT helps the members believe that there will be opportunities for jobs and economic betterment. If the government pursues a stringent policy of repression of such groups committed to change by nonviolent means, dire consequences may ensue. As the International Crisis Group has noted: "If corruption and unemployment continue to grow and the police continue to terrorize people, then in place of state organs, underground anti-state structures will begin to emerge. This will happen not today, but when young people who have passed through underground education in the humiliating conditions of suppression of Islam and children whose fathers sit in prison mature politically. Then an explosive situation will arise."[5]

In March 2004, terrorist bombings in Tashkent and Bukhara clearly signaled that the grievances of Islamic groups were not to be taken lightly. A headline banner read, "3rd Day of Violence Claims 23 Lives in Uzbekistan."[6]

Twenty militants who had been arrested blew themselves up along with their police captors. Suicide bombings occurred for the first time. On several occasions women chased after police. The police then shot the women, who thereupon released the on-off bomb switches and were promptly blown into scattered body parts.

A newly minted group, the Islamic Jihad Group of Uzbekistan, claimed responsibility for the bombings on a Web site linked to al Qaeda.[7] Coming in the wake of the terrorist attack on the Madrid subway system, the Tashkent incidents were quickly labeled by journalists as part of a worldwide attack on governments sympathetic to American policies in the Middle East. In any event, repression of opposition groups has provided fertile ground for recruitment of militant forces in Uzbekistan.[8]

Then, in May 2005, massive violence in protest of the jailing of extremists erupted in the eastern city of Andizhan, resulting in several hundred deaths. The government identified the protesters as Islamic militants and fundamentalists who provoked the government's response as the president continued to enforce the policy to suppress all forms of dissent. While the international community waited for yet another "revolution" in the states of the former Soviet Union, at least initially the government showed little readiness to tolerate opposition to its policies.[9]

The arrival of more than fifteen hundred US Air Force and Special

Forces personnel at an American airbase established in southern Uzbekistan following the events of 9/11 may have triggered some of the anger. Many Uzbeks seeking additional income streams had welcomed the American logistical hub for supporting the campaign in Afghanistan. Yet others did not. The US and Uzbek governments trumpeted this demonstration of solidarity in the battles against Muslim militants, with the Tashkent government welcoming a broad legitimization of the policies of the country—and further frustrating disenfranchised opposition leaders. In this case, US security interests clearly trumped concerns over protection of human rights as the jails bulged with dissidents. And, indeed, it soon came to light that the US military had trained many of the security forces that were carrying out the suppressing of opposition groups.[10] The blatant crackdown on human rights following the Andizhan riots quickly led to the closing of the airbase.

Developments in Uzbekistan underscore that the character and role of Islam are highly dependent on the specific environment where Muslims live. In neighboring states, Islamist groups have different histories and play different roles in shaping the political and social lives of the populations. The efforts of Samuel Huntington and other academics to develop generic paradigms that help explain the role of Islam, as discussed earlier, are commendable, but they must be subjected to ground truth in the countries and regions of interest.

The Uzbekistan case also highlights the short-term and long-term interests of the United States—fighting terrorism today in Afghanistan while promoting political stability in Central Asia for tomorrow. The route to meet today's objective is far clearer than the road to tomorrow.[11]

Finally, a 2004 report from Egyptian scholar Khalid Medani highlights the lack of meaningful jobs as a common thread well beyond Uzbekistan's border that is driving young men toward militancy: "Islamic extremists were able to recruit followers to their organization through the establishment of Islamic welfare associations and the provision of social services, the use of local mosques to preach decidedly military religious sermons, and the use of mafia-like coercive tactics to find employment for young unemployed and underemployed men."[12]

Understanding four issues entwined within the preceding snapshot of developments in the strategically important Central Asian country of Uzbekistan are keys to appreciating the current global situation:

1. implications of rapid population growth
2. conflicting claims for limited land, water, and other natural resources
3. the nexus of poverty, unemployment, and terrorism
4. destabilizing influences of expanding international criminal networks

Insights into each of these areas help to explain the following depressing assessment of the staggering challenges facing the United States:

> Terrorists are plotting to attack the United States from bases in Afghanistan, Indonesia, and Somalia; steal weapons from Central Asian middlemen; raise money by dealing diamonds in West Africa or by shipping money across the Persian Gulf; and finance the schooling in extremism of young boys from the poorest Pakistani households. . . . Rich-country policies and corporate payoffs to corrupt local officials discredit global trade and investment rules, derailing trade agreements and limiting investments, thus depriving millions of opportunities to escape poverty. Global cynicism about America's intentions rises as famine and starvation raise their head again and again.[13]

TOO MANY PEOPLE IN TOO MANY PLACES

It was November 1969. Coffee followed a lavish dinner at a spacious Georgetown residence in Washington, DC. The men were preparing to retire to the veranda for cigars and talk. As usual, problems confronting the world would be on the agenda. The tradition called for the ladies to retreat to the parlor for a discussion of less heady topics—programs for their children and forthcoming meetings of their garden clubs. Remember, this was 1969, when women were still struggling to be heard.

The hostess suddenly interrupted these plans. She boldly announced to the men that the ladies were deeply interested in the topic of the day— control of the world's population growth. The protocol would be changed, and her husband was not to object. All would congregate in the living room.

As I took my place in a posture-perfect chair, a colleague from the US Agency for International Development (USAID) slouched on the couch next to me. Two knitting needles protruded from the inner pocket of his jacket. When jokingly asked whether he did sweaters or shawls, he replied, "Abortions." He was on a nonstop circuit of speech making about the dangers of overpopulation, with his grooved needles demonstrating the simple tools that people with no access to modern birth control methods resort to in desperation.

He was the US government's expert on reducing births in developing countries. He recited to the dinner guests a litany of out-of-control birthrates from around the world. Now that Congress was showering USAID with money, we could all relax, he added. It then became clear that the US government, working through USAID, was serious in its efforts to halt the spiraling growth of populations in a host of developing countries.

At that time, the international consensus was that on all continents beyond North America, Europe, and Australia, urgent and stringent control of population growth was essential. Otherwise hundreds of millions of new faces would quickly consume the inadequate food dividends from the successes of the Green Revolution. Other limits to growth were also of concern—contaminated drinking water, rampant diseases, energy shortfalls, and environmental pollution. They, too, were intimately linked to increasingly dense populations.

The logic for focusing on population control was simple: the more people, the fewer the resources per person, and the less desirable the living space for new arrivals. Of course, some countries needed additional labor to populate their vast territories. But overall, the world's upward birth curve had been so steep that population growth was widely perceived as a threat to life on the planet.

However, when the economists began to delve more deeply into the population issue, they had difficulty finding a good correlation between population growth in poor countries and declines in economic progress. Some experts contended that generalizations were flawed since population problems were country-specific, or even locale-specific. Yet all agreed that population growth needed urgent attention.

Other specialists tried to help the economists. The demographers pointed out that the youth bulge in some populations, the middle-age bulge in others, and the senior citizen bulge that eventually emerges in almost all populations had their pluses and minuses. For example, young brains and strong backs are needed to support a growing cadre of retirees who live longer. However, job experience cannot be instantly replaced, and critical senior personnel should be encouraged to postpone their departure from their professions. All the while, older populations require greater healthcare resources, thereby putting new financial pressure on societies.

The military analysts also entered the debate. Since jobs are often in short supply in economically depressed countries, idle youth will resort to violence, so the conversation went. Also, recruiters for mercenary units have good pickings where unemployment rates among the youth are high. As another military dimension to the discussion, families that had become convinced that fewer children should be the order of the day rebelled when military draft advocates tried to take their lone sons off to battle.

In some Islamic countries, population growth can be explosive. Countries such as Indonesia and Bangladesh are teeming with so many people that the economies have long been stretched beyond reasonable limits. Large foreign aid programs have provided some of the needed relief but also an unwelcome sense of dependence.

A number of crammed African countries are home to rapidly growing and restless Muslim populations. Nigeria, in particular, with a Muslim population of fifty-five million, has become a safe haven for extremist cells and an incubator of anti-Americanism. There, tens of thousands flock to rallies to protest American actions in Iraq and elsewhere, as they blame the Americans and the British for a lingering colonialist bondage in their own country. In other African countries where smuggled diamonds are the currency of terrorists, anti-American sentiments often run high, although the terrorist threat comes less from religion than from idleness, weak institutions, and corruption.[14]

One expert characterizes the Middle East and North Africa as a "long-term demographic nightmare." He predicts that the population will grow from 300 million in 2000 to 650 million in 2050. This growth will exhaust water supplies, force permanent dependence on food imports, and raise the size of the youth population aged fifteen to thirty from 88 million to 145 million. Unemployment already exceeds 25 percent for young males. Thus, an immense wave of future strains on social, educational, political, and economic systems is on the way.[15]

Underscoring how predictions about population trends are uncertain at best, however, another expert points out that the situation is improving thanks to the turnaround in childbearing in the Middle East during the 1990s. Birthrates have fallen in every Middle Eastern country, often dramatically. The resulting "middle aging" of the region should, in this expert's view, diminish the appeal of radicalism, since the population will be increasingly preoccupied with practical issues of inadequate health-care and invisible pensions.[16]

Fortunately, birthrates in many countries are tumbling. From 1975 to 2000, the average number of births per woman per lifetime fell in Indonesia from 5 to 2.5, in Pakistan from 7 to 4, in Nigeria from 7 to 5.5, in Egypt from 6.2 to 3.2, and in Iran from 6.5 to 2.2.[17] The solutions championed by the international community during the 1970s of family planning and educational efforts, a commitment to choice on the issue of abortion, and increased attention to improving the status of women have had impressive results. Developing countries that have lowered fertility and slowed population growth have witnessed higher productivity, more savings, and more productive investments. The population effect on economic growth is clear.[18]

In my frequent trips to Iran, I am repeatedly impressed by the slowly changing status of young women. In 2004 more than 60 percent of new university entrants were women. They simply work harder and receive higher test scores than young men. Even though the bulk of female graduates are expected to become mothers in short order, the women nevertheless increasingly enter the workforce and limit their family sizes accordingly. Indeed, the population statistics reflect a dramatic decline in fertility rates in Iran since the government reversed course after decades of advocacy of larger and larger families.

Of no less importance than the rate of population growth is the increasing concentration of the world's population in cities. By 2015 half of the world's population will be urban. The number of inhabitants in megacities—those fifteen or so cities with populations exceeding ten million—will double to more than four hundred million. Health, education, communication, and other services in many rural areas are so inadequate that even life in an urban ghetto is an improvement. Yet it is precisely in the teeming slums that the most talented "entrepreneurs" too often decide to use their skills and energy to recruit followers of causes hostile to society.

Related to urbanization is transborder migration, with legal and illegal migrants now accounting for more than 15 percent of the population in fifty countries. Migrants seek to move along the following paths:

- to North America, primarily from Latin America and East and South Asia
- to Europe, primarily from North Africa and the Middle East, South Asia, Eastern Europe, and Eurasia
- from the least to the most developed countries of Asia, Latin America, the Middle East, and sub-Saharan Africa[19]

These movements involve several million people annually. They increase social and political tensions and alter national identities. For the developing countries, the migrants who go abroad often relieve unemployment pressure and provide remittances back to their relatives. Also, some migrants will become advocates for policies of their new homelands that benefit their former countries; the Armenian American community that presses for high foreign-assistance levels for its country is a good example. However, many migrants have been among the most talented specialists of the developing countries and represent a substantial brain drain.[20]

As an important example of new migrations, well before the 2005 London subway bombings, European demographers were focusing on the increasing influence of Muslims in European politics. Their growing clout reflects Muslim enfranchisement in several important countries. For example, half of the six million Muslims in France, where the total population is fifty million, are now French citizens. In the year 2000, Germany, with its population of sixty million, began granting citizenship on the basis of place of birth rather than ancestry, and as a result the German-Turks are increasing by more than one hundred and sixty thousand annually. As the Muslim population of Europe doubles by 2015 and the non-Muslim population shrinks by 3.5 percent, the Muslim communities will surely become a potent political force.[21]

The world population will grow by 30 percent in the next twenty-five years. Some analysts take great comfort in a 30 percent increase, which is much better than other predictions of a 60 percent increase. Let us hope that in an increasing number of countries, the population level will stabilize as two-children families become the rule of the day. Already, reports indicate that fertility levels have dropped in more than eighty countries where 40 percent of the world's population lives.[22]

ENVIRONMENTAL SECURITY— PROTECTING STATE INTERESTS AND INDIVIDUAL WELL-BEING

Throughout history, the rights of individuals and of states to resources have been a top agenda item for kings, czars, dictators, and presidents the world over. Clashes over exploitation of fisheries have filled diplomatic agendas for centuries. Struggles over access to water in the Middle East have been common for as long as historians have studied the region. Most recently, Saddam Hussein's efforts to take over Kuwait's oil wells led to the Desert Storm campaign. Everyone wants a larger share of the limited resources of the planet—for consumption or for export earnings.

The Caspian Sea basin is a microcosm of large areas of the world that are plagued by such conflicts over natural resources. These conflicts undermine the interests of states. They devastate the lives of individuals. And, they occasionally trigger armed conflicts. With its broad international outreach, the United States often becomes involved in resource disputes, particularly when oil supplies are at stake.

Nevertheless, violent responses to attempted resource grabs other than land in the Caspian Sea basin and elsewhere have been rare in recent decades. In the basin, countries of the region challenge the claims of their neighbors to offshore oil deposits. They resist construction on the seabed of oil pipelines that could rupture. They protest uncontrolled poaching of the sturgeon stocks. They defend their shorelines from incursions by uninvited ships and unwanted migrants. They complain bitterly about beach pollution from upstream sources as well as oil spillage directly into the sea off the coast of Azerbaijan. All the while, the countries engage in extended negotiations to resolve such issues, often in vain. But those negotiations do usually temper violent reactions and help prevent armed conflict.

Such resource conflicts between the five littoral states of the Caspian Sea have intensified since the collapse of the Soviet Union in 1991. They have not yet led to provocative acts beyond an occasional flight by an unauthorized airplane over a neighbor's territory. Still, the disputes have increased political tensions among the countries.

Four of the states (Iran, Azerbaijan, Kazakhstan, and Turkmenistan) have predominantly Muslim populations while Russia has a significant Muslim community. However, the conflicts have little to do with religion. They are rooted in economic interests and secondarily in domestic and international political commitments to protect the environment according to the requirements of each country.

In 2001 I visited the Iranian coast at the southern end of the Caspian Sea. While touring the marshlands in a speedboat, I was surrounded by lush ecological prosperity and also by the telling tales of ecological destruction from fertilizer runoff. Then, as our craft sped toward the port of Rascht, the color of the sea blackened and marine pollution became painfully evident. The Iranian awareness of the sources and extent of pollution and wildlife destruction along the coast is chronicled in excellent reports by the environmental department of the government of Iran. However, describing environmental degradation is clearly easier than reversing it.[23]

At the sturgeon research center not far from the coast, Iranian scientists had given up hope that oil pollution from Azerbaijan's seabed wells would subside and that sturgeon poaching by all the northern neighbors would be brought under control. The oil tar on the bed of the sea was more than ten meters thick in many "dead" spots, and the sturgeon catch in the Caspian Sea had declined by 80 percent in a decade due to pollution and poaching. The scientists were raising Iranian sturgeon on their inland fish farms with the hope that the fry released into the sea would not travel northward to be "stolen" by others. Rather, the small sturgeon were to circulate in the southern part of the sea near the Iranian coast for a few years as they gradually gained weight and filled with eggs to become profitable caviar catches for Iranian fishermen.

The standoff in resolving serious resource disputes in the Caspian Sea basin causes many diplomatic problems. Yet the likelihood that any of the parties would resort to military actions to press their demands seems low. The US government has had a high profile in the region since the mid-1990s, with a principal motivation to continue asserting its interest in the region's oil. To this end, the United States has vigorously opposed (and distrusted) Iranian efforts to route oil exports from Kazakhstan to Iran, which in turn would export comparable amounts of oil through its southern terminus to Asian consumers.

In a broader geographical context, sharp disagreements over protection and management of natural resources often poison international relations and may even engender mistrust among neighboring states. The United States has had its problems with acid rain drifting into Canada and with western states reducing the Colorado River to a mere trickle of water left for Mexico. The pollution of the Black Sea has turned popular beach destinations in several countries into nearly deserted waterfronts. The death of the forests of the Czech Republic due to air pollutants from Germany in decades past was an unfortunate loss in the heart of Europe, although slow recovery is now under way. Logging of tropical forests in Latin America and Asia has caused dramatic changes in local climates and the erosion of soils along rivers that traverse a number of countries.

The immediately affected individuals—more so than government bureaucracies—are the predominant forces in defining the newly coined concept of *environmental security*. *Environmental security* means *personal* security that is dependent on the environment—both in health and in jobs—as well as security of a nation's resources. When threatened populations maintain pressure on their governments to retaliate against misbehavior of other states, the likelihood of international action increases significantly.[24]

Also, applying international pressure on governments to adopt resource management approaches that are geared to long-term sustainability of resources is achieved through the dozen or so international agreements requiring acceptable environmental policies (e.g., agreements on biodiversity, endangered species, transboundary pollution). A country's failure to comply with such obligations when it is a signatory to the treaties raises questions at international forums as to whether that country can be considered a trustworthy partner in broader contexts. Is a government that dodges its environmental commitments an appropriate participant in international programs, including foreign assistance programs?

The United States often interjects itself into disputes in developing countries over natural resources, sometimes arguing that it is simply helping to ensure enforcement of international agreements such as opposition to logging operations in Indonesia or destruction of marshlands in Central America. Regardless of international commitments, less well-endowed populations resent US preaching over how to manage resources that are thousands of miles from American shores.

Further exacerbating sensitivities of other countries to US advocacy of stringent environmental controls is the refusal of the United States to sign the hallmark international agreements on biodiversity and on global climate change—agreements developed during many years of diplomatic negotiations. The United States has strong scientific and economic reasons for not participating in these arrangements, but it is quite ironic that protecting species and reducing harmful pollutant emissions to the atmosphere are among the top priorities of American officials when discussing environmental issues with leaders of developing countries. This inconsistency is not lost on other governments.

By 2015 more than three billion people will live in countries that are considered to be without adequate water supplies—primarily in the Middle East, South Asia, northern China, and Africa. In developing countries, 80 percent of freshwater resources support agriculture, and a number of these countries are losing their ability to maintain irrigated agriculture at current levels. This development is particularly serious in grain-growing countries where a thousand tons of water are needed to produce one ton of grain.[25]

As to the likelihood of major interstate water conflicts, more than thirty countries receive more than one-third of their fresh water from outside their borders. A potential flash point, for example, is Turkey's program for building dams and irrigation projects that will limit water flows into Syria and Iraq, countries with growing populations. As a second case in point, Egypt is diverting water from the Nile River for its own use, but the Nile is fed by limited sources in Ethiopia and Sudan, which also plan to draw more water.[26]

A critical water-deficient area is the region encompassing Jordan,

Israel, and Palestine, where population growth, unsustainable agricultural practices, and pollution are stretching the limited resources toward the point of disaster. Of most immediate concern is the need for more intensive cooperation in regional water management, a continuing challenge for the three parties. A legal framework for such cooperation was developed in the mid-1990s, but the road to implementation of effective measures has been rocky indeed.[27]

The Palestinians, who are the most dependent on water-intensive agriculture, are literally at the bottom of the barrel, receiving a bare minimum above the per person quantity required for human sustainability. At the same time, Palestine has a population growth rate of about 4 percent. While the predominantly urban population of Israel has a well-developed water distribution infrastructure and receives water around the clock, it, too, has a substantial population growth rate: 3.5 percent. Meanwhile, the Jordanians, also with heavy dependence on agriculture, are overexploiting resources, resulting in significant lowering of groundwater levels and salination of freshwater aquifers.[28]

Of immediate consequence for the United States are, of course, the adequacy and stability of oil exports from the Middle East. Supply and price fluctuations regularly reverberate through stock markets everywhere. Complicating rational decisions by the Middle Eastern governments that dominate the Organization of Petroleum Exporting Countries (OPEC) is a widely held conviction that America's only real interest in the region is access to oil and that intervention in Iraq was driven by the goal of a takeover of Iraqi oil resources.

Sustained economic growth worldwide, along with population increases, is predicted to result in a 50 percent increase in energy demand during the next decade, and the demand for oil and gas will also likely double. With the Chinese economy coming on strong, Asia will replace North America as the top energy-consumption region. Perhaps as little as one-tenth of Persian Gulf oil will be directed to the West, with three-quarters going to Asia. Barring unforeseen circumstances, the Persian Gulf region will continue to be the world's principal source of oil exports, with gas exports coming primarily from both that region and Russia.[29]

Despite this growth in demand, "oil wealth" alone cannot sustain any Middle Eastern country except Qatar, the United Arab Emirates, and, possibly, Kuwait. In particular, as Saudi Arabia's population has grown, its per capita export earnings have declined by 80 percent in recent decades. As there seems to be no end in sight to population growth, this new economic situation poses daunting challenges for regime leaders who had become accustomed to much greater reliance on export earnings.

That said, it would appear that conflicts over natural resources mean only bad news for the United States. As oil demand starts to outpace supply, the United States could easily be perceived as having the single goal of greater control of oil supplies to serve its own needs first. However, this need not be the case.

There are many opportunities for the United States to contribute to the resolution of difficult resource issues, and particularly energy issues, not the least of which is greater energy conservation at home. It has technologies and experience that are in scarce supply in many countries facing resource difficulties. A willingness to share these assets in response to requests from other governments can have a profound effect on attitudes of populations that are being personally injured by poor resource-management policies.

THE NEXUS BETWEEN POVERTY
AND VIOLENCE

Early in his international terrorism career, Osama bin Laden found sanctuary in Somalia. Then he moved to Sudan. Finally he settled in Afghanistan. What did these three states have in common? Most simply, in the new jargon of foreign assistance agencies, they were "failed states." They failed to establish a system of governance that commands respect within and outside the country. They failed to develop their limited economic potential. They failed to protect their populations from either external threats or internal assaults.

These failures are not surprising, for these three countries have long been mired in poverty. The governments had difficulty providing food for their populations, let alone being able to guard their borders and root out bad elements within their populations. And as legitimatized by age-old practices, the rulers believed they had the right to keep for themselves or to distribute to the favored few the limited financial resources that were accumulated through agricultural exports, through illicit trade in narcotics, and through skimming off foreign assistance funds.

As discussed earlier, these and other poor countries have had checkered histories in dealing with foreign colonizers, invaders, and liberators. But once the military campaigns were over and these countries were on their own, they were largely ignored by the international community. For some time, they did not threaten other countries and they were simply bottomless sinks for foreign aid. Even when their populations were subjected to combinations of brutal repression and natural disasters, humanitarian aid packages were viewed as Band-Aids to patch things over until the next crisis.

Now, such benign neglect of the "no-hope" countries by the international community has changed to widespread fear. Most governments finally realize that failed states can become safe havens and recruiting grounds for terrorist organizations. Could the linkage between poverty and support for terrorism be any clearer?

All the while, academic theorists proclaim that poverty is not a "root cause" of terrorism. Terrorists are supposed to have political, and not economic, goals in mind. Many terrorists are well educated. But the "muscle" terrorists are often recruits who have had few advantages in life and who have few alternatives. Of course, terrorists do come from well-endowed regions of the world, as did bin Laden, but even in those areas income disparities often rile frustrated youth to turn to a profession of violence.

What is it like to live in poverty, with access to less than one dollar per day? Illiterate. Malnourished. Suffering from a debilitating disease. No land or capital. A victim of discrimination within your own society. This describes the life of one billion people around the world. Then there are the next two billion people with access to two dollars per day. Few have jobs that offer any hope for the future. But a large number have access to television, a medium that shows them life's other possibilities.

It is unlikely that a large percentage of impoverished people in distant countries could in the near future ally themselves with better-equipped, organized groups in mounting assaults on America. Yet if only 1 percent (an army of thirty million people) were inspired to action, however feeble, the threat would be formidable. The combination of idle hands and television broadcasts of both the good life in America and the reasons to hate America is molding hostile attitudes with serious implications.

In addition, many American interests can suffer from the steady drumbeat of global poverty. For example:

- More than 40 percent of American exports go to developing countries, and poverty in these countries prevents the growth of American markets.
- Poverty and infectious diseases go hand in hand—diseases that do not respect international boundaries and increasingly find their way to the United States.
- Many poor countries are prone to violence, as we have seen in Rwanda, Somalia, and Sudan. Hundreds of millions of dollars from the US Treasury are allocated directly and indirectly each year in responding to humanitarian appeals in the wake of violent outbreaks in such countries.
- Persistent poverty is threatening the environmental carrying capacity of the earth. This includes inefficient use of energy and other natural resources, destruction of agricultural productivity, and irreversible contamination of water and soil resources.[30]

In short, if unattended, global poverty will surely stifle America's economic growth, gradually destroy much of the world's environment, and even incubate hotbeds of anti-Americanism. The argument that terrorists—both rich and poor—are motivated only by political agendas and not by economic betterment of their lot contradicts reality. Of course, economic poverty is but one aspect of the roots of terrorism, which are intertwined with religious, ethnic, social, and political motivations as well.

Poverty might be best described as a "conditioner" of attitudes that prompts groups to resort to violence in response to specific grievances. In some cases, poverty alone may be reason enough to take to the streets in anger. However, when America is in the bull's-eye of protest, a political *and* an economic agenda are inevitably on the table. Just as America's compass points toward economic self-interest, so is the terrorist's needle in search of a greater sharing of the bounties of the planet.

The agendas of groups that resort to violence aimed at American interests lead directly to certain US policies. These policies, when viewed through the lens of the aggrieved, can easily be described as discriminatory. The documentation held up by the "discriminated" to support their accusations highlights the never-ending compilation of media photos and images depicting the miserable living conditions of their brethren in the hellholes of the earth—with the "good life" in America serving as the baseline in measuring the degree of discrimination. While the United States cannot assume responsibility for the adverse impacts of unfavorable geographies, we can initiate policies to assist developing countries in overcoming their plight. This action would immediately contribute to helping establish positive images of America.

In many states, environmental degradation has often been a precursor of violence. For example, lying behind problems in Darfur, Sudan, are two decades of steady depletion of soil productivity due to extended drought and poor land management. Arab nomads have moved to the south in search of habitable lands, some plundering the areas. In the Philippines, uncontrolled deforestation has transformed groups of unemployed workers into insurgents. In Pakistan, degraded croplands force poor farmers to move to the city of Karachi, where shortages and lack of clean water spark violent outbreaks. Thus, environmentalists were thrilled when Wangari Maathai, a Kenyan activist who spearheaded the planting of millions of trees, was awarded the Nobel Peace Prize in 2004.[31]

Underscoring Maathai's results-oriented methods, Geoffrey D. Dabelko identifies preventive action as a critical factor in reducing the likelihood of conflicts rooted in environmental degradation: "Instead of merely reacting to the symptoms of environment-conflict linkages, policy makers should proactively extinguish hotspots by bolstering confidence and building cooperation."[32]

As the global population continues its upward trajectory with 95 percent of the growth in developing countries, there will be a working-age population bulge in many poor areas of the world. In principle, these new hands could provide a great stimulus for global economic growth. But if jobs are not created, the potential for instability, conflict, and assaults on America will only grow.

Again, the correlation between poverty and threats to America could not be clearer. The United States simply cannot hermetically seal itself off from activities in even the most remote states. Weak states where poverty reigns can infect their neighbors with instability. For example, former

Liberian leader Charles Taylor stirred up trouble in Sierra Leone, Ivory Coast, and Guinea. And such despots can threaten a wide range of American interests, which are easily disrupted by conflicts even in distant lands.

INTERNATIONAL CRIME SYNDICATES TARGET AMERICA

No description of the international landscape, which is fueling attitudes toward America, is complete without consideration of the rapidly growing networks of international criminals.

Three years before 9/11, we described the intersections of drug smuggling, money laundering, and international terrorism in *Superterrorism: Assassins, Mobsters, and Weapons of Mass Destruction*.[33] We offered suggestions for intercepting terrorist plots in their early stages and for hardening targets in the United States to withstand their assaults. We warned about the intensive search by international terrorists for technologies that would let them construct their own weapons of mass destruction. And we highlighted how gangsters were laundering tens of billions of dollars through international outposts with the goal of making money by wreaking harm on Americans—particularly schoolchildren who succumb to the temptations of harmful narcotics.

We called for new policies and programs of the US government. Dramatic improvements in intelligence gathering and analysis were at the top of the list. An aggressive counterterrorism role for NATO, which was and still is searching for a well-defined mission, was close behind. The need for stronger measures to reduce corruption among law enforcement personnel both in developing countries and in the United States was highlighted. And a greatly expanded *jobs-first* approach to foreign assistance was singled out as the most important long-term strategy that should be adopted—a strategy designed to win hearts and minds as well as to stimulate economic growth. While we have suffered two massive attacks on the structural icons of America, there is still time to follow the road of broader engagement with populations around the world in need of jobs as the path to a brighter future. Facilitating the creation of jobs abroad will in time pay dividends through more security for America and more international demand for America's export products.[34]

Unfortunately, since 2001, the criminal networks with eyes on America have grown in number and determination. Here is a prediction from America's premier intelligence organization about the future:

> Transnational criminal organizations will become increasingly adept at exploiting the global diffusion of sophisticated information, financial, and transportation networks. They will form loose alliances with one another. They will corrupt leaders of unstable, economically fragile, or failing states; insinuate themselves into troubled banks and businesses; and cooperate with insurgent political movements to control substantial geographic areas. Their income will come from narcotics trafficking; alien smuggling; trafficking in women and children; smuggling toxic materials, hazardous wastes, illicit arms, military technology, and other contraband; financial fraud; and racketeering.[35]

The principal drug trafficking routes that are the lifelines of international criminal organizations and therefore should be of most immediate concern to the United States continue to be the cocaine trails from South America to the United States. They lead through many porous barriers from the Pacific Ocean to Puerto Rico. Yet much of the world's attention has shifted to Afghanistan and the heroin routes to Russia and to Western Europe.

In reality, the United States now "owns" Afghanistan, even though the United Nations tries hard to put an international umbrella over the country. While the role of drug eradication had been assigned to the United Kingdom, the United States couldn't stay out of the fray and has its own parallel program. Why hasn't it been possible to curtail production of opium poppy and reduce the flow? After all, it was the Taliban that promoted the export of heroin, and now their era appears to have ended.

But this analysis is far too simplistic. First, the Taliban certainly promoted drug trafficking and benefited enormously from the profits. Yet they were also able to reduce poppy growing when the international pressure mounted or when the growers threatened to step out of line. Yes, repression occasionally works for the better.

Recent American efforts to encourage farmers to abandon their poppy fields have had little success. Alternative crop production has not worked.

The profit margins realized in converting harvests from the poppy fields into heroin on the streets of Amsterdam are simply too hard to match. Also, the American-backed government of Afghanistan has not been able to crack down effectively on the heroin trade. In fact, the flows of heroin reached an all-time high by 2005.

In examining trade routes, take as an example Tajikistan—a poor country that has gained great strategic importance in recent years. This former republic of the USSR has seven million inhabitants who overwhelmingly embrace the Muslim religion. The country is nestled on the northern border of Afghanistan, with Kyrgyzstan and Uzbekistan as its other neighbors. It is on a direct line between the poppy fields of Afghanistan and lucrative markets in Russia and Europe.

Since the disintegration of the USSR in 1991, the United States has tried to help the country dig out of the hole of poverty—poverty due to miniscule annual incomes measured in hundreds of dollars. The abundant mineral resources in the mountains are not easily accessible and the distance to markets is long. To add to the country's woes, droughts in recent years have crippled agricultural production.

Economic deprivation has opened the gates to anyone with money, and the drug smugglers are on the march. With them have come violent crime, increased rates of HIV/AIDS, and massive economic inequities within the country. Can the Americans be blamed? Since they are perceived as the *real* governors of Afghanistan, they are of course blamed. Washington says the Russian army units still in Tajikistan aggravate the problem.[36] But the Russian units are so thinly staffed with Russians that they hire locals to fill out the ranks. They at least provide a few jobs and they speak a familiar language.

A final example of gangsters fueling turmoil comes from Kenya. In 1986 it took fifteen cows to buy an AK-47 in Kenya. By 2001 the price had fallen to five cows. The price reflected a dramatic increase in the availability of small arms. Power once vested in village elders now belongs to young men with guns.[37] Kenya is a country where the United States has for years been attempting to instill a degree of security and stability. It is the country where terrorists carried out a devastating attack on the American Embassy in Nairobi in 2000.

THE CHALLENGE FOR AMERICA

The problems of population growth and the misuse of natural resources, compounded by pervasive poverty and rampant criminal activity, have kept many countries from moving forward, economically or politically. In the view of hundreds of millions of people, the United States has unfairly become the de facto superintendent of the global commons and thus is expected to solve global problems. The United States has no choice but to adopt a more compassionate view of the lives of others through words and actions. We must adopt a less militaristic role in directing world affairs while we step up our support for international victims of earthquakes and other natural disasters. Only then will the United States be able to counter the growing conviction that military power—from stealth bombers to Kalashnikov rifles—is the way of the twenty-first century and that all the problems leading to the decay of the planet can be traced back to Washington.

As eloquently stated by President Pervez Musharraf of Pakistan, the United States can help in the struggle with poverty. But first Muslims must raise themselves up through individual achievement in their quest for socioeconomic emancipation. Of course, he laments, Muslims are among the poorest, most uneducated, most powerless, and most disunited people of the world. He warns that political injustice combined with stark poverty and illiteracy make for an explosive mix. These lethal ills lead to the propagation of militancy and to extremist terrorist acts. They are cannon fodder in the struggle against terrorism.[38]

Nevertheless, the United States should not be expected to shoulder alone the burden of international peace and stability. As Musharraf has said, the low-income countries must be their own drivers of development. Indeed, America's adversaries may believe that their interests are best served by Americans simply staying home.

Given political, economic, and security realities, only US leadership, in genuine partnership with local leaders around the world, can point toward a more hospitable planet for all nations. As governments and populations in less fortunate countries try to strengthen their muscles to escape from the burden of geographic oppression, the United States can help. How this help is fashioned to serve both US interests and those of the wider world is our primary challenge.

CHAPTER 3

UNDERSTANDING TODAY AND ANTICIPATING TOMORROW

★ ★ ★ ★ ★ *Why Doesn't the US Government Get It?*

When newly appointed secretary of state Colin Powell arrived at the Department of State in January 2001, he was mobbed by civil servants and foreign service officers. They welcomed him with firm handshakes, promising to fully support him. They were convinced that he would return the department to its previous position at the captain's bridge and again steer the foreign policy of the United States. In the preceding years, the department had lost much of its policy leadership role to the Department of Treasury, the Department of Defense, the Department of Energy, and other departments. Secretary Powell was just the person to resurrect the primacy of the Department of State.

For two years, the new secretary stood tall—within the department, in Washington venues, and in foreign capitals. He had his arms around the issues. He understood the interests of other countries. He appreciated the importance of thinking both strategically and tactically. And, of course, he had the ear of the president, at least initially. The retired general hypnotized members of Congress, he reduced critics in the press corps to lone voices with no listeners, and he dazzled the American public. When Colin Powell spoke, people paid attention and they acted in accordance with his advice.

During my single personal encounter with Secretary Powell in March 2002, I found him to be remarkably well informed and enlightened as to *long-term* US interests. We discussed expansion of US-Iran scientific exchanges, although the timing could not have been worse for garnering US support for such programs. The cleric-led government was putting down protests on several university campuses over restrictions on expressing political dissent. Meanwhile, CNN was reporting new allegations by the international community about Iran's support of terrorism. Also, authoritative evidence concerning Tehran's efforts to obtain nuclear weapons had just appeared in the press.

Under these circumstances, it was far from clear why the United States should share its scientific wherewithal with a regime with such unacceptable internal and foreign policies. Yet Powell's reaction when hearing about proposed new exchanges between the United States and Iran was affirmative. "Such programs are a terrific idea," he responded with considerable enthusiasm. "We have our problems with Iran today, but we must look to the future. And the scientists will play a key role in the transformation of the country."

THE BLUNDER AT THE UNITED NATIONS

In February 2003, Colin Powell made one of the few blunders in his otherwise fine career of public service. But this was a huge blunder: he made the case for the existence of weapons of mass destruction (WMD) in Iraq to the United Nations. The repercussions from this presentation will continue for years to come. The political fallout from the episode promises long-term debilitating effects on multilateral approaches to promoting peace and stability, on US relations with Muslim countries, and on America's global image.

President Bush chose Powell to make the case to the public that Iraq posed an immediate threat to the United States and to the world. Powell had, in fact, participated in key White House discussions of the evidence—which, to some, was less than convincing and perhaps was presented to Powell in a devious manner—that Iraq had ready-to-use weapons of mass destruction. There he listened to CIA director George Tenet advise the president that making the case of the Iraqi threat would be a "slam dunk." When the president called upon Secretary Powell to present the evidence in New York—in preference to Secretary of Defense Donald Rumsfeld or National Security Advisor Condoleezza Rice—Powell dutifully accepted the challenge to speak for the administration about the purported imminent danger.[1]

The fault for Powell's misstep may well have rested with others, but he had to take responsibility, even if he was snookered. At the United Nations, he used his talent, his popularity, and his charisma to mislead—knowingly or unknowingly—the assembled representatives of many governments as well as an American television audience concerning the military threat from Baghdad. There, in front of dozens of cameras that beamed his speech around the world, he made the following assertions:

- We know from sources that an Iraqi missile brigade outside Baghdad dispersed rocket launchers with warheads containing biological warfare agents to various locations.
- We have first-hand descriptions of biological weapons factories on wheels and on rails, and we know that Iraq has at least seven of these mobile biological agent factories.
- Saddam Hussein has the wherewithal to develop smallpox-laden weapons.
- We have a human source who corroborated that movement of chemical weapons occurred at an Iraqi site.
- Iraq today has a stockpile of between 100 and 500 tons of a chemical weapons agent.
- Saddam Hussein has made repeated covert attempts to acquire high-specification aluminum tubes. Experts who have analyzed the tubes in our possession agree that they can be adapted for centrifuge use.[2]

However, the world soon knew that CIA director Tenet, who supplied this analysis, was wrong, dead wrong, in his view on weapons of mass destruction being hidden in Iraq. Even if Powell had reservations about the evidence, he had repeated the false allegations in a manner that supported the zealous reliance on this distorted evidence by those around the president. Since then, criticism has been escalating, as exemplified by the following statement by Kenneth M. Pollack, former CIA analyst and member of the National Security Council staff: "The intelligence community overestimated the scope and progress of Iraq's WMD programs. The administration stretched those estimates to make a case not only for going to war but for doing so at once."[3]

While at the time Powell may have thought that he was being honest and forthcoming in his assessment of the threat of weapons of mass destruction, his fiery words gradually unraveled. Within a year, he had become discredited in the eyes of many governments as a reliable spokesman of the facts. The skeptics quickly assumed that his future statements, or, indeed, statements of any US government spokesperson, would be simply fabrications designed to support US policies.

Colin Powell made three fatal mistakes in preparing his remarks for delivery at the United Nations. First, he ignored much of the advice of his own skeptical analysts within the Department of State who warned about faulty intelligence—the distorted intelligence that was being fed to the president. He did take some of his staff's advice and declined to repeat allegations of the CIA and some administration officials that Iraq was seeking uranium ore from Africa. But he did *not* heed other reservations of his analysts.[4]

At the same time, credit should be given to the analysts at the Department of State for daring to challenge the views of hundreds of experts in the fourteen other government intelligence organizations. The department's analysts were accustomed to thinking outside the box, particularly when firm facts inside the box were sparse. They simply would not accept a flawed product of "groupthink," a disease that has long plagued the intelligence community.[5]

Groupthink has been described as "a process in which a group can make bad or irrational decisions as members of the group attempt to conform their individual opinions to what they believe to be the consensus of the group—they do this by examining few alternatives, gathering information selectively, responding to pressure to conform with the group or withhold criticism, and collectively rationalizing the situation."[6] In this particular case, a very large "group" of intelligence analysts seemed bent on showing senior officials how they could document assertions that were dominating the Washington political scene, dismissing sources with contrary views as either deliberate liars or poorly informed.[7]

Powell's second mistake was relying on highly questionable sources for the information he presented: an Iraqi chemical engineer, an Iraqi civil engineer, an Iraqi major, an Iraqi in a position to know, an Iraqi eyewitness, and an Iraqi military officer. Did he really know anything about those sources? Obviously he did not know enough. Most turned out to be unreliable dissidents who were determined to discredit Saddam Hussein so that they or their friends could join with the US military forces as the Americans took over the reins in Baghdad. As Walter Pincus of the *Washington Post* put it, these sources were not concerned as to whether they were completely accurate in their stories as long as they were convincing as to the evil intentions of Saddam Hussein.[8]

The CIA analyst who was the only American to have interviewed the key source for the story of the mobile biological weapon laboratories had attempted to set the record straight as to the "smoking gun" that was soon to be unveiled by Powell. The analyst had repeatedly alerted his supervisor that the source, code-named Curve Ball, was an unreliable drunkard. He then pointed out that the corroborating sources were known to be fabricators. But his supervisor told him that no one was interested as to whether Curve Ball knew what he was talking about. And, as it turns out, Curve Ball didn't.[9]

Finally, Colin Powell turned to the British intelligence services to buttress his case without an adequate check on the reliability of *their* sources. Indeed, the international exchange of intelligence information had become so frantic that source reliability became unimportant. At the United Nations, Powell stated in support of his case, "The fine paper that the United Kingdom distributed yesterday describes in exquisite detail Iraqi deception activities." In short order, alert British journalists reported that much of the contents of the paper were simply lifted from a ten-year-old article in the journal *Middle East Review of International Affairs*. "Wasn't this assessment a little out of date?" they asked.[10]

Compounding his misstep at the United Nations, for more than one year Colin Powell refused to acknowledge that he was wrong and that he had misled the American people and the international community. Perhaps he was simply too loyal a soldier to admit an error that was largely the fault of others. However, such an admission of error, when the real facts became clear, surely would have been the wise course in promoting the interests of the United States. Instead, the inaccuracies of the story unfolded through the testimonies and writings of on-the-ground inspectors, initially dispatched by the United Nations and then by the United States. Soon an array of outspoken US government insiders also challenged the conventional wisdom prevalent in the intelligence community.[11]

It is indeed regretful that in some ways Powell became the personification of what went wrong with US governmental decision making at the turn of the twenty-first century. This approach gave short shrift to those in Washington and within other governments whose assessments of threats to international security differed significantly from White House views. As a consequence, the faulty basis for intervening in Iraq certainly incited unprecedented resentment toward America in dozens of Muslim countries and seriously undermined US credibility around the globe.

America now faces the challenge of regaining the respect and, in many cases, the trust of others. Efforts to transform the hostile views of America's opponents to more favorable attitudes require candor and forthrightness in governmental pronouncements. When facts are blurred, government officials should not substitute their own versions of the story. Of course, governments must often make judgments on the basis of a paucity of factual information about developments abroad. Yet official statements should be clearly and appropriately qualified. Misleading or deceptive statements are unacceptable.

A special challenge is to gather intelligence that will support both defensive and offensive actions to thwart plots of terrorism. The task requires a far better understanding of the roots of discontent underlying the hatred preached by Osama bin Laden and others of his ilk. Only then will America be able to design and implement effective policies and programs to reduce animosities that if unchecked could lead to more devastating consequences.

BETTER INTELLIGENCE FOR BETTER NEAR-TERM DECISIONS

Other intelligence failures with enormous international consequences illustrate extensive weaknesses in the US intelligence infrastructure prior to 9/11. For example, the United States failed to detect preparations for

India's testing of five nuclear warheads in 1999. The oft-cited reason for the failure was the ability of Indian specialists to cleverly conceal their massive activities in the Rajasthan Desert. Every three days, when an American reconnaissance satellite passed over the testing area, all equipment was out of sight. By working in three-day spurts, India was able to deceive the world, according to this theory.

Having spent five years as a participant in carrying out nuclear tests for the US Department of Energy in the Nevada desert, I have difficulty accepting this explanation. The number of vehicles, the sprawling lattice-work of cables, and the large size of the specialized equipment would have been difficult to conceal. Perhaps there are many tunnels in the terrain surrounding the Indian test site where the equipment could have been quickly hidden, and perhaps hundreds of Indians equipped with graders and rakes constantly smoothed new indentations in the sand. But as detonation time approaches, especially at a facility where testing has been in abeyance for many years, the overall levels of all types of activity at the facility and in the surrounding areas increase dramatically. There should have been many clues of the impending tests.

Whatever the reason for the intelligence breakdown in detecting test preparations that could have led to international political pressure on India to forestall the tests, the CIA decided to reorganize various offices following the intelligence lapse. The reorganization was intended to reduce the likelihood of repetition of this type of intelligence miss. However, one cannot help but become cynical about such restructuring when the new structure included promotions for several key CIA officials who purportedly had been responsible for the intelligence breakdown.[12]

Two other intelligence errors during the late 1990s further underscored the serious long-term impact that mistakes could have on the world's opinion of the United States. As part of the NATO air campaign against Serbian aggression, the US Air Force erroneously bombed the Chinese embassy in Belgrade—a mistake based on use of out-of-date maps. Clearly, this did not sit well with Beijing. Also, in northern Africa, US Navy missiles fired from afar destroyed an aspirin factory in Sudan that was mistakenly identified by American intelligence as a facility for producing chemical weapons. This error was widely resented not only in Sudan but in many neighboring countries as well.

Mistakes happen. But if the hair triggers controlling American firepower were relaxed, it should be possible to reduce the frequency of mistakes. Despite the temptation to fire back immediately when attacked, more deliberate assessment of intelligence information that avoids mistakes in times of crises can reduce the likelihood of creating even more enemies of the United States.

Following 9/11, the calls for reform of the American intelligence services were loud and determined. They certainly resulted in dramatic increases in budgets for various government agencies. New contracts were negotiated with computer firms to help "fuse" information available to different agencies. Elaborate schemes were devised to "connect the dots" whenever there were enough information-laden dots to connect. Unfortunately, as we have seen, the admonitions for better intelligence did not improve judgments concerning the threat of weapons of mass destruction in Iraq.

Of special concern has been the atrophy of HUMINT, or HUMan INTelligence capabilities. HUMINT involves agents on the ground in dangerous environments, penetration of hostile organizations, and working with defectors. While the massive communication-intercept systems and reconnaissance satellite systems of the United States have been working efficiently, former CIA director Tenet and others have repeatedly underscored that interpreting cryptic messages and analyzing snapshots from space in the absence of on-the-scene HUMINT confirmation provide incomplete and sometimes misleading information.[13]

The 9/11 Commission established by Congress to investigate the intelligence lapses that contributed to the success of the terrorist attacks on 9/11 brought an unprecedented degree of public scrutiny to the workings of the intelligence community. The commission listed ten missed opportunities for the intelligence agencies to uncover components of the 9/11 plot, such as the neglect of information concerning flight training of al Qaeda pilots in the United States. The public testimony of the CIA and FBI intelligence analysts, together with reports based on hundreds of interviews, exposed to the unforgiving lights of television the limitations on America's ability to acquire and interpret reliable information both from abroad and from within the United States.[14]

The testimony before the commission also underscored the importance of steps under way to improve the situation—particularly efforts to recruit intelligence analysts with expertise in the geographic areas of concern. Even so, the small number of intelligence specialists with Arabic language skills is still troubling. Cross-assignments of specialists from one agency to another were put into place to address a second key weakness, namely, the lack of coordination among government agencies.

The three commission recommendations that received the greatest attention in Washington were the following organizational "fixes":

1. The president, with the concurrence of the Senate, should establish the position of an intelligence czar, who would act cooperatively with, but independently of, the CIA. This recommendation was accepted, and a director of intelligence is now in place.
2. The Congress should consolidate the responsibilities of its many committees involved in intelligence oversight. This recommendation has been more difficult to implement.
3. The Counterterrorism Center, which coordinates collection and analysis of terrorism-related intelligence, should be moved from the CIA to an independent organization subordinate to the intelligence czar, and the center should have new authority to establish intelligence collection tasks. While the center was moved, the extent of its authority quickly became controversial.

In sum, the dangers posed by terrorism have finally become the top priority of intelligence collectors and analysts.

A number of successes in containing al Qaeda were recorded by the US intelligence community shortly after 9/11, particularly in Pakistan. Why was there a sudden upsurge in successes when prior to 9/11 the CIA was largely a bystander in the country? A former CIA operative stationed in Pakistan wrote in August 2001:

> Westerners cannot visit the cinder-block, mud-brick side of the Muslim world—from whence bin Laden's foot soldiers mostly come—without announcing who they are. No case officer stationed in Pakistan can penetrate either the Afghan communities in Peshawar or the Northwest Frontier's numerous religious schools and seriously expect to gather

useful information—let alone recruit foreign agents. A US official overseas, photographed by and registered with local intelligence and security services, can't travel much, particularly in a police-rich country like
Pakistan, without the host services knowing about it. American intelligence has not gained and will not gain Pakistan's assistance in pursuit
of bin Ladin. . . . And non-official cover officers (NOCs) haven't really
changed since the Cold War. We're still a group of fake businessmen
who live in big houses overseas. . . . Operations that include diarrhea as
a way of life don't happen.[15]

Clearly the operating environment in Pakistan changed dramatically after
2001. The massive American presence in Afghanistan had an enormous
influence in eliciting Pakistani support of US intelligence operatives—
from the president down through the ranks of the Pakistani intelligence
services. The local officials simply did not know which American shoe
would drop next. They certainly didn't want to be on the receiving end of
an American military offensive in uncontrolled parts of their country.

In addition, the US intelligence community became less risk-averse.
After a decade of trying to avoid casualties among its covert operatives at
all costs, the CIA and the Department of Defense again recognized that
important clandestine operations are inherently dangerous—and necessary.

While much attention has focused on al Qaeda, the CIA was quick to
recognize that it was not the only immediate terrorist threat that must be
addressed. Whether inspired by al Qaeda or born solely from their own
roots, many other terrorist groups consider the United States as Islam's
greatest foe. Some of these groups are just as extremist and just as well
equipped as al Qaeda, according to the CIA.[16]

For example, the CIA has long believed that small international
extremist groups have spun off from al Qaeda. They operate throughout
the Middle East and elsewhere. A second level of threat comes from yet
smaller local groups with domestic agendas. Sometimes they work with
international terrorist organizations interested in their countries. These
groups are not necessarily creatures of bin Laden. They usually have
autonomous leadership, they pick their own targets, and they plan their
own attacks. However, they, too, are focused on the heartland of America
as their ultimate objective.[17] The bombings in Bali, Istanbul, Madrid,

London, Egypt, and elsewhere certainly seem to confirm this assessment, which poses daunting problems for the intelligence community.

Added to this challenge are the concerns of the Defense Intelligence Agency (DIA) of the Department of Defense, which has a broad charter to collect and analyze intelligence of military significance. The DIA has emphasized the importance of intelligence about activities in "ungoverned spaces" that terrorists use as their bases of operations. The southern Philippines, remote Indonesian islands, rural areas of Burma, and still-unknown hideaways in Africa and South America are examples of such areas. Ungoverned spaces include enclaves in densely populated cities, perhaps the most difficult environments to penetrate. Presumably the agency intends to increase surveillance of activities in all of these locations—a tall order indeed.[18]

Given these new perspectives, the scramble for more money and more people is on. The US Congress suddenly has become very receptive to requests for larger budgets for intelligence activities, which have grown to more than $40 billion annually. Indeed, Congress is very loose with the pocketbook when its members run scared. Make no mistake: Congress has become truly fearful that new intelligence breakdowns will allow additional attacks on the mainland of the United States.

In keeping with past tradition, the intelligence agencies always seek funds for new technologies, even if the payoffs from such expenditures are difficult to forecast. Espionage agencies have listening devices from football-field size to pinhead dimensions, but they want more. Communications among spies have shifted from radio transmissions to quick-burst electronic signals bounced off satellites, but the systems need fine-tuning. Digital cell phones and underground fiber cables complicate the interception of foreign messages, thus penetrating these communications is a priority. But, as noted, sophisticated technology without agents on the ground and trained analysts to interpret acquired data is not sufficient to protect the United States.

Despite the changes implemented after 9/11, the US government nonetheless continues to damage its reputation with intelligence failures and biased reports. One example of a US government report that seriously undermined the credibility of America was released in April 2004. The Department of State issued its annual report, *Patterns of Global Ter-*

rorism, which blacklists terrorist organizations around the world and cat-
alogs terrorist incidents during the previous year. The department
announced a sharp decline in incidents in 2003 and proudly trumpeted the
achievements of the administration in addressing the terrorist threat.

Without delay, however, congressional staffs uncovered errors in the
report. The number of incidents was actually much higher than reported.
Charges were made by Democratic politicians of manipulation of the data to
boost the image of the administration in an election year. Voices from abroad
attacked the entire report as yet another display of arrogance of the US government. And even more damaging, some foreign critics argued that certain
US military actions in Iraq should also be cataloged as acts of terrorism.

In June 2004, the State Department released a revised version of the
report, showing that the number of worldwide terrorist incidents had
indeed substantially increased rather than decreased in 2003. The CIA
accepted responsibility for the errors. The agency blamed antiquated
computer facilities and personnel shortages. The CIA vowed to fix the
system to prevent future blunders, reviewing all aspects of the system—
the computer programs, the interagency process for recording incidents,
and the quality control over the process.[19]

The Department of State and the CIA vehemently denied that the
administration had applied pressure to distort the figures in the original
report. However, they did not mention the key issues in preparing annual
reports on global terrorism when they vowed to establish a better system
for generating data. These issues are

- the vague and controversial definitions of terrorist organizations
  and terrorist incidents
- the reliability of sources of information that are used in characterizing terrorist organizations and in counting incidents
- the uncertainties in the weights given to different types of sources
  (e.g., defectors, open publications, clandestine agent reports, etc.)
- the rigor of the procedures for resolving differences among the
  assessments of different government agencies

In 2005 the Department of State released the next version of its
assessment but this time decided to omit statistics on the grounds that the

data were flawed. To an aggressive press, this tactic seemed designed to hide the fact that the United States was losing the struggle with terrorism despite President Bush's repeated declarations of victory after victory. Several weeks later, the National Counterterrorism Center released its own data that showed a dramatic increase in the number of terrorist incidents, but the Department of State continued to exude optimism over the prospects for success in the "war on terror."[20]

What will be the roles of spies in the decades ahead? What types of espionage can help increase the quality and quantity of information available for decision making at the top levels of government departments and for preparing essential reports? Will clandestine intelligence collection continue to be a cloistered activity, immune from all but the most pro forma oversight and decoupled from other information-gathering activities?

Spying reached its zenith during the Cold War. In future years, with so many types of threats coming from so many different directions and orchestrated by so many different groups, there will surely be a resurgence of spying. The country with the best information will continue to have advantages, not only in attacking the new battlefields of terrorism but also during trade negotiations and other diplomatic interactions where insights into opponents' objectives and tactics are crucial.

Internationally, it makes sense to increase intelligence sharing as countries mobilize against the threat of terrorism. The circuits leading to Interpol and other international organizations equipped to help track down unsavory characters are surely overloaded already. However, many governments are not willing to share some of their sensitive information with others.

Nevertheless, expanded data sharing is vital. Greater attention must be devoted by all countries to ensure that the level of confidence in the accuracy of shared information is made explicit. The US government has much to offer in data exchanges. But it must convince governments skeptical of US motivations that its information is valid and that shared information will not be misused.

A long-running debate in Washington has centered on the advisability of analyzing publicly available information, often referred to as *open-source* information. For example, is information on the Internet a treasure trove of intelligence information or simply volumes of unsubstantiated data and conjecture? At present, in the search to uncover information concerning military tactics, the Internet probably leads to no more than 1 percent of the information of importance, according to one estimate.[21] As to discerning political and economic trends, the percentage is undoubtedly much higher, given the extensive information now being posted by government departments and respected scholars.

Occasionally, Internet information helps in near-term threat assessments. A highly publicized case involved the Web site of a group of priests in a monastery in Kosovo. During the height of military confrontations there in the late 1990s, these priests posted on their site each day the latest movements of Serbian troops on the roads that they could view from the monastery. The extent to which the anti-Serbian forces benefited from this information is not clear, but this Web site demonstrated that in one case, parties in the midst of violence were able to provide important information even when military operations were already under way. However, this has been an exceptional situation—at least until wireless Internet connections become more commonplace and roadside watches become easier to organize.

Open-source information should be used for establishing starting points for mounting expensive covert collection efforts. Yet historically, many government analysts do not take such information seriously. If the information is not marked "secret," then too often it is considered of questionable relevance. Despite this skepticism, however, open sources often provide the most reliable predictions for long-term assessments of the future.[22]

Intelligence agencies will continue to perform especially well in dealing with immediate threats—the whereabouts of foreign troops, indicators of preparations for terrorist attacks, activities of international criminals, and transit routes of drug traffickers. Other organizations, within and outside governments, will often be more important sources of information in looking to the long-term: rumblings in poverty-stricken areas; reactions to American policies abroad; and newly emerging alliances among groups with hostile agendas at the international, national, and local levels. It certainly makes sense for the president and his advisers to hear directly from scholars, business leaders, and others with firsthand experience in the hot spots of the world.

COLLATERAL DAMAGE FROM INTELLIGENCE COLLECTION

At the same time, unsavory intelligence operations, when uncovered, can quickly ruin America's reputation. In May 2004, for example, photographs documenting the gross misconduct of American military intelligence operations in Iraq rocked the world. Entire populations of many Arab countries and hundreds of millions of residents of America's traditional allies were appalled by the US Army's "intelligence body shop"—the infamous Abu Ghraib jail in Baghdad where American military handlers degraded, mutilated, and killed Iraqi citizens in efforts to extract information from them. Then, with no convincing evidence to the contrary, the world assumed that similar American-run body shops could be found in Afghanistan, at Guantanamo Bay, and elsewhere. A particularly damning characterization of events in Baghdad was the statement by an American general who had investigated conditions there: he reported that the unusual aspect of the activities was simply that they were photographed.[23]

Among the images repeated around the clock on almost every television station throughout the Arab world were photographs of

- a hooded and wired captive being threatened with electrocution
- male and female US soldiers laughing while posing over a pyramid of naked detainees
- a female US soldier dragging an Iraqi with a leash around his neck across the prison floor
- the body of a dead Iraqi packed in ice

Coupled with the pictures were excerpts from an investigation by another US Army general that highlighted

- pouring of phosphoric liquid and cold water on detainees
- beatings with broom handles

- sodomizing of detainees
- inciting dogs to bite captives
- unexplained killings of prisoners

In the words of this general, these were "sadistic, blatant, and wanton criminal abuses."[24] Some of the abused prisoners had nothing to do with the fighting in Baghdad. They were simply picked up in wide-ranging US Army sweeps of streets in tumultuous areas of the city.

The responses of US military leaders to the revelations were appalling. A primary concern of the chairman of the Joint Chiefs of Staff was the Pentagon's need to pressure CBS to delay release of the photographs for more than one week so the military could be in a better position to cope with public reactions. He denied any knowledge of the substance of three internal army investigations dating back nine months that documented the abuses. The commanding officer of the military jail at the time of the abuses simply said that she was unaware of the atrocities, since military intelligence authorities had assumed responsibility for the "prisoner-softening" operations. Other Pentagon apologists cited brutal atrocities by Iraqi insurgents, as if the United States should mirror their behavior. Almost all of the military brass immediately blamed the problems on a few young crazies who were out of control. And the military investigators were promptly isolated from the press.[25]

Finally, the international furor became so loud that President Bush held a damage-control interview with reporters from a Dubai-based television station and an American-sponsored Arabic language station. "I want to tell the people of the Middle East that the practices that took place in that prison are abhorrent and they don't represent America. . . . They represent the action of a few people."[26]

These words were hardly sufficient to dampen the increasing outrage from the near-simultaneous release of additional investigative reports of abuses in other prisons. Critics noted that the president did not "apologize" for the abhorrent action. Also, the problem was not a single, isolated incident as implied by the president. Abuses that took place at different times and at different locations were uncovered. It was hard for any observer to conclude that culpability did not extend all the way to the highest levels of the Pentagon.[27]

The reaction throughout the Muslim world was swift, with demonstrations and threats toward America surging to an all-time high. Many Muslims who had accepted earlier statements that the US intervention in Iraq was essential to liberate the oppressed population of the country quickly changed their views. In short order, they swelled the ranks of doubters of US policy pronouncements. The skeptics in the United States and abroad had always considered the Americans to be conquerors, not liberators, in Iraq, and now they could label them as torturers as well. "If you wanted to write a script as to how you undermine the credibility of the United States in the Middle East today, you couldn't have done a better job," said Hisham Melhem, an Arab reporter commenting on the *Jim Lehrer NewsHour* about the Abu Ghraib prison scandal. "If you have any illusions about winning hearts and minds in Iraq and in the Arab world, you should forget them."[28]

Adding fuel to the fire of anger was the fact that many of the abuses took place in Saddam Hussein's most feared jail, a symbol that should have been demolished long before the incidents.

Torturing prisoners is but one intelligence activity with adverse side effects that poison attitudes toward America. Clandestine agents operating overseas are not bound by the same rules that govern their behavior, or the behavior of anyone else, in the United States. In their profession, criminal acts are not only tolerated but also sometimes encouraged—robbery, looting, and even assassination. Also, of course, bribery and spreading of propaganda have long been tools of the trade for those who need not worry about accountability. A flurry of objections can be expected not only from foreign governments and their citizens but also from Americans when covert activities do not go as planned and secret operations are exposed to the world.

Following the misbehavior of US Army personnel in the prisons of Iraq, there is a growing conviction abroad that the Americans will stop at nothing to get their way. They will not be deterred by the need to kill their opponents once an intelligence operation has been initiated. This is the bottom-line conclusion for many people around the world.

On this side of the ocean, Muslim visitors to the United States, as well as Muslim Americans, are often extensively grilled by airport security personnel and even by officials of US intelligence agencies. Particularly egregious encounters find their way into the press. Such incidents are then broadcast around the world.

Islamic radicals in the United States who are plotting destructive actions have been uncovered on a number of occasions, thus screening of suspicious individuals is necessary. At the same time, such profiling gives credence to the growing impression that intelligence agencies prey on law-abiding Muslims without adequate reasons. There is no choice but for Americans to learn how to live with this conflict between security and the rights of privacy. All the while, the US government must try its best to explain to the world the seriousness of the dilemma.

America should neither lower its guard at home nor dismiss the clones of James Bond abroad. The clamor about the importance of human intelligence cannot be ignored. Homeland security must and will continue to tighten. Intelligence activities in war zones are obviously essential. However, intelligence activities—whatever the justification—must be undertaken with great care, recognizing that revelations of such activities will take an increasing toll on the image of America.

Oversight by elected bodies must provide an adequate link between the secret side of government and the people who guard against misuse of power, presumably the US Congress. That link has repeatedly been shown to be so weak that each intelligence operation runs the risk of undermining the very principles on which Western democracies have been built.[29] Human rights advocates are now clearly focused on unacceptable behavior of American undercover agents, whatever the cause and whatever the anticipated payoff from illegal activities. Together with Congress, they should be able to play a constructive role in establishing reasonable limits of behavior for undercover operatives.

EARLY WARNING OF IMPENDING VIOLENCE

As explained earlier, current aspects of global turmoil—from demographic changes and resource conflicts to unemployment and famine—are creating a significant negative impact on the stability of nations and societies. Several US government departments and agencies recognize the importance of looking a decade or more into the future to anticipate these and other destabilizing trends, and their new interest in "early warning" is certainly commendable. An *effective* effort to anticipate and respond to troublesome signals would be a welcome change to the past emphasis of the US government on quick fixes for reacting to today's problems.

As has been painfully demonstrated in the Middle East, no quick fixes are available to modify the underlying basis for deeply engrained hostile attitudes toward America. But analytical capabilities to understand the fundamental factors that contribute to such attitudes can be improved. Early warning of impending trouble spots provides a chance for developing fixes that will be sustained over the long haul to the benefit of both foreign countries and the United States. The role of the United States may simply be to raise red flags and to encourage conflict-resolution efforts by other parties. Or, the United States may be invited by the parties that are involved to take an active role in dispute resolution.

The US Agency for International Development (USAID) has long recognized that unless it anticipates internal conflicts in developing countries and takes steps to contain them, it will not be able to do its job in strengthening the capabilities of the poorest societies to survive, let alone enjoy economic progress. Also, early indications of foreign incursions must be addressed. Pressures in Washington for quick results in alleviating poverty have always been a strong driver of the agency's programs, thereby reducing the effort devoted to paving the way for the future in addition to solving today's problems.

The immediate problems are, of course, huge. In addition to well-known poverty conditions, violence in many countries has led to more than fourteen million international asylum seekers, while twenty-five million people have been displaced and are homeless in their own countries. Killings by child soldiers, gross mistreatment of women, and harassment of humanitarian relief workers have become standard scenarios in many regions. It is no wonder that USAID tries its best to address the key factors that lead to conflicts, for example, youth unemployment, unfair competition over land, and corrupt political and financial institutions at both the national and local levels. Of course, the activities of transnational criminal organizations and terrorist networks aggravate all of these factors.

While the causes underlying outbreaks of wars and lesser conflicts are quite specific to individual countries and regions where turbulence erupts, USAID has developed the following generalized template of characteristics to evaluate when assessing trends in specific countries:

- grievance and greed as incentives for violence, and particularly bitterness over monopolization of limited resources and unjust governance
- access by militant groups to financial resources and to sympathetic officials that can support violent outbreaks
- globalization that threatens state sovereignty, permits arms flows, and fosters criminal networks
- inadequate capacity of the state to constrain opportunistic elite behavior by reducing incentives, blocking access to resources, and limiting international influence
- windows of vulnerability when states are particularly weak, such as during contested elections, in the wake of economic shocks, or following natural disasters[30]

The concept calls for USAID, upon recognition of warning signs, to support conflict resolution or other types of programs that will reduce tensions and eventually lead to the prevention or settlement of disputes. While programs that will change threatening trends are difficult to design and implement, the stakes are simply too high not to take action. As the importance of preventive action becomes increasingly obvious, the likelihood that USAID will have more resources to address dangerous situations in their early stages of development seems good.

Also deserving mention is the effort of the CIA's National Intelligence Council (NIC) to look ahead. The NIC serves as a CIA think tank. Every five years the council predicts the likely developments of international significance for the next fifteen years. The council has a major outreach program to involve hundreds of experts from many countries. As an example of its forecasts, in addressing the Middle East in 2015 the report of 2000 predicted:

> No single ideology or philosophy will unite any one state or group of states, although popular resentment of globalization as a Western intrusion will be widespread. Political Islam in various forms will be an attractive alternative for millions of Muslims throughout the region, and

some radical variants will continue to be divisive social and political forces. . . . By 2015 much of the Middle East populations will be significantly larger, poorer, more urban, and more disillusioned. The problem of job placement is compounded by weak educational systems producing a generation lacking the technical and problem-solving skills required for economic growth.[31]

The importance of the media in creating images of America abroad and in providing Americans with firsthand views of international developments has reached new heights. The CNN and Al Jazeera TV networks have been leaders in providing opportunities for hundreds of millions of people to view snapshots of America and to obtain information from trouble spots in the Middle East. Now dozens of other Western and local stations are transmitting breaking news and other material to populations throughout that region.

When a crisis erupts, no intelligence brief can compete with a live picture that will have lasting impacts on the White House and on Capitol Hill. Of course, detailed analyses by American embassies and by other commentators quickly fill in details. They usually provide different perspectives to information-hungry audiences in Washington and in other capitals.

In a striking new departure from past reluctance to allow reporters to be on the front lines, the Pentagon's decision to embed American reporters within combat units of the US Army during the march to Baghdad in 2003 was brilliant. The correspondents felt like (and were) participants in the battles. Many had sobering experiences that enhanced the quality of their reporting. Complaints about limitations on movement and embargoes on reports were few in number. The world surely experienced much of the march to Baghdad from ground level through their reporting.

Today, some of the best books on international crises are being written by correspondents. Their on-scene experiences provide captivating reading, filling in details that can dramatically affect the viewpoints of readers. Their hard-hitting bestsellers are highly significant supplements to the more scholarly works of academics who spend lifetimes studying different areas of the world.

Another valuable source of information for government officials and ordinary Americans is the broad base of experiences of international business travelers. Business representatives break bread with important political figures around the globe. And they provide hard-nosed analyses of the economic realities in most corners of the world.

The Department of State has taken a special interest in the American business community. Many years ago, the department established the Overseas Security Advisory Council (OSAC) based in Washington, with embassy-supported overseas councils springing up in a number of countries. The objective of these councils is to help international travelers, particularly private company employees, cope with increasing security risks, and much of the OSAC dialogue is directed to this end. At the same time, the experiences of American business abroad are so rich that often the information provided back to the US government through OSAC and other channels is the most authoritative information that exists on country-specific developments.

In addition, thousands of American academics in universities and think tanks assiduously search through databases of all types to help students, policy officials, and the public comprehend the significance of new and forgotten incidents everywhere. Many have specialized knowledge about regions of the world and collectively they seem to cover almost every topic that could possibly be of interest in Washington. Some belong to diaspora communitie, such as those of the Iranian Americans in Los Angeles and Washington.

Almost all intelligence agencies recognize the value of tapping this vast resource, hence the number of advisory committees to various departments and agencies continues to grow. The Department of State has the most imaginative program. Every week, the department sponsors several meetings involving two or three dozen government officials and carefully selected academics on specific topics of current interest. These meetings are highly informative, and few attendees are disappointed in their content.

A focus of one of the programs, for example, has been Yemen, a country adjacent to Saudi Arabia with an impoverished population of nineteen million people. There, recent American foreign policy has been excessively tilted toward combating terrorism that may be rooted in the country, with less concern given to the side effect of trampling on human rights. In 1998 saboteurs mounted an attack on the US naval vessel *Cole*, which was moored in Aden harbor, and retribution has been a strong motivation for US aggressive antiterrorist activities in Yemen.

Academics, recently invited by the Department of State to speak on trends in Yemen, pointed out that Yemen is a unique Muslim country—a country where rivalries between the Shiites and the Sunnis are seldom an issue. They noted that, while the government is autocratic in many ways, the population engages in a wide variety of informal democracy activities—vibrant debates, protest demonstrations, public criticism of the regime—and Yemen's civil institutions are models for the region. The American researchers underscored that US policy toward Israel stirs up far more anti-American resentment than the US intervention in Iraq, noting that many influential Yemenis believe the intervention in Iraq was simply a ploy to strengthen the Israeli position in the region. They also emphasized that the leadership of the country shows great respect for the United States for two important reasons—US foreign assistance funds and demonstrated US readiness to intervene when neighboring Saudi Arabia or Eritrea attempt to challenge the territorial sovereignty of Yemen. Finally, having lived in the villages and taught in the schools, the same academics provided penetrating insights as to the increasing educational opportunities for girls and the growing professional role of women.[32]

Perhaps this overview of Yemen offered few new insights for the several longtime professional Yemen watchers within the government. Even so, academic views are often important validation of the government's perceptions of developments in foreign countries of particular importance for US foreign policy. Conversely, some of the comments of the academics raise doubts concerning conventional wisdom about developments in Yemen.

Those seeking to understand foreign lands must also occasionally retreat to the library. No intelligence analyst, foreign correspondent, or political scientist could have rivaled the eloquence of a historian in prophetically explaining (in his book found on many a library shelf) the state of affairs in the Middle East in 2002:

> The blame game—the Turks, the Mongols, the imperialists, the Jews,
> the Americans—continues and shows little sign of abating. For the gov-

ernments, at once oppressive and ineffectual, that rule much of the Middle East, this game serves a useful, indeed an essential purpose—to explain the poverty that they have failed to alleviate, and to justify the tyranny that they have intensified. In this way they seek to deflect the mounting anger of their unhappy subjects against outer targets.

If the people of the Middle East continue on their present path, the suicide bomber may become a metaphor for the whole region, and there will be no escape from a downward spiral of hate and spite, rage and self-pity, poverty and oppression, culminating sooner or later in yet another alien domination. . . . If they can abandon grievance and victim-hood; settle their differences; and join their talents, energies, and resources in a common creative endeavor, then they can once again make the Middle East, in modern times as it was in antiquity and in the Middle Ages, a major center of civilization. For the time being, the choice is their own.[33]

Finally, a wellspring of information not to be overlooked is that of the polling services. As noted earlier, several highly reliable polling services have provided, in recent years, penetrating, and often shocking, insights into the attitudes of many levels of populations in volatile regions of the world. Some polls are funded by the US and other governments, others are supported by foundations, and still others operate on a commercial basis. For those who doubt the level of international animosity toward America, simply consult any of the polling services. A good starting point is the Pew Research Center, easily accessible on the Internet at http://people-press.org.

Knowledge is power. Appropriate use of valid information can translate into good use of other types of power. But faulty or inaccurate information—as we have seen—can misdirect all types of American power with devastating consequences. If, as suggested earlier, Washington accepts "reducing global turmoil" as the overarching objective, positive results can be achieved if we take certain steps. By paying attention to authoritative information regarding the interests and aspirations of populations throughout the world, the US government can begin to develop policies that take these critical factors into account, thereby stemming the tide of anti-Americanism while at the same time serving US interests.

CHAPTER 4

STRENGTHENING TIES WITH THE DEVELOPING WORLD

★ ★ ★ ★ ★ ★ ★ ★ *We Can Do Better*

In May 1973 I arrived in Indonesia, the world's most populous Muslim country. Local headlines in Jakarta trumpeted a heavyweight boxing match to take place in the fall at the Senayan Stadium. Indeed, it was a championship match, featuring Muhammad Ali. I was no fan of professional boxing matches, whether they were fought in Las Vegas, in Madison Square Garden, or even in Jakarta. Besides, I had never heard of Ali's opponent, a rugged Dutch pugilist named Rudi Lubbers.

The excitement in the sweltering city over the publicity that accompanied the match was remarkable. Legalized mayhem would be a brief respite for the country—a much-needed release valve for pent-up frustrations of a population beleaguered by persistent poverty. Lubbers responded well to the need for a significant break in the daily routines of the population: he lasted twelve rounds in the ring before succumbing to the heat and to the blows of Ali.

During my visit to Jakarta and to distant provinces of Indonesia, I focused on introducing modern technologies to a desperately poor economy that needed all the stimulation possible. The technologies included the use of aerial remote sensing to guide logging activities in uncharted forests, installation of acoustic sensors on fishing vessels to help map the most promising paths to undiscovered fishing grounds, and more efficient radio transmitters to upgrade distance education programs in isolated villages. I had spent many months convincing colleagues at the

US Agency for International Development (USAID) in Washington that these advanced technologies could be helpful in raising the standard of living in Indonesia. But they thought my ideas were far-out for a country where much of the population was illiterate and living well below the poverty level.

My colleagues reluctantly acknowledged that such technologies could be helpful, at least theoretically. However, they were more interested in slowing the rampant corruption in Indonesia that skimmed off external money made available through trade or aid into the pockets of a favored few. Surely, any assistance to increase logging and fishing activities would end up benefiting companies owned by relatives of the leaders of the regime, they warned. Also, as long as access to education remained unfair and skewed in favor of the elite, any investments in hardware for distance education would inevitably line the pockets of friends of the ministers, they added.

Nevertheless, my colleagues did not object to my unusual activities as long as I agreed to emphasize the importance of "income distribution" in my meetings with senior Indonesian officials. It seemed like a reasonable trade-off if I were to minimize objections within USAID to my continued advocacy of new approaches to development assistance. Such approaches were important since they enabled technological leapfrogging over at least some of the barriers to better lives in the developing world.

My first official meeting was with the Indonesian minister of finance. He was the focal point for all external assistance programs. I dutifully raised the issue of income distribution: "What steps are being taken by the Indonesian government to ensure that benefits flow fairly to the poor when distributing the government's available resources?" The answer was quick and to the point. "My good friend, if we had income to distribute, we would distribute it equitably." This response was certainly a dodge of the question. But the point was clear: Indonesia was and remains a poor country.

Indonesia is a particularly pertinent example of a country at risk for radical activism where US policies have resulted in increasing anti-Americanism. It is not only the fourth-most populous country in the world, trailing only China, India, and the United States; it is also the nation with the largest Muslim population—87 percent of its total population of 210 million. The principal island is Java, which is the size of the state of New

York. It alone is crammed with more than 105 million inhabitants. Despite large inputs of US foreign assistance across several decades, both the government and the population have become increasingly hostile to the aggressive American policies implemented in the past few years. This is unfortunate, since the events after 9/11 had fostered much sympathy for America and Americans.

Indonesia's economy has been steadily growing in recent years. Unfortunately, despite its abundant natural resource base, it is not growing fast enough to accommodate the increasing number of new job seekers. Twenty million Indonesians were unemployed in 2004, and the number continues its unrelenting upward trend. Prior to the end of 2004, economists had estimated that the economy needed to grow by 7 percent, an unrealistic goal, just to keep the ranks of the jobless in check.[1] Then the tsunami disaster occurred, and all predictions were discarded.

USAID has recorded some impressive foreign assistance successes on the island archipelago, such as increasing rice production and slowing the spiraling birthrate. In 2001, with a new administration in place in Washington, USAID shifted its emphasis from agriculture and population control to education, decentralized and democratic governance, and employment creation. The new US management team believed that these areas housed the engines of economic growth. Yet the prospects for major economic advances are still not bright. The international aid budgets of the World Bank, USAID, and other donors are simply not commensurate with the task, and even the massive influx of international assistance following the tsunami tragedy was quite inadequate.[2]

Indonesia's situation is fairly typical of the challenges facing many developing countries today: a long history of international aid projects with a mixed record of success and a legacy of corruption; internal political struggles between various ethnic and/or religious groups; and increasing frustration over the ever-widening gap between their economic progress and that in the developed world, especially in the United States—a frustration that manifested itself in terrorist bombings targeting foreign tourists on the resort island of Bali in 2002 and again in 2005.

The 2004 tsunami, dreadful as it was, offered an opportunity for the United States to come forward and make a difference in the lives of Indonesian victims and others who found themselves in the massive wave's swath. The catastrophe led Secretary of State Colin Powell to state that in all his years of military service and his involvement in many relief efforts, he had never witnessed such devastation. The death toll was in the many tens of thousands. Hundreds of thousands of people required immediate evacuation from coastal areas.

Many international heroes, including Americans, rushed to the scene to help with the rescue and relief efforts. Unfortunately, the American response started badly when President Bush announced a US commitment of only $15 million, a paltry sum by any measure. This led to accusations that Americans were "stingy," further fueling resentments against the United States and suspicions as to its intentions. The misstep was quickly corrected with the announcement of a commitment of $350 million, which included funds diverted from other assistance programs around the world. American naval units were soon on the way to the region with water, food, and other supplies to be delivered by helicopters, and American relief personnel were on the ground assisting with evacuation of low-lying areas, medical services, distribution of food, and construction of shelters.

Even then, despite the crying need for assistance, the Indonesian government repeatedly announced its intention to terminate dependence on foreign disaster-relief teams within several months. Former presidents Bill Clinton and George H. W. Bush tried their best to convince Indonesian victims that they were not forgotten as the two repeatedly visited the critical areas to help mobilize additional support. Like leaders of many governments, some Indonesian politicians tend to be very suspicious of American intentions when military forces have become involved, even when those forces participate in such humanitarian efforts as aiding in the immediate aftermath of the tsunami calamity.[3]

Indonesia has long been a country holding many opportunities for the United States to improve lives while winning hearts and minds. Foreign assistance is a powerful instrument in promoting a more favorable image of America by demonstrating genuine concern for struggling populations. Regrettably, higher popularity ratings traceable to foreign assistance are often doused by perceptions of America's determination to colonize the world through its economic and military dominance. As the tsunami efforts show, assistance must be carefully designed to be effective and it should be accompanied by other policies that help—and do not threaten—populations in dire straits.

PERSISTENT POVERTY AROUND THE GLOBE

Clusters of millions of poor people are barely surviving in dozens of countries. More than one billion people live on the equivalent of less than one dollar per day, and three billion live on less than two dollars. Of particular concern are the twenty-five million people who have been displaced within their own countries, often with no lifelines for help. Such displacements due to wars, droughts, or other internal catastrophes can last from years to decades.[4]

The linkages among poverty, terrorism, and US national security are becoming clearer with every passing day, although poverty, in and of itself, cannot be blamed for the rapid rise of global violence. Poverty does feed a sense of social injustice and anger, particularly among the youth. While the downtrodden may not take to the streets en masse and lead violent protests, they may become sympathetic supporters and even foot soldiers of those who do.

Accompanying persistent global poverty is the pervasive frustration with unrealized ambitions for development. In Algeria, for example, French support of the education sector was supposed to lead to prosperity. Instead, armies of unemployed grow in numbers commensurate with stalled economic progress. The oil of Nigeria was to bring about an economic boom across the country. Instead, political and economic chaos dominates the lives of the people. They remain mired in desperation as the new influx of cash leads to major benefits for only a few officials and collaborators in key positions. All the while, in many countries where economies should be on the rise, growing populations with increasing consumer appetites quickly use up any new money that may appear—with little heed to investing in the future.

Meanwhile, the worldwide migration from rural to urban areas is relentless. Cities harbor most of the existing jobs, better services, and simply more action. The urban tinderboxes where disenfranchised youth crowd together in frustration are growing in number and turbulence. In self-defense, well-established city dwellers have no choice but to live increasingly in fortified compounds where they feel secure and able to keep the less fortunate at bay.

Are the development processes backed by the United States and other donors a major stimulus to urbanization and all its unfortunate side effects? Yes. Excited by reports of new funding from abroad—funding that inevitably flows through the cities—and by prospects for a better life, the youth simply will not remain on the farms. However, once in the cities, young people with high hopes quickly become disenchanted with low-paying or no-paying jobs. They form all types of groups, from labor associations to criminal gangs, which overwhelm creaking and over-centralized bureaucracies that cannot control them.

Is misdirected foreign aid fertilizing the roots of terrorism? Yes. Foreign aid can give excessive power to the rulers of countries, and these divisive effects are sometimes the most significant impact that is left behind when programs come to an end. Well-designed and well-delivered aid is essential. Traditional approaches to foreign aid that are usually focused on immediate rather than long-term impacts must give way to efforts that not only respond to today's realities but also reduce the incentives for hatred and violence in the long term.[5]

EVOLVING DEVELOPMENT STRATEGIES

For decades, economists specializing in development have advocated four approaches to alleviate suffering in desperately poor countries. They rightfully call for (1) more foreign aid, (2) greater debt relief, (3) reduction of tariff and other barriers that hamper developing countries' access to international markets, and (4) increased foreign direct investment. Of course, money is not the sole answer to alleviating poverty, but it is an essential ingredient. At the same time, stronger local institutions are needed to ensure that income from all sources is used wisely. There must be local buy-in to the approaches that are advocated by purveyors of aid, and these strategies must be ones that realistically can be sustained when foreign financial infusions end.

Would even economic miracles be adequate to cool off potential hotbeds of violence in the poor countries? Perhaps. In poor countries, economic "progress" is almost always measured by the general populace in miniscule wage increases of tens of dollars per year. It is difficult to see how such baby steps will make a difference for the vast majority of people currently in poverty. Nevertheless, there is no alternative for the United States in trying to make a difference.

Frustrated by intransigent economies in countries of strategic importance or of humanitarian concern, the United States has for a number of years slowly switched its emphasis from support for economic progress to support of democratic reform as the first step in building viable states. Installing democracy is now emphasized in every presidential statement concerning assistance to poor countries. While promoting the reform of governance structures through persuasion and training is politically attractive in Washington, and cheaper than investing in production infrastructure, the economic return on democratic reform by itself is seldom obvious. It is economic betterment that is first and foremost on the minds of impoverished populations.

Accompanying this shift in emphasis to promoting democratic reforms, the United States began to revise its lists of other priorities for foreign aid, beginning in the late 1990s. First, control of HIV/AIDS moved to the top of the list. Most recently, based on experiences in Afghanistan, Iraq, and violence-torn Africa, the United States has elevated internal security as an essential condition for economic growth nearly everywhere. Designers of foreign assistance efforts are responding to the needs of desperate people by supporting healthcare and internal security programs, as well as democratic reforms. At the same time, it is essential that economic growth not be pushed aside, whatever the difficulties in stimulating employment and improving productivity.

In May 2004 a group of America's leading experts on international development issued a compelling statement about the dangers from international neglect of the plight of states that are weak and failing:

> A common thread runs through the disparate [often terrorist-related] crises that form the fundamental foreign policy and security challenges of our time. These crises originate in, spread to, and disproportionately affect developing countries where governments lack the capacity, and sometimes the will, to respond. In the most extreme cases, these states have completely failed, as in Afghanistan, Haiti, or Somalia. In many others, states are not failed but weak. Governments are unable to do the things that their own citizens and the international community expect from them: protecting people from internal and external threats, delivering basic health services and education, and providing institutions that respond to the legitimate demands and needs of the population.[6]

The group suggested several radical new departures for US policy. First, they concluded that consolidating the currently fragmented responses of the US government to the threat of extremism was important enough to warrant establishment of a cabinet-level government agency that could assume leadership responsibility for policies and programs directed toward developing countries. This agency would fold together selected activities currently under the purview of the Departments of State, Defense, and Treasury; USAID; and several other small government-sponsored organizations. Second, they argued for a new office within the apparatus of the National Security Council to oversee all other relevant activities in addition to those folded into the new department. Also, they called for increased US assistance to support the police and military forces of stressed countries in the Balkans, the Middle East, and in Africa to help those governments secure their territories and protect their people. [7]

Clearly, we must reflect on some of the lessons learned in providing assistance to more than one hundred countries since World War II—particularly lessons during recent years—while also examining new ideas that are now on the table. Both successes and failures abound, and an overriding reason for success has been *local commitment* to the objectives of specific projects.

Even with this rich history, American politicians and development specialists, in their zeal to find magic bullets, too often forget that most issues on the current agendas of international and national assistance agencies have been there for decades—and for good reason. For example, more than thirty years ago, and even longer, donor governments recognized that strengthening local institutions—policy institutions, technical institutions, and educational institutions—was the key to sustainable economic growth. Yet today, the demand for quick payoffs in two to three years from aid programs often precludes the possibility of US support for the slow process of institutional development that usually takes a decade or longer. Also, experts have long recognized the importance of encouraging the evolution of a local private sector and of not preempting private-sector options. Yet it is usually easier politically for aid agencies to provide funds to governmental institutions, however inefficient, than to support private-sector programs that may be riskier in the short term but show more significant potential in the long term.[8]

ADJUSTING FOREIGN ASSISTANCE IN THE POST–9/11 ERA

If the United States is in a war to win hearts and minds, and it must be, the US government should fully embrace USAID as one of the strongest weapons in its arsenal. It should mobilize its forces around a revitalized agency for funneling assistance around the world rather than inventing parallel tracks through less experienced entities. Hundreds of millions of people have benefited from USAID programs conducted during the last fifty years. Local participants in successful USAID programs are vociferous advocates of the American way of life, and USAID project alumni can be found working in the offices of presidents and ministers, serving as leaders of industry and academia, and enriching intellectual communities in almost every developing country.

Following 9/11, US funds flowing through USAID increased dramatically as reported by the administrator of the agency in 2004: "We are a nation under threat and at war. Not only are the directions of foreign aid dramatically new, but the commitment is dramatically large. The annual budget at USAID has risen from $7.9 billion prior to September 11 to $14.9 billion in 2003."[9]

These ringing words should have inspired the Washington crowd of USAID supporters to rejoice in the newfound wealth of the agency. But at the same time, the crowd was witnessing a fragmentation of responsibilities for activities in developing countries to more than forty different departments and agencies of the US government, with USAID in control of only half of the government funds for development assistance programs. Thus, the enthusiasm was muted by visions of the interagency squabbling that was certain to arise in every country where USAID had been the dominant agency for decades.

Also, the new funds for USAID may have little impact in reducing endemic poverty. This increase and subsequent ones have been earmarked largely for reconstruction programs—with limited short-term employment opportunities—in Iraq, Afghanistan, and other war-torn countries. Also, as usual, large amounts of the budget are regularly headed for other "strategically important" countries, particularly Israel and Egypt, where assistance budgets are tied more to political alliances than to relative needs of the people.

Finally, much of the funding has been controlled by the more than two hundred special programmatic earmarks attached to the appropriations by the US Congress and by the administration. This is not to say that earmarked funds can't make a difference. However, they frequently complicate the rational allocation of assistance. Such imposed programs may not achieve local buy-in, with a much-reduced likelihood of effective local participation in the programs and program impact. In short, the common belief that USAID controls the destiny of the funds it receives is far from reality.

The administrator also noted that in 2002 the president had declared that international development would share center stage with diplomacy and military defense in US foreign policy. For example, USAID would help fortify weak states by ridding them of corruption. In addition, the agency would assist marginalized populations in gaining control over their limited property, which has been an easy target for confiscation by the ruling elites.[10] However, it is unlikely that USAID can really muster the political clout to stand shoulder-to-shoulder with the Department of State and the Department of Defense.

In countering a common perception that has plagued USAID for decades, the administrator adopted a defensive tone: "Within the beltway, we are accused of being unfocused, dissipating our energies and taxpayer monies in an array of ineffectual programs and projects. On the other hand, we are accused of being overly focused, operating under constricting paradigms and simplistic assumptions about democratic nation building. But in the nations where we operate, we are broadly recognized as one of the premier agencies of development in the world."[11]

For many years, USAID has been an undervalued asset of the US government, berated by critics within and outside the halls of Washington. Too often it is considered simply as a repository of money for politicians, diplomats, and Beltway bandits alike to use for their pet projects. It seldom receives adequate credit for its stunning accomplishments that date back to the Green Revolution, to the establishment of a superb technical education infrastructure in India, to the stimulation of cutting-edge technologies in Korea, and to the successful assault on diarrheal diseases in South Asia.

USAID has been trying to reinvent itself to cope with the challenges of the twenty-first century. As a starting point for a new vision, USAID in

2002 agreed to develop a joint policy and program strategy with the Department of State. In principle, it makes sense to fold together foreign policy objectives and foreign assistance objectives. However, USAID was a weak partner in the first round of planning. Almost from the beginning, the agency was overpowered into embracing programs that have little to do with its traditional core mission of alleviating poverty and promoting sustainable development. In short, the plan centered on diplomatic and security goals and not on international development objectives. Take the following goals, for example:

- Resolve local and regional conflicts to preserve peace
- Prevent terrorist attacks against the United States, our allies, and our friends
- Protect the homeland by securing our borders and infrastructure
- Reduce the threat of weapons of mass destruction
- Minimize the impact of international crime and illegal drugs
- Assist American citizens to travel, conduct business, and live abroad securely
- Increase understanding for American values, policies, and initiatives
- Ensure a high-quality workforce in the United States

These are all worthy objectives, but what do they have to do with USAID's mission of international development? Very little. The remaining goals are more on-target for USAID:

- Strengthen world economic growth while expanding US business opportunities
- Improve health, education, environment, and other conditions for the global population
- Minimize the human costs of displacement, conflicts, and natural disasters

But where is agriculture? What happened to job creation in developing countries? Aren't transportation and communication more critical than ever in reducing the gaps between rich and poor? In short, USAID's mission was pushed into the background. Clearly the plan should be revised. Some of the authors of the plan have already moved on to other assignments, and a new team surely can do better.[12]

In January 2006 the administration announced that the administrator of USAID would also serve as a deputy secretary of state. The idea is to ensure that both organizations will be working from the same script in increasingly important countries. This is seemingly an attractive goal. But does this mean that USAID will become simply a mechanism to address short-term foreign policy objectives, with long-term challenges of strengthening institutional capabilities of developing countries pushed completely into the background? It certainly seems that way.

Already, the agency's guidance to its overseas missions and program offices dwells excessively on political topics—particularly on building democracy within every country where USAID operates. This is a significant issue, but it too often takes the spotlight off the core challenge for USAID—stagnant economic growth in poor countries on every continent.

While USAID has often received high marks from recipients for many of its programs, its insistence on determining the foreign aid priorities of host countries (driven in large part by the aforementioned earmarks) and its reliance on high-priced technical advisers who are often not useful to host countries greatly deflate the value of its investments. A rule of thumb, repeated to me over many years by senior officials of a number of recipient countries, estimates that two-thirds of USAID funds designated for a specific country will be spent ineffectively on American advisers and on meaningless analyses and supporting activities. Yet one-third of the budget is better than nothing, and USAID has indeed created beneficial impacts, so the program should go forward, argue the local officials. Imagine the results if USAID's full budget had been effectively used over many years.

Even with all its inefficiencies, during the 1960s USAID led the way in constructing dams, highways, power plants, and other infrastructure facilities that are vital in providing developing countries with basic services. In the 1970s USAID was the world's leader in strengthening economic planning capabilities and in establishing modern universities in distant lands. In the 1980s USAID recognized the importance of harnessing America's research capacity to address nagging problems of disease, malnutrition, crop productivity, and other challenges in tropical areas. In the 1990s USAID was in the forefront in harnessing the power of the Internet and in highlighting practical approaches to improve health and environmental conditions. All the while, the agency played an indispensable role in responding to humanitarian disasters on all continents—floods, famine, earthquakes, and other types of catastrophes. Now, in the twenty-first century, the agency must keep all of these areas on its screen while also addressing new challenges triggered by globalization and unprecedented levels of violence.

Finally, the USAID leadership has long recognized the significance of private financial resources flowing to the developing world. Through its Global Development Alliance, the agency is creating hundreds of public-private partnerships that draw on corporate resources, technology, innovative talent, and on the nonprofit sector's understanding of development issues and ability to deliver assistance in the field. Participants include, for example, CISCO, Home Depot, IKEA, and the World Wildlife Fund.[13]

HIGH EXPECTATIONS: THE MILLENNIUM CHALLENGE CORPORATION

In January 2004 the US government established the Millennium Challenge Corporation (MCC) with an initial budget of $1 billion for the first year and plans to increase the annual budget to $5 billion per year by 2006. Conceived in the early days of the Bush administration by a small planning group led by the Department of State, the MCC is pursuing a dramatic new US approach to international development—a significant addition to other international assistance efforts, such as the programs of USAID. It is too early to judge the effectiveness of the MCC. While the MCC is off to a slow start, early indications are that the concept has hit highly receptive chords in developing countries and that the bang for the buck that it achieves will likely be higher than the impacts of other US development programs carried out in recent years. The principal downside of the concept is that the organizational responsibility for the new approach was not given to USAID, where the program should have been housed.

What is new, and why are the prospects for success high? Several characteristics set the MCC apart from traditional US development assistant programs.

- **Sufficient funding**: The likelihood of lasting impacts in the countries where it supports programs is reasonably high.
- **Local priorities**: Each participating country designs and develops the program that it wants to promote for funding from the MCC. There are no US congressional earmarks on the funds available for the program, giving the countries broad latitude in choosing their own priorities. The MCC staff claims that it will be neutral and not try to influence the determination of priorities. Of course the program that each country develops must make sense within the overall development strategy of the country and must be able to produce concrete and meaningful results.
- **Local responsibility for program management**: Once the program is approved by the MCC, the funds are transferred per an agreed-upon compact with the host government. The local government then takes full responsibility for managing the funds appropriately as well as carrying out the program efficiently. Funds are *not* channeled through American intermediary organizations, which would require a portion of the funding to cover the expenses of the intermediaries.

To promote accountability and equity, the MCC insists that each program proposal receives the endorsement of a broad segment of both the governmental and the nongovernmental communities in the recipient country. Also, proposals are expected to provide for coordination with related programs of other donors, while being consistent with the overall development plans of the country.

The MCC board initially selected sixteen countries as eligible to apply for MCC financial support. They were considered to be following appropriate paths to creating good governance, developing human resources, and pursuing sound economic policies. In the language of the MCC, they were "ruling justly, investing in their people, and establishing economic freedom." The countries are all in the low-income bracket with an aggregated per capita income average of less than $500 per year.

These sixteen countries are to be joined by additional countries in the next several years. Several dozen "threshold" countries have been identified and are on the waiting list. The threshold countries are required to be either (1) countries qualified in terms of their development policies with somewhat higher per capita incomes than the original group of selected countries, or (2) lower-income countries needing modest improvements in their approaches to governance, economic policies, and/or investments in people.

This new departure, which shifts priority setting from the US Congress to the recipient countries, is long overdue. USAID should attempt to mimic the approach of the MCC to the largest extent possible. If the MCC is as successful as hoped, in time the entire foreign assistance effort might be patterned after this approach.[14]

But what are the dangers that could destroy this initiative?

- **Less money than promised**: Congress could limit the funds made available to the MCC so much that the likelihood of significant impacts is dramatically reduced. In fact, Congress has already reduced the requested funding for 2005 on the grounds that there are still unused funds in the pipeline.[15]
- **Resumption of congressional earmarking of funds**: The administration must absolutely veto such an appropriation bill, since the first earmark will open the floodgates for more to follow.
- **Mishandling of funds**: One or more of the recipient countries could be irresponsible in the handling of funds. Congress and the administration should not overreact to such a development by hamstringing the entire program. The violating countries should be promptly dropped from the program.
- **Reduction in funds for USAID**: The administration is already reducing USAID funds, according to the USAID mission in Mongolia, an MCC country. Such a step alienates those governments and people, fostering opinions that the US government often lies and is now reneging on its commitment of using the MCC as an "additional" funding stream. Such reductions blatantly undercut the pledge that the MCC was designed to increase the foreign aid budget by 50 percent, and they should not be tolerated by Congress.

INADEQUATE US CONTRIBUTIONS TO INTERNATIONAL DEVELOPMENT

For many years, the paltry US financial contributions to international development have been repeatedly criticized by other donor governments and by nongovernmental organizations. Of the twenty-two principal donor governments, the United States allocates the smallest percentage of its gross national income (GNI) to international development. The United States reported its contribution as .14 percent of GNI in 2003 compared to an average of all the donors of .41 percent and the UN target of .7 percent. Of course, the GNI of the United States is by far the largest in the world. Therefore, even its small-percentage commitment of resources exceeds in absolute terms the contribution of any other country. Specifically, the United States reported a $15.8 billion annual contribution of the total $68.5 billion for all donors, approximately 23 percent of the total.[16]

These percentages are debated each year at the Development Assistance Committee (DAC) of the Organization for Economic Cooperation and Development (OECD) in Paris. The industrialized countries try their best to put a good face on their foreign assistance efforts, but the developing countries that are recipients of foreign assistance are never impressed—convinced that their slow growth is a legacy of colonialism coupled with their locations in resource-poor areas of the world. Also, according to critics within developing countries, the industrialized countries are doing their best to exploit whatever oil, timber, and even wildlife that some poor countries have inherited.

The validity of the numbers denoting US foreign assistance contributions as well as the reported numbers of others are questionable, almost always erring on the high side. For example, the United States in the past has included in its estimates funds used for helping Russia dismantle its missiles. Is this really development assistance? Many donor countries are notorious for including costs incurred to promote business interests of their companies, projects that have little relevance to positive impacts on development. Also, few countries highlight the fact that much of their declared aid is in the form of consultants from their own countries with little transfer of cash that could be more effectively used by the recipient countries.

Further adding to the confusion, the numbers used by the United States in characterizing its foreign aid commitment vary considerably from report to report and speech to speech. Even the best US government analysts have difficulty explaining which programs are included and which are excluded when reciting the Overseas Development Assistance index, the standard used by the OECD. Still, there is no doubt that, based on per capita income, the US government is at the bottom of the list of donor countries ranked in order of their generosity.

Is foreign aid the only measure of commitment by the wealthy countries to bettering conditions in the poor countries? For decades, US government officials—sometimes characterized as foreign aid "apologists"—have been saying that other measures are equally important.

The Center for Global Development works with *Foreign Policy* magazine to promote an elaborate index that takes into account many policies of governments that help poor countries. The index is in a state of evolution, but as of 2004 it included additional indicators covering such areas as "tied aid" (a negative indicator reflecting required purchase of goods and services from only the donor country) and positive indicators reflecting promotion of trade, foreign direct investment, environmental performance in the recipient country, contributions to peacekeeping and humanitarian efforts, and technology research and development that could have relevance to developing countries.[17]

How does the United States rank in this forum? The result is better than being dead last: seventh of twenty-one donors in 2003.

If this type of analysis seems questionable to many experts in the United States, the developing countries view the effort simply as an excuse for low levels of foreign aid. Nevertheless, the concept has some merit. A number of policies of the industrialized countries that are based primarily on domestic considerations have ramifications that extend to even the poorest countries of the world. However, changing these policies is usually a more difficult task than increasing the levels of foreign assistance. Furthermore, the needs of developing countries will likely not be decisive factors in decisions concerning adjustments.

Since its inception, the United Nations has been a forum where developing countries can vent their economic frustrations. They often attribute their problems to the unfairness of industrialized countries: the wealthy countries have established a global economic system that ensures they will control the bulk of the planet's bounty. These countries see increased foreign aid as the major way to correct the system that is in place.

In the early 1970s I visited New York City as a US government representative participating in debates of the UN Economic and Social Council over how developing countries could obtain access to technologies developed by the world's industrialized countries. At this meeting, the tropical and desert countries simply wanted a clear statement of their right to participate in technological progress. The industrialized countries were determined to protect their inventions.

The objective of the session was to draft a resolution that would reflect the common interests of all. No votes were to be taken since the document was to be a consensus document. Seven weeks later, a short resolution emerged, as word after word was changed multiple times to reflect the views of delegates from more than one hundred countries. While the experience was no doubt frustrating for all and achieved little, the global community must be sensitive to the importance that developing countries attach to such participation at the world's discussion and voting tables.

During the 1990s the delegates to the United Nations launched new efforts to solve the nagging issues of international development as the twenty-first century approached, including the establishment of Millennium Development Goals. The idea is to enlarge global commitments to reducing poverty by stressing mutual responsibilities of both the poor and the rich countries. Poor countries are to improve governance and to mobilize and manage resources more effectively and equitably. Wealthy countries are to increase foreign aid, debt relief, market access, and technology transfers—familiar themes for decades but still areas of overriding concern.

The internationally agreed-upon Millennium Development Goals are as follows:

- Eradicate extreme poverty and hunger
- Achieve universal primary education
- Promote gender equality and empower women
- Reduce child mortality
- Improve maternal health
- Combat HIV/AIDS, malaria, and other diseases
- Ensure environmental sustainability
- Develop a global partnership for development

More specific subgoals, to be achieved by 2015, have been established within each category. For example: reduce by half the proportion of people who suffer from hunger, eliminate gender disparity in primary and secondary education, reduce by two-thirds the mortality rate among children younger than five, and cut by 50 percent the proportion of people without access to safe drinking water.[18]

All governments agree on the worthiness of these goals. At the same time, most donors complain that they cannot obtain enough funding from their legislative bodies to live up to their commitments to achieve the UN targets. Also, most acknowledge that the overall contribution of $69 billion annually recorded by the OECD is about one-third of the amount that is needed to achieve the Millennium Development Goals.

For decades the industrialized countries have shirked their financial responsibilities to back their political commitments with their pocketbooks. This lack of past action is now coming back to haunt all countries. Accommodating the stream of displaced refugees, warding off the spread of infectious diseases, and countering terrorism rooted in poor countries are costing much more than would the cost of preventive measures in decades past.

Recognizing the seriousness of the problem, the leaders of the eight most economically powerful nations (the G8) in June 2004 renewed their pledges to support achievement of UN goals, this time focusing their attention on the power of entrepreneurship in eradicating poverty. They reported that annual personal remittances of immigrants to help families and small businesses in their homelands exceeded $100 billion and they pledged assistance in facilitating such remittances. (As one example, émigrés in the United States send $6 billion annually to the Philippines.) They called on the multilateral regional development banks to improve business conditions and increase technical assistance for entrepreneurs. They highlighted the importance of establishing financial conditions for affordable housing and water supplies, emphasizing the need for financial transparency in the private sector that supports such activities. They urged expanded access by small groups of entrepreneurs to microloans.[19]

Many of the G8 countries are responding to this agenda. While in some cases there is simply a repackaging of existing programs to fit the new agenda without increases in financial commitments, the pressure is on all of the countries to do better. With each G8 summit, the seriousness

of the problems of poverty and the linkages of poverty to the security
interests of all the G8 countries become clearer.

THE SPECIAL CHALLENGE OF THE
MIDDLE EAST

In 1959 the United Kingdom, Turkey, Iran, and Pakistan established the
Central Treaty Organization (CENTO). While primarily a security
alliance, CENTO was also intended to bind together these countries in
common efforts to promote the economic and scientific development of
the region. The predecessor organization, the Baghdad Pact, had dis-
solved as Iraq went its own way following the replacement of a pro-
Western government in Baghdad in 1958. The other four members moved
the headquarters to Ankara and continued their cooperation.

I was a US government observer at meetings of CENTO during the
1970s. My role was to promote the scientific interests of the United States
within the CENTO framework. Even though the United States was not a
CENTO member, it provided considerable financial support for CENTO-
sponsored activities. Science had become a mainstream interest of
CENTO.

My task was easy. The interest by CENTO members in access to
American science and technology was off the charts. The modest cooperative programs to provide such access were repeatedly hailed as a success
by members at CENTO meetings. The programs provided opportunities
for Pakistanis, Iranians, and Turks to study in the United States and scientific equipment for them to use when they returned home.

Even though CENTO disintegrated in 1979 due to political turmoil in
the region, the short life of the organization left a positive legacy of goodwill toward the United States. The programs demonstrated the power of
American science and technology in commanding international respect
for openness and objectivity—values that are cherished in the United
States.

The CENTO program was but one of hundreds of regional and
country-specific initiatives supported by USAID in the Middle East over
many years. While the largest USAID expenditures by far have been

directed to Israel, other initiatives have been of great importance and impact. USAID support for the American University in Beirut, for example, is believed by many graduates and observers to have changed the course of history by providing a highly respected American presence that touched many countries. Alumni of the university are in senior positions throughout the region. Their scholarship, their courage in living in Beirut in difficult times, and their commitment to peace are reflected in many local initiatives.

Even during the most tumultuous waves of anti-Americanism in Lebanon, the mortarboards of American University stirred indelible memories of the generosity and noble objectives of the American people.

Turning to other countries, USAID programs in Turkey have supported the development of several important universities and other research and education institutions that today make up the human resources infrastructure of the country. In recent years, Jordan has become a favored recipient of USAID projects since the government has been both an enlightened force for democracy and a responsible custodian of Western funds. As a different kind of example, Egypt has long received large amounts of US aid, with the funds intended to demonstrate American fair-mindedness in addressing both sides of the Israeli-Arab split. While the US Government Accountability Office regularly uncovers inappropriate diversions of USAID funds in Egypt, the programs have nevertheless been an influential force in convincing many prominent Egyptians that Arab needs are not forgotten amid the turmoil in the Middle East.

Since 9/11 the US government has scrambled to demonstrate in a more highly visible manner to the Muslim world that its concerns about the future of the region go well beyond a military presence. Many US pronouncements have heralded new USAID programs, although in truth some have been in development for some time. Other initiatives are actually funded by significant increases in the financial contributions to the region. Unfortunately, this sudden generosity on the part of the United States, oriented toward short-term impacts, reflects the simplistic view that throwing money at the problem will somehow offset the rage fueled by military actions and continued military presence in sacred lands.

In June 2004, along with the renewed pledges to support achievement of UN goals, the G8 released its overall plans for promoting reform in the

Middle East. Perhaps the most important announcement was the intention of the G8 to establish a Forum for the Future, whereby ministerial-level representatives from the G8 and the countries of the Middle East would discuss on a regular basis a range of issues. The G8 plan emphasizes political reform but recognizes the importance of economic growth, business-to-business contacts, and cultural exchanges. This broad agenda is to provide an umbrella for many specific activities supported by different G8 countries.[20]

These initiatives ring well in Western capitals. However, they are a far cry from the promise made by foreign ministers and other leaders of the Western countries at the World Economic Forum held at the Dead Sea just one month earlier. There, an objective of creating one hundred million new jobs during the next ten years for the young people of the Middle East was established.

In response to the G8 plan, many ongoing Western projects—some quite small—have been packaged together with new starts, perhaps to give the appearance of a larger initiative than has actually been offered. The United States in particular continues to be hesitant in its approach to some Middle Eastern governments—conflicted by a desire for far-reaching transformations coupled with an interest in maintaining useful relations with many governments that have not committed to democratic reform. Also, some Arab governments may resent being saddled with a grand plan developed without true region-wide consultations. For this reason, the Forum for the Future is indeed important, and *patience* must be the byword in developing meaningful cooperation. New infusion of funds is also important, but in this political tinderbox great care is needed lest misdirected monies simply foster greed, and even disrespect, for America.

An omnipresent factor inhibiting enthusiasm among Middle East states for grand transformational plans of the West is the refusal of the United States to discuss Israel's security issues. Even though security dominates much of the remainder of the G8 agenda, this topic is conspicuous by its absence in the approach in the Middle East. The United States knows that the immediate reaction to any mention of security would be placing on the table for discussion the Israeli-Palestine peace process.

In the words of two astute Western observers, "The attempt to launch a new initiative without discussing the peace process is a triumph of abstract logic over political reality."[21] But the United States has difficulty in fending off assaults on its policy in other forums. The emotions are so high on this topic that US negotiators rightly consider that they have a better chance of success in other areas by keeping the peace process off the discussion table.

THE ROAD AHEAD

Can international development assistance make a greater difference in the lives of impoverished people? Yes, but only if the United States, the leader in the field, upgrades its approaches. As former USAID administrator Andrew S. Natsios stated in the *International Herald Tribune*, "The world is sharply focused on terrorist threats blasting apart our sense of security from New York to Madrid to Indonesia to Baghdad. The twisted minds of a tiny group exploit the growing divide between the globalized and non-globalized world, the East and the West, Muslims and Christians, democracies and dictatorships. If we really intend to help people in the developing world, it is time to review and renew our approach to foreign aid."[22]

Poverty reduction has traditionally been and should remain the number one objective of foreign assistance. The key to significant poverty reduction is economic growth. Sustained growth depends much more on a developing country's own policies than on foreign aid. Still, foreign assistance can play a crucial role as long as America is both generous and hardheaded—rewarding success and accountability but remaining intolerant of lukewarm local commitment and creative financial diversions. All the while, foreign assistance should be coordinated with but not dominated by efforts to protect US economic and security interests abroad.

Several interrelated adjustments of the US approach to foreign assistance are on the table and should be embraced by the US administration and Congress:

- **Establish a new cabinet-level department**: As discussed earlier in this chapter, consolidate the international development programs of a number of US government agencies under one roof and ensure that other relevant programs that remain in their current organizational configuration join in a consolidated march toward development successes.

- **Overhaul the Foreign Assistance Act**: Originally written in 1961, the amended version of the act now contains an excessive number of targets—thirty-three objectives and seventy-five priorities. Also linked to the act are many stifling personnel and procurement regulations, earmarked funds for pet projects of politicians, and buy-America provisions for purchase of goods and services regardless of the appropriateness of American designs for introduction in distant lands. These barnacles must be scraped off the reconfigured hull of a newly launched foreign assistance Ship of Hope.

- **Spread the concepts of the MCC**: Emulate as rapidly as possible in other foreign assistance programs the concepts that undergird the MCC, particularly those programs administered by USAID.

- **Strengthen USAID**: Recognize more widely the unique experience and capabilities of USAID and promote new legislative mandates that strengthen the agency rather than erode its leadership role or micromanage its activities. This should be the goal whether the agency is folded into a new cabinet department or remains a separate agency affiliated with the Department of State.[23]

These initiatives will help ensure that increased financial commitments will be used more wisely and effectively. They will go a long way toward restoring the reputation of the United States as a compassionate but realistic advocate of international peace and prosperity. At the same time, more effective foreign aid programs can reduce poverty, improve prospects for employment, and lead to more stable governments in many areas of the world.

CHAPTER 5

EDUCATION AND JOBS

★ ★ ★ ★ ★ *Preparing for a Satisfying Life.*
Is It Possible?

Global leaders and experts alike recognize that education is a key, perhaps the most important key, to developing a more peaceful world. Only a world of the informed will be able to reconcile the many conflicting interests with strong political and cultural roots within various communities. Without an educated population, no country will be able to advance economically in a world where globalization has become both a necessity and a reality.

The United States should be in the forefront in promoting access to learning. It has recorded many impressive achievements in promoting international education. Beneficiaries of these efforts in nearly two hundred countries are truly fans of America. But the scope of these successes pales in comparison with the enormity of the challenges of education confronting an impatient world divided by different political, economic, and cultural interests.

CHALLENGES TO EDUCATORS IN TURBULENT CHECHNYA

Grozny is the capital of Chechnya, a tumultuous Muslim enclave of one million inhabitants, tucked away in the northern Caucasus region of

Russia where civil insurgencies have raged for the past decade. With fighting and weaponry the order of the day, educators view school and after-school programs as alternatives to young people taking to the streets. For the rector of the Grozny State Pedagogical College, funds to purchase a wrestling mat so his physical education department could stage tournaments on a regular basis are as important as support for the regular curriculum. "Replace the nightly duels of Kalashnikov automatic rifles with evening wrestling matches! Let the restless young men release their pent-up energy in the gymnasium and not in the streets!" he exclaimed during our discussion of a possible grant from a program that I was administering in 2003.

Together with colleagues in Washington, DC, and Moscow, I had organized in 2003 a program of small grants, financed by the US National Academies, to Chechen educators that would help them make modest improvements in their programs. Six grants, totaling $20,000, were awarded in response to proposals from administrators, professors, and teachers in Chechnya. The rector mentioned above was the recipient of one of the grants. From his perspective, the level of funding was large, but by international standards these small grants barely qualified as serious assistance activities.

At the time, fighting was at a high point between the security forces of the Moscow-backed administration in Chechnya, who were supported by massive Russian military units, and bands of Chechen insurgents, who had sporadic support from international mercenaries. Nevertheless, with the grant and the help of his friends in Chechnya and Moscow, the rector was able to purchase a large mat, head gear, and gym shoes for the wrestlers. We were indeed pleased when we saw photographs of the first match with an eager crowd cheering for their favorite athletes.

Several American academics challenged us as to whether wrestling qualified as a suitable college subject and whether it was an acceptable activity for an "education" grant. Those at the State Pedagogical College had no questions as to the importance of learning how to channel physical energies. My American colleagues and I agreed.

We awarded a second grant to a school where Chechen pupils from ages seven to fourteen held classes in a bombed-out building with crumbling walls and no electricity, water, or roof. The teacher proposed construction of a small cultural museum that would acquaint the pupils with their heritage. Students from nearby schools could also visit the museum, which would be located near the center of Grozny.

Once the grant funds arrived in Grozny, work began at a feverish pace. The teacher and her pupils cleaned out the mounds of dirt and broken concrete slabs from a corner of the building. She arranged for the purchase of construction material for a roof, walls, and doors as the framework for several rooms in this destroyed concrete structure. Local carpenters then built a modest exhibition hall of connecting rooms.

Photographs of the opening ceremony documented the inauguration of the museum as a significant local event. Fortunately, it was held during a pause in the regular bombings and sniper fire throughout the city. The volunteer labor that contributed to the effort was indeed impressive. The grant funds were devoted simply to buying and installing needed construction material.

These two grants were the most successful in our modest program. They provided useful insights into the priorities of educators in Chechnya—at least at that time. The challenges faced by Chechen educators are probably a microcosm of the frustrations and difficulties in helping children and young adults in many ravaged areas of the world to become self-sufficient. Self-sufficiency through education is an essential goal. If the "Americans" are associated with such noble efforts, particularly in times of crisis, a by-product can be the positive, long-lasting image of the United States as a friend and supporter of better lives around the globe.

The grant proposals prepared by Chechen educators gave priority to the interests of students. They were not directed to the needs of the educators themselves even though teachers in Chechnya had received skimpy pay, few supplies, and no training for a decade. Perhaps with a long-range vision of the future, the needs of the educators should have taken priority. However, in Chechnya, the immediate welfare of children *is* the future. They are the priority, and their teachers are prepared to struggle to help them without delay as best they can.

My Russian and American colleagues and I also organized a Russian-Chechen-American conference on education held in 2002 at the Russian

Black Sea resort of Sochi, which is three hundred miles from Grozny. The vice premier of Chechnya, who was responsible for education, reported at the conference that the two governmental priorities for reconstruction were security and children. Judging from the subsequent enthusiasm in Grozny and Moscow over the small grants described earlier, she was certainly correct and she was good to her word in helping us promote the interests of the children. It was indeed unfortunate—yet a sign of the times—that she was nearly killed by a bomb detonated in the main building of the Chechen administration about eight months after the conference. Following five months in a Moscow hospital, she retired from politics, turned over her education portfolio to others, and left Chechnya.

In Sochi, we were reminded that the United Nations Educational, Scientific, and Cultural Organization (UNESCO), in 2001–2002, had sponsored preparation of an excellent report on the conditions of education in Chechnya—preschool through secondary levels. Despite the fighting, local authorities and educators were able to carry out an authoritative study of how the education system had collapsed in the mid-1990s but was slowly recovering as education remained a priority of parents. Optimism for a better future permeated the results of surveys and informed the many recommendations for action by the international community. Among the sobering findings were the following observations, as the school system began to function after a near-total shutdown a few years earlier.

- **Unsatisfied demand**: The demand for preschool education was ten times the capacity of existing kindergartens. At the primary through secondary levels, overcrowded facilities were in atrocious condition but nevertheless functioned for the 50 percent of the children who could make it to school.
- **Lack of space**: Overage students and repeaters were increasing in number. As student retention levels improved, overcrowding became even more severe.
- **Physically and psychologically damaged kids**: More than one-third of the pupils were disabled and needed special attention, with some of them (e.g., orphans and children of displaced families) not eligible for government rehabilitation programs. In addition, the

psychological condition of children could be described in words and phrases such as "terrorized," "reserved disposition," "cautious behavior with adults," "retarded speech development," "poor imagination," and "absence of emotions."

- **Emphasis on bilingual**: Chechen-Russian bilingual capability was a defining feature of educational and social development of students, beginning in preschool.

In addition to the need for continued rebuilding of the physical infrastructure, three priority tasks for further restoration and development of the education system were identified by UNESCO: to provide (1) specialized education to remote villages through correspondence courses, (2) Internet centers to overcome information isolation, and (3) training and retraining of teachers. These recommendations were seemingly straightforward. However, implementation in the near term would require large investments, since working telephone lines were scarce and transportation services were close to nonexistent.

The report also recognized that attitudes toward cultural traditions, based in large measure on child-adult interactions, were a critically important area that should be addressed. In this regard, festivals, competitions, exhibitions, and simple meetings were considered a necessary form of social therapy complementing classroom activities. Several of the small grants that were mentioned earlier addressed some of these concerns.[1]

Chechnya is an unusually turbulent Muslim area. The roots of the current confrontations with Moscow date back many decades. Since the early 1990s educators have been caught in a cross fire between a Moscow-imposed regime backed by a sometimes brutal Russian army, and local renegades who are a combination of separatists, economic bandits, and terrorists. All the while, the bulk of the population has simply wanted to lead peaceful lives.

The end of the conflict in Chechnya is not in sight. The Russians have ruled out any level of independence for the Chechens. A short period of quasi-independence followed an inconclusive war (referred to as the First War) between Moscow loyalists and Chechen separatists during the 1990s. An election endorsed by Moscow was held at that time. Avowed separatists won the election.

Then the new leadership failed tragically at state building. Kidnapping for ransom of Russians by Chechens in Moscow and other distant cities became routine. To a considerable degree, warlords took over. Soon thereafter, the secularism of the past gave way to the beginning of efforts to establish an Islamic republic that encompassed neighboring territories as well. The schools barely functioned.

Moscow was not keen on merely watching what it considered a steady deterioration of the situation with no reversal in sight. Thus, when Chechen militants invaded the bordering Russian republic of Dagestan in the late 1990s, the Russian army quickly backed the Dagastanis and the Second War erupted. Violence reigned in many regions of Chechnya until the Russians gradually reestablished strong control, but local insurgents were determined to continue the battle indefinitely. They took the battle to Moscow where they set off explosions in apartment buildings, in airplanes, on crowded streets, and in the subway system. They took nine hundred hostages at a Moscow theater, a terrorist act that ended in hundreds of deaths.

Then in September 2004, schoolchildren were thrust into the midst of a horrific manifestation of the Russian-Chechen conflict. Thirty vicious terrorists, perhaps emboldened by heavy doses of narcotics and armed with grenade launchers, mines, explosives, and automatic weapons, seized a school in the Russian town of Beslan not far from the border of Chechnya.

More than twelve hundred children, parents, and teachers were celebrating the first school day of the year. The hostage takers herded all but a few lucky escapees into detention areas in the school. They demanded that Russian military units withdraw from Chechnya and that thirty Chechen militants captured earlier by the Russian Army be released.

The tragedy ended on the third day. Russian Special Forces stormed the school following the detonation of an explosive device in the building, and the hostage takers shot and killed a number of children trying to flee the explosion. More than three hundred hostages, primarily children, died. Another seven hundred were hospitalized as fires ignited, gunfire rang out throughout the complex, and part of the school's roof collapsed on hundreds of hostages. Russian authorities reported that all hostage takers were killed with the exception of one captured militant. As the Russian children were treated for all types of injuries in local hospitals and clinics, in Moscow medical facilities, and at home, the traumatized families tried to absorb the devastation of their shattered community. Now hundreds of children face a future with haunting fears and anxieties while hundreds of others lie in local cemeteries.[2]

Looking to the future, neither Russian withdrawal from Chechnya, nor peace talks involving the insurgents, nor UN intervention are acceptable to the Russian government. President Vladimir Putin, with support from the Russian people, will not negotiate directly or indirectly with rebels who dispatch terrorists. At the same time, Moscow's efforts to carry out dialogues with many parties in Chechnya—those considered not to have been associated with terrorism—will probably continue. Apparently, the Russian government believes that with the help of the large Chechen diaspora in Moscow and with greater Russian allocations of financial resources for reconstruction in Chechnya, the Russian-backed administration in Grozny will slowly improve security, remove dissident elements, and gain credibility in the republic.[3]

Meanwhile, human rights activists in the United States and Europe violently oppose Russian policies in Chechnya, advocating Chechen independence as the only solution to the continuing violence.

Since 9/11 the US government has gradually accepted Russian efforts to squelch the violence emanating from Chechnya as part of the global "war on terror." However, the Kremlin considers the United States an ambivalent partner. Russian officials are particularly disturbed when US leaders suggest that Russian violations of human rights in Chechnya are the major cause of the violence. They simply cannot understand how the US government can back Israel's strong military efforts to fend off Palestinian suicide bombers while not unequivocally backing Russia's efforts to contain Chechen insurgents.

As to the potential role of education in helping to eventually cap the violence, universal education throughout the USSR was a priority during the Soviet era. This tradition of educational achievement still permeates much of the education community in Chechnya. Can education become a peaceful rallying point for many elements of a divided population? Can children begin to prepare for productive lives under such difficult conditions?

Clearly, the problems are overwhelming. As of 2005 half of the children of the republic tried to study at home. For them, the trek to a functioning classroom was either too long or too dangerous. The other young people who were fortunate enough to attend organized classes did so under unbelievably difficult conditions—no toilets, no heat, no lunches, no books, and no assurances that classes would not be abruptly terminated.

A start toward a revitalized education system has been under way since the late 1990s. The tens of thousands of teenagers who have never attended a single organized class should be included in education efforts lest they remain fertile targets for international recruiters bent on increasing terrorism in Chechnya or elsewhere. The hope is that education will not only prepare young people to play constructive roles as they mature but that education also will effectively bring together children from families of different political persuasions.

Peace will come slowly, if at all, to Chechnya. An important factor in peace building is a well-informed and tolerant population in Chechnya and in surrounding areas. Education is a most promising route to tolerance that takes into account political and economic realities, the desires of various people of Chechnya, and the inalienable human rights of all.

Violence in Chechnya has clearly been one of the most critical problems facing Russia since the disintegration of the Soviet Union. While Russia is determined to resolve this problem without outside political interference, education provides an entry point for the international community to be of help. Humanitarian assistance has flowed into Chechnya from European organizations for a number of years, with the United States providing limited food and medical supplies. What is more humanitarian than providing facilities for children to learn? As was demonstrated by our small education grants, the US government could win enormous respect from Russians and Chechens alike with modest investments in this area.

EDUCATION AS A KEY TO GLOBAL HARMONY

For decades the United States had been in the lead in promoting advanced education opportunities around the world. It is still the world's most popular destination for international university students. However, its role in helping to build educational institutions abroad has been declining as the pressures for immediate results from US government investments in collaborative activities increase.

Of course, education takes many forms and is shaped by family values, by religious tenets, and by cultural mores. Whatever the form, education can help societies avoid the ravages of hatred. No one is born prejudiced against other people. One path to a safer world is to prevent development of such prejudice, and education is a critical prophylactic. International education endeavors can play a special role in helping to temper violence.

Enriched education efforts include the development of esteem and respect for others of different backgrounds, in addition to the basics of reading, writing, and arithmetic. They nurture interpersonal relations based on mutual benefits. Effective learning programs offer a framework for appropriate behavior while fostering a decided preference for coping with adversity through means other than violence. The challenge is to transform such principles into programmatic reality.[4]

Half a million foreign students from almost every country study each year at US institutions of higher education. The American models for university and college education clearly have become the envy of the world. Thus the discussion of educational pathways for turning international animosities toward America into global respect begins with commentary on the power of higher education.

American concepts of university education are exported in whole and in part to foreign countries through international students and visiting faculty members from abroad who subsequently gain positions of prominence in their home countries. These concepts include, for example, (1) approaches to structuring the requirements for academic degrees, (2) design of curricula for specific subjects, and (3) encouragement of two-way interactions between educational institutions and government departments. Also, they extend to faculty councils, student organizations, and other aspects of campus life.

Examples of the influence of the American education model are manifold. Former communist countries have dramatically changed their undergraduate and graduate degree programs to mirror the US bachelor-master-doctorate model. Almost all countries are trying to enhance the scientific research capabilities of universities as emphasized in the United States so that students in the natural sciences have opportunities for significant laboratory experiences. Also, foreign educators recognize that the United States leads in transforming social sciences from theoretical discussions of abstract concepts into applications of research findings that are relevant to everyday problems.

As the foreign alumni of American institutions continue to disperse around the world, the international linkages between American and foreign universities and colleges, their departments, and their individual laboratories grow. Indeed, thousands of international partners in higher education seek US government funds for carrying out all types of joint programs. Their proposals are so numerous that most cannot be funded. However, the proponents of collaborative activities, in the United States and abroad, have become very resourceful in finding alternative financial sources when the US government does not come through.

Among the most important US government-financed exchange activities is the Fulbright Program. This program has supported two hundred and fifty thousand participants during the past fifty years and has become well institutionalized on a global basis. Fulbright committees are working in many countries. These committees both choose foreign participants to travel to the United States and help place American participants in their countries. The program is recognized in the United States and abroad as supporting only high-quality proposals for serious international efforts in research and teaching. Selection for participation in the program rightly reflects a level of scholarly achievement that deserves international recognition.[5]

An interesting experiment in transporting the American university model to the Middle East is under way in Qatar, hardly a poor country financially but still an emerging country intellectually. The country's emir, urged on by his activist wife, is determined to make the capital city of Doha the higher-education center of the Middle East. Already the Cornell Medical School, Texas A&M University, and Carnegie Mellon University have established campuses there, and several other American universities are in line to do the same. The country's leadership is fully committed to the American approach to higher education and is determined that students in neighboring countries will recognize the advantages of enrolling in Doha's universities.[6]

FOREIGN ASSISTANCE AND HIGHER EDUCATION

For decades the US Agency for International Development (USAID) set the world standard for well-designed assistance programs to help strengthen universities abroad. In Nigeria I witnessed firsthand how the "American" university—the University of Nigeria—managed to maintain high standards under difficult economic conditions twenty years after termination of its support by USAID. American colleagues had imparted to their Nigerian counterparts an infectious enthusiasm for teaching, which was evident even as the faculty gathered up the unused stubs of chalk at the end of lectures to ensure they would not be stolen. They simply could not stop talking about their experiences in America where not only was the chalk more plentiful but education objectives also coincided with their own.

As another example of the long-term importance of well-designed assistance programs, USAID helped establish in Afghanistan forty years ago an engineering faculty that produced graduates who could readily obtain employment in many countries of Europe if the working conditions were not quite right in Kabul. At Cornell University, an anchor in the United States for the program, I learned how American engineering departments benefited from interactions with well-trained Afghan colleagues. Graduates even now are occasionally encountered in Kabul.

Similar stories can be repeated for USAID-supported activities in a wide array of disciplines—from business management to health sciences to agriculture—in dozens of countries.

Unfortunately, in recent years USAID's programs to support the development of universities abroad—or even to retain contact with universities it helped establish—have declined dramatically. Nevertheless, two programs remain strong.

First, USAID provides significant financial support to a number of US agriculture-oriented universities that work jointly with counterpart universities in developing countries on specific agricultural issues—livestock, aquaculture, peanuts, and soil management, for example. Paired universities in the United States and selected countries carry out both educational and applied research programs to enhance the capabilities of the local universities while solving specific production-oriented problems. The best of American agricultural research, which often means the best of the world's research, is on display and commands respect everywhere.[7]

In another effort, USAID has long supported a program titled American Schools and Hospitals Abroad. The agency provides funding for equipment, supplies, and other institutional needs to more than a dozen overseas universities and secondary schools. Embedded in the early histories of these institutions was a strong American presence. The idea is to strengthen these outposts of American education in ways that continue to help bridge the gap between American values and approaches and the particular problems and priorities of the respective countries.[8]

USAID has also been vitally concerned with economic planning and assessment capabilities of countries where the agency operates. Indeed, economic analysis has long been considered the cornerstone of development. For four decades USAID has supported many economic-oriented research and training activities targeted both at improving policies at the highest levels of government and at strengthening pedagogy at universities and colleges. Unfortunately, this focus on economics is rapidly being lost.

In other areas of social sciences, USAID's efforts—and indeed the international efforts of the entire US government—have been weak and spotty at best. In Russia and Central Asia, several American private foundations have stepped in and are now supporting social sciences initiatives at a few universities. Among the types of university competencies that are of interest to foundations and that are also relevant to countries beyond Russia and Central Asia are the following:

- continuity of cultures in modern society
- communications across the Eurasian frontier
- tolerance in contemporary civilization
- security, conflicts, and cooperation
- state, society, the individual, and culture
- power: states, society, and individuals
- problems of modernization of a state[9]

Recent problems in promoting higher education within the foreign assistance program are illustrated by a personal experience in August 1996. At that time, I headed to Bosnia with high hopes of building bridges among the Serbian-, Croatian-, and Bosnian-dominated universities in a country steeped in fresh memories of ethnic cleansing. The Internet provided a powerful linkage tool, and officials of USAID and the World Bank urged that I explore practical details of the idea of using the Internet to facilitate positive relationships among the three ethnic groups. Sporadic fighting among the groups was continuing, and the Holiday Inn where I spent several nights in Sarajevo was full of the bullet holes similar to those I would later see punctuating the many bombed-out buildings in the area.

It was not easy to engage university colleagues in constructive dialogues at the Holiday Inn or in other shattered buildings of the city. But university professors of all three ethnic groups professed a readiness to at least experiment with a demonstration project on noncontroversial subjects in the natural sciences. Could they usefully share expertise and then supplement local experience with commentaries from Western specialists who would agree to participate in the experiment?

We were never to find out. Upon my return to Washington, the same officials of the World Bank and the US government informed me of an abrupt change in policy: university-level education was no longer a priority. All funds available for rebuilding the education sector in Bosnia were redirected to the immediate rebuilding of destroyed and damaged public schools. The immediate priority as winter approached was the providing of temporary shelters for children. Yes, ethnic reconciliation through shared programs at the university level was interesting. But that task should be left to others, stated reconstruction officials.

With no public or private funders in sight, I reluctantly abandoned an idea with great potential. It could have contributed to reducing hostilities among feuding parties while also shining a light on the positive role that the United States could play in addressing one of the most difficult issues in war-torn areas.

OPPORTUNITIES IN DISTANCE EDUCATION

In Iran more than four hundred thousand students are enrolled at Payame Noor University, headquartered in Tehran. This "Distance Learning University" is not equipped with the online programs the term implies when used in the United States and elsewhere. However, it has more than two hundred well-staffed study centers throughout the country, which distribute standardized texts to be used as part of its system of organized learning for students unable to study at traditional campuses.

Access to the programs of the university is remarkable. Every secondary school graduate in the country—male or female—is entitled to enroll and attend classes at one of the study centers. While almost all of the best students go to the more traditional universities, hundreds of thousands of second-tier students (or those without the necessary resources to access other universities) attend the distance education sessions in the study centers. The university also provides a second chance for interested residents of Iran who were not able to attend university at the usual age.

In short, the university gives almost everyone an opportunity to enroll, even holding specialized examinations to admit students who have not completed high school. These and other "provisional" students who fall below the normal admission line must meet certain achievements during their first year or they are not permitted to continue. A large percentage of the enrollees have been provisional students, and many have succeeded in graduating.

The size of this massive distance education effort at a single university, based primarily on self-instructional textbooks prepared by the university staff for home study, surprises most educators who visit Iran. The country began experimenting with distance learning in the early 1970s when a few correspondence courses were offered, and in 1988, when a specialized university was established. This university blossomed from an initial enrollment of five thousand to its current size. The university offers associate, bachelor, and master degrees in a large number of programs. The doctoral degree is offered in Persian Language and Literature.[10]

Colleagues at Sharif University in Tehran are also deeply involved in distance education, pushing toward the online-education components so popular in the United States and elsewhere. They are developing an electronic framework for a distance education effort that initially will link the Tehran campus of Payame Noor University with the study centers. The hope is that eventually students will have the capability to tap into the system electronically from home or from nearby workplaces.

At the same time, Sharif University has been developing electronic-based education programs for its own students, who are the cream of Iran's talent pool. The university has a relatively small target audience that benefits from its considerable intellectual resources. In short, Sharif University is determined to have a digitized world-class program for its students, wherever they may be.[11]

One American expert has noted the similarities in the visions for distance learning in Iran and in the United States. In both countries distance education is being designed to support the following admirable goals:

- make educational resources available throughout the country
- serve students from every socioeconomic class
- ensure that learning experiences from afar are of comparable if not better quality than on-campus experiences
- provide high-quality courses and degrees at affordable prices
- prepare students for good jobs at competitive salaries, jobs that will have a positive effect on development of the country[12]

A number of countries in the Middle East are experimenting with distance learning. The government of Jordan, for example, announced plans in 2002 to begin to introduce distance learning programs throughout the country's public and private colleges. The plan is eventually to award masters' and even doctoral degrees. As to the technologies to be introduced, the concept calls for large Internet components and satellite teleconferencing. While all types of students are expected to participate in the programs, the initial participants have been largely working professionals.[13]

Such enthusiasm for distance learning should be tempered, however, by the experiences of skilled teachers in the field. For example, according to a leading American advocate of distance education in commenting on the early days of digitized systems:

> Faculty often took lecture materials used for face-to-face presentations and simply put that on-line. The first-generation classes were often inferior to in-class versions, but the material was in electronic form and could be used by students at any time. Over time the faculty would supplement these courses with more graphical materials and even simple animations. It soon became clear there were problems. The course was not really adapted to the needs of the distance education student, and many resources were not truly integrated into the course. Furthermore, the faculty realized that the amount of work and the expertise needed to make a major improvement was significant.[14]

In sum, distance education is expanding rapidly as countries seek new ways to use the Internet to reach populations that cannot come to central classrooms at prescribed times. The United States has pioneered many novel approaches in this field. This focus is surely one wherein American experience can be invaluable in facilitating education objectives in developing countries. The United States has the relevant technological wherewithal, and American institutions have undertaken innumerable efforts to improve the means of conveying messages that make a lasting impression on students in all types of disciplines.

PREPARING FOR EMPLOYMENT

During recent years, support of primary education in poor countries has become the priority of the US foreign assistance program. Such basic education is, of course, essential if young people are to cope with everyday needs. At the same time, simply coping is not enough. Indeed, no issue is of more critical importance in creating societies that enjoy economic progress and global stability than meaningful jobs for young people—jobs that are challenging, jobs that are rewarding, and jobs that provide income.

Secondary and university education are key stages in the development of employable skills. In poor countries, *general* secondary-level education is seldom the best approach for the majority of pupils. On the contrary, secondary education should be very much oriented to employment realities. Such an orientation may mean increased emphasis on vocational training, covering a wide range of practical skills, and on work-study programs. As to university training, the American emphasis on basic-science literacy and humanitarian studies is frequently inappropriate in areas where jobs are scarce.

Effective employment-oriented training programs are not easy to organize in poor countries. There are few mentors, and it is difficult for students to find practical experience of relevance to the interests of the small private sectors. Moreover, successful job-training efforts that are sponsored by governments are relatively few in number. Once there is a demand for skilled engineers and workers, however, training mechanisms can easily follow.

Obviously, the best way to increase job opportunities is to accelerate economic growth—which has long been a primary objective of developing countries. The beginning of the twenty-first century saw a new burst of enthusiasm worldwide for small business development, microcredit programs for individual entrepreneurs, and locally based service industries oriented mainly to the agricultural and industrial sectors. The US contribution to job creation, which can be a meaningful antidote to development of anti-American extremism, is most effective if programs with multiplier effects are emphasized. It is essential to establish strong cadres of teachers at universities. It is also important to support development of local policies that encourage expansion of industry and service activities. These two strategies are usually far more effective in the long run than focusing on the plights of individual schools at the primary and secondary levels.

As the interest of developing countries in reaching global markets with goods and services from developing countries climbs, new opportunities for American educators to play important roles in job creation emerge. The World Bank, with its careful analyses of global trends, is optimistic that large numbers of jobs can be created in poor countries. However, both financial resources and management expertise are extremely important in opening new investment horizons that will lead to employment opportunities, and stronger education programs are essential in developing such expertise in the view of World Bank officials with whom I met in June 2004.

If developing countries are to be successful in their international forays in search of trade and aid, they must play by the international ground rules. They should understand how Western economies, which are the dominant force in globalization, operate and they must emulate Western practices if they wish to compete internationally. They should understand contract law. They should appreciate the significance of intellectual property and the ways to protect it. They must adopt international accounting standards. They must respect, appreciate, and ultimately follow the ground rules for international trade being established by the World Trade Organization. Thus, they urgently need well-trained specialists—the *MBA globalists* of the twenty-first century.

In this area, American universities have much to offer. The foreign demand for entry into American business schools is increasing every year. Even the virtual business schools that operate through Web sites are drawing large numbers of applicants. At the same time, many American universities have opened thriving affiliates of their business schools throughout the developing world. The outreach of the University of North Carolina in Thailand is a good example.

However, educators are wise to heed an important caveat when promoting Western business acumen in countries that are suspicious of American motivations: They should concentrate on the international dimensions of doing business while recognizing the reality of the way business currently operates in many parts of the world. Internal business practices within other countries may be inefficient. They may be devoid of economic rationalization. They may be corrupt. Indeed, their practices may be repugnant to outsiders who are used to following certain codes of business ethics.

However, such practices will not be easily changed, and American criticism and preaching may have a boomerang effect in turning local officials away from US approaches. What seems to the outsider to be a country's inappropriate policies or inexcusable tolerance of gross mismanagement often reflects internal acceptance of long-established practices. Tax evasion and favors for government services, for example, may be so deeply engrained that attempts by outsiders to make immediate change will only result in bitter controversies. Then, too, corporate America—although it has made strides in complying with new laws governing accountability and transparency—is likely to be viewed as having little room to talk when it comes to ethical business practices. Hence, all the more reason for US educators working abroad to resist launching a *direct assault* on practices they find intolerable or inequitable—for example, inadequate rights of minority stockholders, patent infringement, or the other inappropriate practices noted earlier. Such assaults may quickly end their welcome in foreign countries.

Rather, it is preferable to concentrate on explaining the impact of such practices on the interests of Western investors and international financial institutions. By compelling developing countries to focus on the international dimensions of doing business, US educators can help foreign leaders appreciate the need to clean up their internal approaches. Even the most hostile critics of American "economic imperialism" will have difficulty challenging the motivations of the United States in helping other countries understand the full dimensions of the global market.

From another perspective, multinational companies, including those headquartered in the United States, should be recognized for their contributions to job creation. Some voices in the United States and abroad criticize multinational companies operating in developing countries for paying too little attention to the welfare of local populations. Sometimes there are well-founded concerns as to whether salary levels are adequate, whether working conditions are satisfactory, and whether multinational corporations have a commitment to environmental preservation.

At the same time, many companies make unique contributions in developing local labor forces. They provide significant jobs, including jobs that require modern skills. These skills are often imparted to employees through training programs established by the companies themselves. A lack of applicants for jobs offered by multinational companies is seldom a problem. By local standards the jobs are very attractive.

Working conditions may not always be up to the standards of the industrialized countries. However, the first step to achieving international endorsement of working conditions is simply to have jobs that are attractive to the local populations.

A few years ago, I visited a highly automated electronics assembly plant in Malaysia owned by a US-based multinational company. I was startled to learn that only two years earlier, 60 percent of the workforce had been living in remote villages with little opportunity for advanced education or employment other than low-productivity farming. Yet, as if by magic, the economically deprived but nevertheless industrious young people had been transformed into a highly reliable workforce. What I was witnessing was the result of on-the-job training. With newly acquired skills, these new employees serviced robot-driven production lines and carried out quality assurance tasks under the watchful guidance of a handful of more experienced specialists. Where are they now? Some have undoubtedly moved on to more responsible positions both within and outside the company.

The company continues to provide jobs where none existed before. While some companies are rightly cited for unsavory business practices, others, such as the one responsible for the transformation of this Malaysian workplace, can make positive contributions to the development of local technical capabilities.

As noted in chapter 4, through the Global Development Alliance, USAID has cofinanced with US companies many programs designed to increase private-sector development and thereby increase job opportunities in developing countries. For example, Shaffer and Associates, a Louisiana-based firm, is constructing a sugar plant in Mali. USAID is financing the research needed to identify the most productive sugarcane varieties and to ensure that environmental standards are met. In Indonesia, USAID and industry are teaming to educate low-income farmers in remote areas about cocoa production practices and connect them to buyers. Masterfoods (formerly Mars) has agreed to buy high-quality cocoa through contracts that permit growers to reap the rewards of their effort. [15]

Finally, any discussion of employment issues in the Middle East must also address the role of the foreign workers, and particularly the hundreds of thousands who are in the Persian Gulf states. Indian, Pakistani, Asian, European, and American workers are seemingly everywhere. In Qatar, for example, 75 percent of the population is made up of foreign workers and their dependents. Foreign workers bring much-needed skills and many strong backs to the region. Also, foreign workers can be dismissed and sent home when economies weaken.

What is the impact of these foreign workers on employment opportunities for local residents? A common rejoinder is that most local residents are only qualified to perform uninteresting low-level tasks. But as populations grow and the economic pie is sliced more thinly, the permanent displacement of many foreign workers seems inevitable. For some countries, release of foreign workers now can serve as a stimulant to the development of an indigenous capability, which will help ensure economic stability in the long term. At the same time, foreign workers must adjust to the requirement to shift to other countries where their skills are in shorter supply.

There is no easy solution to reducing unemployment. In many countries where international agencies play an important role, a shortage of interpreters is a chronic problem and English-speaking schoolteachers and university professors often abandon their professions for higher pay as interpreters. Another shortage area is the construction industry. Flying in foreign construction crews to countries ravaged by violence or natural disasters is too often a short-term fix rather than the basis for long-term economic betterment. Skilled carpenters, plumbers, and welders, for example, are usually in short supply. For education efforts to have impacts in many countries, the United States and other foreign donors should put job creation in the forefront of their activities, and the developing countries themselves must do the same. Otherwise, these countries will not only have great difficulty in raising their standards of living, they will also risk becoming dangerous recruiting grounds for groups seeking idle young muscles for their acts of terrorism and violence.

THE IMPORTANCE OF PRIMARY AND SECONDARY EDUCATION

Recall my experience in Bosnia where support by US officials for higher education was pushed aside in the immediate aftermath of the war. The relocation of schoolchildren dominated US and other foreign aid programs following the cessation of fighting in Kosovo. The importance of providing educational opportunities for schoolchildren cannot be denied. In war-ravaged countries where much of the population ends up in refugee camps, primary education faces many challenges beyond simply having an adequate physical infrastructure. Nevertheless, failing to recognize the comparable significance of maintaining the cadres of university instructors who are already in place, as discussed above, has consistently been a mistake in the zeal to promote primary and secondary education.

Even in developing countries that are not in the midst of violent upheavals, primary and secondary education face a lack of classrooms, inadequately trained teachers, poor training materials, and parents who are uncertain as to the future opportunities for their children. While the conditions in Chechnya described earlier may seem extreme, situations in many other countries are also harsh.

The US Congress has responded to the international appeals that no child should be left behind, even in the poorest countries. In 2004 Congress earmarked $400 million as a down payment for meeting the education components of the UN Millennium Development Goals (described in chapter 4). Presumably, much of the US investment will be directed to teacher training. Insofar as the programs become entangled with differing philosophies on how children are best prepared for life, suspicions can be cast on the real motivations of US assistance efforts.

Congress has embraced approaches to international education advocated by the 9/11 Commission. The Senate, in particular, has actively promoted efforts to improve education in the Middle East through provisions of basic education tools such as textbooks and the construction of local libraries.[16]

All the while, USAID has responded to congressional pressure and has shifted most of its education resources to supporting primary and secondary education. Two arguments for reducing the emphasis on higher education are (1) universities serve primarily children of wealthy parents, which is unfair to less-fortunate families, and (2) Americans will continue to connect with universities in developing countries through many channels, whereas USAID is almost alone among American institutions in financing primary and secondary education activities abroad. The counterarguments, however, are no less compelling: (1) there are hundreds of thousands of neglected primary and secondary schools, and USAID's education budget of one-half billion dollars annually will have little impact in improving education at the primary and secondary school levels, particularly when USAID is compelled to give most of its funds to expensive American advisers; (2) the World Bank and other donors are investing hundreds of billions of dollars into primary and secondary education with much of the funding going directly to institutions in developing countries; and (3) primary- and secondary-education capabilities are not particularly strong assets of the United States, particularly when compared to its higher education assets.[17]

No one questions the importance of providing bricks and mortar for facilities where young children can gather and learn. When it comes to developing curricula and establishing the conditions for learning, however, questions arise. Does the United States have high-quality and relevant experience to bring to the table?

Yes, but we need to be careful. Thousands of American schools do a wonderful job in working with parents to launch rewarding lives for children. However, many schools are obvious failures, particularly in poor neighborhoods. There are many negative perceptions of American primary and secondary schools at home and abroad. Any experts who are sent overseas to share the best of the American experience must be very carefully selected for their assignments. They must be highly qualified and motivated if they are to overcome such perceptions and make a positive difference in the lives of young people on other continents.

In my view, USAID and Congress are currently misguided in considering the support of primary and secondary education to be far more significant than support of university-level education in developing countries. They will probably continue this politically popular emphasis, but they need to be constantly reminded that it is at the university level where a broader range of American interests can be most effectively promoted. Many highly visible successes have resulted from American support of international higher education. While the impact of a thriving university begun from scratch with US assistance cannot be quantified, local testimonials in dozens of countries attest to the payoff from such investments. The United States' universities have indisputably strong assets—reputation, experience, variety, and relevance. The requests of the future leaders of developing countries for cooperation are continuing and unequivocal.

Since the US government will continue to provide considerable support for primary and secondary education in developing countries particularly in Muslim countries, a few comments on these efforts are in order.

UNDERSTANDING THE MADRASSAS

During the past several decades, the role of *madrassas*—schools that highlight Islamic studies—has increasingly brought dismay to political leaders in the United States and Europe and has raised new challenges for the international education community. Madrassas offer a heavy introduction to the teachings of Islam although they have different structural and doctrinaire characteristics in different geographical areas:

- Some madrassas operate at the primary-school level. Others enroll secondary-level students as well.
- Some concentrate nearly exclusively on religious teachings. Others give great weight to secular subjects.
- Some are morning-to-evening schools. Others offer after-school courses to supplement studies in secular schools.
- Some are publicly financed. Others are strictly private undertakings.
- The interpretations of the Koran that undergird the teachings vary significantly.

Thus, any generalizations about madrassas must be viewed with caution.

Immediately following 9/11, international attention focused on the seeds of anti-American hatred that had been planted in some madrassas around the world and particularly in madrassas in Pakistan. Documentary films, television broadcasts, and photographs of journalists have reported in graphic detail how pupils sit in their classrooms in some madrassas for hours on end repeating Koranic verses. According to the reports, many pupils do not understand the Arabic language, let alone the meaning of the verses. Nevertheless, they eagerly add their shouts of angry epithets aimed at the "infidels" from the West, and particularly those invaders from America.[18] The words of a nine-year-old at a Pakistan madrassa financed from abroad are telling indeed: "I could have been like the others in the refugee camp with no clothes and no food. . . . Muslims are the best in the eyes of God, and we must make it the same in the eyes of all men by force. . . . When I grow up, I intend to carry out jihad in every possible way."[19]

The international community has repeatedly clamored for Pakistan to close down the extremist madrassas. Ironically, some schools had been supported by the United States as a small countereffort to Soviet occupation of Afghanistan in the early 1980s. Many receive financial support from benefactors in Saudi Arabia—with promulgation of the extreme tenets of the Wahhabi branch of Islam being the quid pro quo for continued funding.

Political leaders in Pakistan and other Muslim countries have responded to the calls for retribution and violence echoed in the madrassas by issuing their own condemnations of the teachings of extremism that lead to terrorist acts. They claim to have clamped down on financing the hate-filled madrassas that are often linked to international banking channels with abundant funds in lieu of barren donation boxes in public places. Unfortunately, little has changed at many of the most threatening madrassas.

To be sure, in 2003 the Pakistani police responded to the orders of the Pakistani president to close many highly visible Koranic schools that preached violence. One police inspector informed me that he had personally placed large locks on the entrances to sixty schools and banned the imams from returning to these centers. But he acknowledged that the crackdown affected only a small number of the thousands of incubators of anger and violence, including many located in remote outposts where less than a dozen pupils were enrolled.[20]

Of course, in Pakistan and elsewhere, thousands of "good" madrassas focus on important religious tenets that should be embraced and promoted. But "bad" madrassas that relentlessly preach the need for a holy war have graduated between seventy thousand and one hundred thousand pupils from about seven thousand schools at both the primary- and secondary-school levels since 1998 in Pakistan alone. They are indeed worrisome; in fact, some have been described as "jihadist factories." They are training many recruits for dissident military forces. Some military leaders both in South Asia and in the West see devotion to jihadist activities as the most powerful weapon of poor Muslim nations.[21]

The recruitment of students at the madrassas, as well as at mosques and orphanages, to join the ranks of extremist groups is in some cases entangled with international political agendas. For example, Pakistani militants have attempted to shift perceptions of the struggle with India over Kashmir from a territorial dispute to a battle with India over Islam. They point to the eight Indian consulates in Afghanistan where clandestine agents focus on Pakistan with the full support of an Afghan president hostile to Pakistan. This encirclement effort is, in their view, clear evidence that India is pressuring its Muslim neighbor from all directions, and thus a strong and sustained response rooted in the Pakistani education system is essential.[22]

Many madrassas in Pakistan have a distinctly international flavor, particularly at the secondary-school level. The crackdown on madrassas in Karachi after 9/11, for example, encouraged some young boys to migrate to schools in Bangladesh where extremist preaching apparently was not well controlled. At the same time, the number of foreign students in Pakistani madrassas, particularly outside Karachi, has steadily increased. Students come from Malaysia, Indonesia, Thailand, and the Philippines, and a number of sons of Afghan veterans from past border conflicts with Pakistan have enrolled, sometimes on Pakistani government scholarships.[23]

Looking at education on a broader geographic scale, most poor countries with large Muslim populations have significantly increased access to primary and secondary *public* schools in recent years despite the paucity of governmental funding and the shortages of suitably located schools. At the same time, the steady deterioration of the quality of education in many public school systems that are overtaxed with burgeoning populations is evident. In particular:

- Government investments in education remain low.
- Shortages of qualified teachers are omnipresent.

- Teacher training is limited and often ineffective.
- Learning materials and textbooks are in short supply.
- Weak administrative capacity at the national and local levels is usually the rule.[24]

One of the strengths of *Islamic* schools, including many good and bad madrassas, is that they are usually more physically accessible than public schools, despite the progress in access to public schools as noted earlier. They often provide educational opportunities in areas where no public schools exist. Some of these schools combine religious studies with secular subjects or, indeed, with the entire public school curriculum. Generally, the quality of education in nonreligious public schools, however poor, is better than the quality in Muslim schools that offer secular subjects. Both types of schools suffer from a shortage of teachers qualified to teach mathematics and other secular subjects.[25]

As public school systems become stronger and more accessible in Muslim countries, more parents choose public schools but often add religious classes in other settings at the beginning or end of the day or during the weekend. Still, many other parents continue choosing to send their children to Muslim schools. They believe that the experience is the only way to reaffirm, strengthen, and preserve their children's identity with Islam. The following list provides an idea of the estimated numbers and types of schools in Pakistan.

Secular and Religious Schools in Pakistan	
Secular schools	288,519 (1)
Students	15,753,610 (1)
Madrassas operating under the Religious Education Board	6,528 (2)
Students	1,197,427 (2)
Other Extremist Madrassas	7,000 (3)
Students	100,000 (3)

[1] For 2000, USAID estimate, 2004
[2] For 2002, USAID estimate, 2004
[3] For 2004, Department of State estimate, 2004[26]

How can education in Islamic countries continue to serve the needs of populations for both modern curricula and for activities that help preserve their identity? At the top of the list of priorities for Muslims is the imperative to strengthen *both* public education and Islamic education.

As a start, all schools should be registered with governments and become subject to some degree of oversight. The goal of mainstreaming Islamic schools into the national education system would help them provide more interesting alternative-education choices for families. Steps toward standardized curricula would seem to be a step in the right direction.

Also, increased international investment that does not fall into the hands of irresponsible financiers is required to broaden access and improve quality almost everywhere. As an example, in 2003 the Bush administration committed more than $100 million to help Pakistan's education system provide alternatives to the "bad" madrassas. The idea was simple, perhaps too simple: build up a stronger public school system, which is in and of itself a good counterbalance. This commitment of $100 million rested on two somewhat uncertain assumptions, however: (1) that the Pakistan Education Sector Reform Strategy, intended to reduce extremist education, is sound, and (2) that the public schools will not promote intolerance and extremism as is doled out by the militant madrassas. The hope is that the additional funds for the national program will be helpful in tempering extremist education.[27]

The United States will continue to be involved in supporting primary- and secondary-education efforts in Islamic countries and regions and particularly in those countries where militant Islam has a strong foothold. The US government considers the issue too important for the United States not to be involved, even though we may not be playing to our greatest strengths. Teacher training will probably be the primary activity that the United States supports. However, American specialists should recognize that there are disagreements within the Muslim world as to how Islam should be practiced, preserved, and promulgated; disagreements that have implications for teacher training. To avoid being accused of siding with one or another faction of Muslim societies when addressing controversial tenets, specialists dispatched by the US government to work in this field need to be guided by universal values—

and specifically values embodied in UN declarations—that all Muslims can embrace.

Also, the United States must accept the reality that access to "appropriate" education will not necessarily dissuade vulnerable youth from joining terrorist groups. Such groups may promise immediate gratification in contrast to the long time needed to reap the benefits of formal education. Nevertheless, education with balanced teachings should be an important component of efforts to redirect youth from temptations of violence to commitments to responsible behavior. Militancy is military might gone askew. Civility is education gone right.

SPECIAL NEEDS OF YOUNG GIRLS

In Yemen, Dutch foreign-aid officials have long recognized why large clusters of young girls don't go to school. There are no toilets for the girls. The costs of appropriate clothing, while low, are also an inhibition, and the lack of female teachers detracts from an inviting environment. But the toilets have been the primary concern of parents and their daughters alike for decades. Therefore, the Dutch launched a major program in 2002 of constructing bathroom facilities in schools to enhance the appeal of education to young girls throughout the country.[28]

More than 180 countries have signed on to the UN Millennium Development Goal that calls for a quality basic education for every boy and girl by 2015. However, the road to this goal is long, expensive, and full of potholes akin to the facility problems in Yemen. The young girls will have the most difficulty responding to this clarion call to provide children with a fair start in life, particularly in countries where, for centuries, females have not acquired equal status to males in society. Of the 104 million children ages six to eleven who are not in school, 60 million are girls. Of the 150 million children who *are* in school but who will drop out prior to completion of the primary grades, 100 million are girls.[29]

The benefits of education for both boys and girls seem obvious. They often include, for example, higher wages for the graduates, more productive farming for the villages, and faster economic growth for the country. For the girls, the benefits also include smaller and more sustainable families, a decline in infant mortality, reduced HIV infection rates, reduced domestic violence, and more participation in the political process. According to the World Bank: "When one takes into account all its benefits, educating girls yields a higher rate of return than any other investments available in the developing world."[30]

At the same time, strong economic barriers explain why girls stay out of school even where appropriate facilities exist. Parents are less willing to pay the costs of schooling—which may include attendance fees and the costs of transportation, clothing, and safety—for girls than for boys, since boys are expected to become income earners. Also, having girls in school means they are not available to fulfill their domestic roles, which are not optional vis-à-vis the dictates of Muslim cultural traditions.[31]

For young women who can make it through primary and secondary school, some compete quite well for available student positions at many institutions of higher education. In dozens of countries, more women than men are enrolling. While in the aggregate females still lag behind male enrollees at universities, in some Muslim countries they are actually surging ahead.

In Iran, for example, well over 60 percent of the new university enrollees are women. Why? Women believe they have a level playing field with men, and they simply focus on one area where they believe they have an equal chance: merit. However, when it comes to advanced degrees, women continue to lag far behind as tradition calls for many to become mothers and homemakers before they become "too old" in the eyes of their societies.[32]

That said, the United States should use all of its diplomatic muscle to encourage countries around the world to ensure that girls have equal access to education. It's the key to controlled birthrates and the achievement of many more elements of stable and growing societies. When it comes to large foreign assistance efforts, the United States should build this case in urging other donor countries to make major contributions as well.

NEXT STEPS

In looking ahead, a final example concerning the challenges of education underscores that educators in most regions of the world will follow their own paths with or without American involvement in their activities. Tatarstan is a feisty republic of Russia with a significant Tatar majority among its population of five million people. The population is determined to maintain its cultural identity through reliance on the Tatar language throughout the education system, despite the practical problems it presents.

During a visit to a Tatar secondary school in the provincial capital of Kazan in 2003, I was very favorably impressed by the high level of student achievement in a variety of subjects, particularly in the natural sciences. Islamic studies were relegated to after-school classes for children of interested parents. The teachers and pupils at the secondary school were well attuned to the importance of a secular education, and their school days were packed with subjects studied in the West.

Despite the limitations of textbooks prepared in the Tatar language, the school administrators of Tatarstan were determined they would not return to reliance on Russian as the language of instruction. This approach in effect excluded Russian children from attendance at Tatar schools, and they were accommodated at other schools. Both Russian and English were taught as second languages at the Tatar school. School officials knew that for pupils eager to participate in regional and global activities, fluency in these languages was essential.

The plan was to have the Tatar language eventually replace Russian in the universities as well. Initial steps had already caused difficulties and protests from the Russian minority in Kazan, home to several excellent universities. A particular difficulty was the use of the Tatar language in studying scientific subjects, and even the Tatar students opposed such an idea.

Here, the jury is still out on how this effort to retain traditional cultural roots will fare. The attempt to couple the forces of cultural tradition with the recognition of the importance of secular education in a globalized world is admirable.

We have addressed only a few aspects of education in Muslim regions of the world and the potential for broadening the international dimensions of such education. Limited financial support for international education will continue to be provided by the US government, by private organizations, and by American educational institutions themselves. Foreign students will find other sources of financial aid to take advantage of the outstanding capabilities of American universities.

At the top of American priorities should be education programs that help mitigate growing hatred toward the United States throughout the Muslim world—programs that expose young people to the best aspects of American society. In practice, this may mean having sensible US visa policies for prospective foreign students from turbulent countries who wish to enroll at US institutions. It may mean greater recognition of the payoff from educational partnerships supported through foreign assistance efforts. Or it may mean new approaches to using modern technologies in broadening access to science, engineering, and other types of instruction throughout the world.

Programs that generate job opportunities to utilize the skills of graduates of educational institutions are needed everywhere. Developing countries must be prepared to participate in the global economy if they are to experience significant increases in job opportunities; and such participation demands the skills of the MBA globalists of the twenty-first century. Also, many of the jobs will be in the private sector. More well-designed partnerships involving international companies are key to providing job opportunities in developing countries.

Education alone cannot solve the problems of economic development. However, without strong educational underpinnings, few countries will prosper. The United States can benefit in many ways by being an active proponent and participant in international education. The face of America will certainly be seen as more sympathetic as increasing numbers of foreign students enjoy the benefits of the American educational experience whether it be here or in their home countries.

CHAPTER 6

UNCORKING THE
NUCLEAR GENIE

★ ★ ★ ★ ★ *America Can Have the Bomb,*
but Many Others Cannot

Riding a donkey across one of the highest golf courses in the world was an exhilarating experience. At more than nine thousand feet above sea level were well-tended greens, sand traps, and even ball-washing stations at several tees. But the donkey paid little heed to the swings of the occasional golfers as he dutifully plodded upward along the tourist path skirting the steepest fairway. He was intent on reaching the highest point and then returning his passenger to the restaurant at the eighteenth hole.

A golf course on top of a mountain was but one of the many marvels of Kashmir, with millennia of history preserved in its temples, its ancient ruins, and its sprawling gardens. Bargaining for freshly woven shawls and carpets, gathering medicinal herbs, and paddling through marshes covered with lotus and unique Asian flora had long been signature attractions of this rich, green mountain region straddling the border of India and Pakistan. In years past, trout fishing in the streams added for the visitor a sporting alternative to swinging golf clubs. All the while brilliantly plumed kingfishers flitted atop the lotus leaves, imperiously keeping watch over their kingdom.

Few experiences have been as memorable for me as living for a week on Dal Lake on a houseboat christened *New Buckingham Palace*. Each houseboat was in reality a flotilla of two boats. The passenger boat had sleeping quarters (in my case, two bedrooms and two bathrooms), a living room, a dining area, and, at both ends, open porches with lounging chairs. A kitchen boat was tethered to the mother boat, since cooking and feasting were round-the-clock pastimes. Local merchants paddling smaller boats called shikaras showered visitors with flower petals each day at the crack of dawn while peddling fruits and vegetables and even watercolor paintings. Who would not want to extend such a vacation by a second week or even a month?

THE ROOTS AND CONSEQUENCES OF NUCLEAR ARMAMENTS IN SOUTH ASIA

A one-week seminar on the potential contributions of Indian industrial companies to strengthen the science departments of Indian universities was the basis for my visit to Kashmir in 1979. The seminar participants slept on houseboats and gathered each day at discussion sites on the waterside. Also, we had opportunities to meet with the provincial governor and other local officials who proudly talked about the contributions to national development made by their own university in Srinagar, the capital of Kashmir.

At the time of the seminar, the likelihood of the region becoming a flash point that could ignite nuclear devastation of incomprehensible magnitude was in itself incomprehensible. Nuclear capability was far from anyone's mind. But Kashmir was destined to become a political cauldron that could threaten to trigger a lethal mushroom cloud.

The seminar participants quickly learned that the territory of Kashmir had been contested by different ethnic groups even before India and Pakistan won their independence from Great Britain in 1947. Also during our stay, we witnessed street demonstrations in support of rival Kashmiri politicians, each side boasting a large cadre of determined supporters. Even so, the following report of developments directly linked to Kashmir in 1998 would have seemed like a fantasy twenty years earlier: "In May 1998, India announced that it had exploded five nuclear devices. Two weeks later Pakistan boasted of six nuclear explosions of its own. . . . Suddenly the prospect loomed of a nuclear war in South Asia that could kill millions and irradiate a quarter of the globe. . . . The international community could not stop two major countries from crossing the nuclear line."[1]

Conflicting claims over Kashmir may not have been the only irritant in Indian-Pakistani relations in 1998. However, they were a major cause of tension between the two neighbors. As to the timing of the Indian tests, some observers contend that political aggression toward India by the government of China was the spark. Whatever the trigger, these tests and the Pakistani tests that followed sent relations between these two neighbors to a new low.[2]

Ethnic turmoil has plagued Kashmir for decades. Under the India-Pakistan partition plan developed by the British in 1947, Kashmir was free to accede to India or to Pakistan. Kashmir's maharaja wanted to stay independent but eventually decided to accede to India. He signed over key powers to the Indian government in return for military aid and a promised referendum on future governance of the region. The concept of a meaningful referendum quickly faded into the background, and a never-ending territorial dispute has since triggered two India-Pakistan wars.

The first war erupted in 1947 before the ink was dry on the formal state partition documents. As one of its earliest acts of peacemaking, the United Nations was on the scene and supervised the establishment of a cease-fire line. This Line of Control divided the region into a northern area administered by Pakistan and a larger southern area administered by India.

The second war broke out in 1999. This brief but bitter conflict erupted when Pakistan-backed forces infiltrated India-controlled territory in the southern area. Fortunately, under international pressure, the fighting subsided in a few months.

Then in 2004 the two countries unveiled a peace map after months of lengthy negotiations. A cease-fire along the Line of Control was again in effect, and by mid-2005 the president of Pakistan and the prime minister of India claimed they had reached accord concerning the conflict. Bilateral talks over nuclear risk reduction were also under way. How long this good news would last was uncertain, since old habits die hard in South Asia.

Then a shattering earthquake erupted in the region in October 2005, killing more than eighty thousand people and displacing more than two million people from their homes. The only positive outcome of the devastation was the working together of Indian and Pakistani troops to provide relief efforts to those who had lost everything. While the region needs many years to recover from this tragedy, we can only hope that the situation will cast nuclear rivalries into the background.[3]

The continuing danger of nuclear action demands that the US and other governments relentlessly encourage both India and Pakistan to take every possible step to resolve permanently the political standoff in Kashmir. Fortunately, many Kashmiris consider America to be an honest broker when it comes to Kashmir. Given Indian and Pakistani sensitivities to any outside interference, the United States will likely serve more as a facilitator than a mediator.[4]

Further complicating the South Asia nuclear scene was the revelation in 2003 that Pakistan, with its newly born nuclear capability, had for many years been the home of dangerous nuclear proliferation behavior. The following report summarized the situation that shocked many governments. "In 2003, news emerged that a network of scientists, engineers, and middlemen from Pakistan, Switzerland, England, Germany, Sri Lanka, and Malaysia had for years sold nuclear bomb designs and equipment necessary to produce nuclear weapons. Buyers included North Korea, Iran, Libya, and perhaps other states. This development raised the specter of a "'proliferation Wal-Mart.'"[5]

At the center of these nefarious activities stood Dr. Abdul Qadeer Khan. A talented metallurgist, he has long been the most celebrated bomb designer in Pakistan. Indeed, he is revered as the father of the "Islamic" bomb since Pakistan became the first Muslim country to have one. But Khan was indiscriminate about his customers and he did not seem to be plotting against the adversaries of Islam.

Khan's secret procurement in the mid-1970s of centrifuge designs for the Pakistani nuclear program from a shady Dutch industrial consortium highlighted his early activities, which eventually spread around the globe. This particular technology was an essential key to Pakistan's successful weapons program. Today, this enabling technology remains high on the acquisition lists of other states that aspire to achieve nuclear status.

In the mid-1990s, Western intelligence agents learned that Khan had organized a shipment of centrifuges through Dubai to an unknown destination. In exchange he supposedly received two suitcases containing two million in cash for services rendered. Then in 2003 components of additional centrifuges, which were manufactured in Malaysia, were discovered on a German freighter bound for Libya. The Pakistani government acknowledged that Khan brokered the deal, though it denied any government involvement.

In view of the enormous public support for Khan within Pakistan, the president of the country simply issued a sharp reprimand to Khan and removed him from the post of adviser to the prime minister. He was a privileged scientist operating on his own, explained the president. Khan was consumed by greed and took advantage of his position to accumulate wealth for building private villas throughout Pakistan, the president added.

Could such an operation really go unnoticed by the government? Probably not. First, the Pakistani army keeps close watch on the nuclear weapons complex. While its loyalty to the president is always in question, to assume that the army neither saw nor reported unusual activities to the president, or perhaps to his opponents, is hard to believe. Second, Khan's activities were simply too extensive to go unnoticed by his fellow workers. There were too many scientists engaged in related activities for outsiders to believe that none had reported irregularities. Finally, relevant reports of Western intelligence agencies were passed to Pakistani counterparts on more than one occasion and certainly raised questions as to Khan's activities.

If Western governments were suspicious of Khan many years ago, why were there no formal overtures at the highest level to the Pakistani government to stop his activities? Indeed, the rejoinder of Pakistan's president to Western accusations of lack of action by his government to destroy Khan's network was along the following lines: if the Americans suspected Khan years ago, they should have told the president, and he would have investigated.[6]

AMERICA'S TARNISHED NUCLEAR REPUTATION

South Asia's nuclear volatility in the midst of political turmoil emphasizes the vital importance of responsible stewardship of nuclear weapons and nuclear material that can be used in weapons. The United States must be the chief international steward.

Actions by the international community, and particularly the United States, on many fronts are essential to encourage a rollback of nuclear weapon capabilities in South Asia and elsewhere. Of course, necessary action also includes steps to reduce tensions between India and China, which has a formidable arsenal of nuclear weapons at the ready. But first and foremost, the United States, as the world's leading nuclear power, has a responsibility to clearly and irrevocably demonstrate its own readiness to lead a reduction of nuclear weaponry on a broad scale.

Indian politicians have for decades complained publicly and privately about the nuclear discrimination policy of the United States, which contends that only a favored few can have nuclear weapons. Critics refer to this policy as "nuclear apartheid." They ask, "Why is it that not only the United States but also the Soviet Union, the world's largest communist country, could develop nuclear weapons with the approval of the United States; but India, the world's largest democracy, could not?"[7]

The international community has had no choice but to legitimatize retention of nuclear weapons, at least temporarily, by the five countries (the United States, England, France, Russia, and China) that had them before 1970, at which point there was agreement on the need to reduce the world's nuclear arsenal with the signing of the Treaty on the Nonproliferation of Nuclear Weapons (known as the NPT). To sweeten the bitter taste for the have-nots in this deal, the five nuclear-weapon states pledged to help the other countries use atomic energy for peaceful purposes, as the five countries worked to reduce their nuclear inventories. In the eyes of many leaders, however, the United States has not exhibited a willingness to consider giving up this asset, even by the end of this current century. To them, America's intention is to keep the rest of the world in a state of fear, or at least intimidation, forever, by maintaining overwhelming nuclear superiority.

Progress in reducing the weapon stockpiles has been painfully *slow*. After nearly half a century of disarmament negotiations, more than twenty-five thousand warheads remain in the combined inventories of the United States and Russia, while the other three original nuclear-weapon states have hundreds for their own use. Pronouncements by US government representatives heralding the *rapid* pace of disarmament in recent years are viewed as disingenuous at best and deceitful at worst by many governments around the world.[8]

When the nuclear have-nots hear that twenty-five thousand warheads remain, they have difficulty understanding why they should stay on the sidelines while the nuclear powers continue to stall on their commitment to work toward complete disarmament. In 2002 the United States and Russia agreed to reduce the number of *operationally ready* strategic nuclear weapons on each side from a previously agreed-upon level of six thousand each to between seventeen thousand and twenty-two thousand each by 2012.[9] Then in 2004 the US administration announced that the United States would reduce its total nuclear stockpile by 50 percent by 2012. These are admirable steps. But even assuming Russia will also eventually agree to reduce its stockpile by 50 percent, more than six thousand warheads will still remain in each country's possession.[10] What is the point of such a large reserve? How many spares are needed? Surely this number can be reduced to a lower level without decades of delay.

More than 180 countries have endorsed the NPT. But India, Pakistan, and Israel would not sign on. North Korea signed and then in 2004 backed out of its commitment. These four countries are determined to have their own nuclear arsenals whatever the political costs of noncompliance. Iran signed the NPT, but Washington worries that it may soon become yet another nuclear-weapon state.

Clearly the United States, with its command of both military and civilian components of nuclear technology and with its awesome military and economic power, has a special responsibility to spearhead international efforts toward a world safe from self-destruction. In the near term, this responsibility means promoting and supporting international nonproliferation efforts to keep the nuclear genie in the bottle. The United States is certainly focused on that task in its efforts to halt nuclear activities in North Korea and Iran.

The longer-term perspective causes much of the irritation. The United States should demonstrate more forcefully its intentions to work both unilaterally and through international agreements toward a world free of nuclear weapons, a world that will use rather than abuse the power of the atom. Such a weapons-free world may not be realized in the next fifty years, but elimination of all, or nearly all, nuclear weapons should be the ultimate goal. Months of progress now can shorten the time line by years in the future.[11]

The duplicity in US policies is obvious to other countries. More balanced approaches to the control of nuclear weapons are essential. However, the time is short. Only the United States has the political and military clout to lead the world down a path of peace and reconciliation that is not punctuated with nuclear booby traps. A secure tomorrow requires action today.

MISUSE OF DANGEROUS NUCLEAR MATERIALS

Several nuclear threats confront the entire world: first and foremost is the possibility of deliberate detonations of nuclear weapons with far-reaching effects similar to those so vividly demonstrated decades ago at Nagasaki and Hiroshima. Second, so-called dirty bombs laden with radioactive material packed around high explosives are a more likely but less destructive terrorism threat in the immediate future. These devices, nevertheless, hold the potential for killing dozens of people from the blasts of the high explosives, while causing major economic and social disruptions as they contaminate large tracts of dense urban areas. Third, the possibility of sabotage of nuclear facilities looms on the horizon, while memories of the effects from the Chernobyl accident still linger in the minds of residents of many countries of Europe.

Unfortunately, evidence is accumulating that terrorist groups are increasingly focused on all three of these dimensions of nuclear destruction. The Aum Shinrikyu cult in Tokyo tried to obtain uranium from mines in Australia. At al Qaeda training camps, crude drawings of nuclear devices have been uncovered. And, illicit trafficking in radioactive material is increasingly linked with terrorist groups.

Turning first to nuclear weapons, terrorist groups justify their efforts to obtain these powerful weapons as a necessity to redress the imbalance between the destructive capabilities of American-led forces of colonialism and their own limited capabilities to protect oppressed people. They are not preoccupied with the sophistication of the weapons that they obtain. They simply want devices that will work and can be transported undetected to selected targets.

In addition to freelance terrorists, "rogue" states might buy, steal, or otherwise obtain ready-to-use weapons, from the former states of the Soviet Union, for example, or from the international nuclear black market. I heard rumors in Moscow in the early 1990s of attempted purchases by foreign mercenaries of weapons from Russian military commanders who had fallen on hard times. Also, there was talk of attempted thefts of weapons based in Central Asia. As far as is known, these particular rumors were not substantiated by any transfer of weapons.

Throughout the 1990s much attention in the West focused on the possible use by terrorists of small Soviet nuclear devices, referred to as *suitcase nukes* or *suitcase bombs*, which might have been lost during the disintegration of the USSR. Considerable uncertainty surrounds estimates as to how many and what type of suitcase nukes the USSR actually produced. The Soviet armed forces surely had some types of small nuclear weapons for use in artillery shells and underwater mines, as did the US armed forces. They were probably light enough to be hand-carried by saboteurs. Whether they were electronically encoded—and therefore impossible to detonate without access to passwords—and how long they would continue to work before they needed recharging remain unanswered questions outside the Russian Ministry of Defense. But the mere idea that a terrorist group might possess a suitcase nuke, however imperfect, has stirred anxieties in Washington and other capitals.[12]

An alternative to illicitly acquiring ready-made weapons is for a rogue state or a terrorist group to build its own nuclear weapons with the assistance of another Abdul Qadeer Khan. A primary constraint in this regard is the difficulty of acquiring weapon-usable fissionable material, and particularly, highly enriched uranium (HEU). As previously noted, Pakistan succeeded in developing a centrifuge capability to transform readily available natural uranium into HEU, but less-skilled basement terrorists would probably try to acquire uranium that has already been processed into HEU on the black market.

While in Moscow in 1997, I learned of twenty-three attempted thefts from Russian facilities of small amounts of HEU, which had occurred from 1992 to 1994. Few attempts have been reported since then, probably due to restoration of stringent security measures that had deteriorated sharply in the chaos that followed the breakup of the Soviet Union. Fortunately, most of the reported plots were foiled at the outset by the Russian security services.[13] However, the world may not know until it is too late if other undisclosed plots succeeded.

Many years ago, Iraq was on course to create a nuclear device. The Israelis became very concerned about this effort, and in 1981 Israeli bombers, presumably with a green light from Washington, knocked out Iraq's nuclear research center. But the logic that bombing the center would set back Iraq's weapons development program was fundamentally flawed.

It has now come to light that the Israeli attack had just the opposite effect. Saddam Hussein was so incensed by the air strike that he and his aides decided to devote more resources to the nuclear weapons program and hide the program from the outside world. Fifteen years later international inspectors uncovered significant results of his increased efforts, although he was still some distance from having a nuclear weapon.[14]

In another region, North Korea's nuclear weapons program has long been on the watch list of many governments. In 1996 there was optimism that since a nuclear agreement—more accurately called an Agreed Framework—had been reached between the United States and North Korea, Pyongyang would give up its weapons program in exchange for desperately needed economic assistance. This hope faded in the late 1990s.

In 2004 negotiations involving Japan, China, South Korea, and Russia, as well as the United States and North Korea, were initiated to increase the international pressure on Pyongyang to forgo its weapons ambition. However, the North Koreans soon walked out of the talks, insisting that bilateral discussions with the United States were the appropriate forum to discuss the issues. Then in September 2005 they returned to the negotiating table, and the six participants agreed to a somewhat ambiguous approach. Would North Korea finally give up its nuclear program? While the six-party talks may have succeeded in extracting limited commitments from the North Koreans, the road to positive action seems long indeed.

Finally, the military orientation of the nuclear program of Iran is also a front-burner issue for the international community. President George W. Bush famously labeled Iran, along with Iraq and North Korea, as members of the "axis of evil." An important common denominator for these three states was their apparent intention to develop nuclear weapons. Realistically, the circumstances in the three countries were so different that this common branding was of limited use in the US approaches to dealing with each one.

America's most dangerous nuclear adversary may be a technically savvy terrorist group working clandestinely with sympathizers within a rogue government. Not only could such sympathizers offer a safe haven for the group, but they could provide machine shops and other small facilities that would be difficult to hide from the outside world without such collusion. Also, such sympathetic governments might provide banking channels, thereby allowing the terrorist group to circumvent the ever-tightening international clamps on their financial lifelines. Thus, the United States needs to build effective relationships with as many governments as possible, even if certain policies of some governments are anathema to the United States. The stakes of hidden nuclear facilities are simply too great for the United States to deny itself access to any government.

Many Armageddon scenarios have been written about the pulverization of urban areas from a nuclear bomb attack. In addition to devastating effects from the huge blast that would result, greater firestorm effects than previously recognized are now also predicted. One scenario of a nuclear bomb exploding over the Pentagon describes how the neighborhood where we live, less than one mile away, would fare: "Light from the fireball would melt asphalt in the streets, burn paint on the walls, and melt metal surfaces within a half second of the detonation. The interiors of vehicles and buildings would explode into flames. The blast wave and the 750-mile-per-hour winds would arrive, tossing burning cars into the air like leaves in a windstorm."[15]

But those residents wouldn't be the only ones headed for permanent rest at nearby Arlington Cemetery. Virtually no one in an area of about fifty square miles would survive.[16]

While the explosion of a nuclear device is one of the greatest dangers to humanity, the threat of a dirty bomb has also moved to the top of the priority list of counterterrorism organizations. Such a device, often called a radiation dispersal device (RDD), would consist of conventional explosives packed together with radioactive material, which is then spread across vast areas when the device explodes. The immediate death toll would be attributable primarily to the blast of the explosive material, such as powerful Semtex or C-4 concoctions or even TNT or dynamite, but intensive radioactive contamination might contribute to additional deaths in the long term as well. This delayed impact would be particularly worrisome if the contaminated area is not immediately evacuated.[17] At the same time, the psychological impacts and economic losses could be huge as the word spread that there had been a "nuclear" attack, triggering evacuations of large urban areas for uncertain periods of time.

The heightened threat of this type of weapon lies in the easy availability of radioactive material. During the past fifty years, *millions* of ionizing radiation sources have been distributed worldwide for legitimate and, indeed, critical use. *Thousands* of ionizing radiation sources are used in radiotherapy units in hundreds of cancer clinics. More than twelve thousand new sources are introduced each year for use in industrial radiography. Large numbers of sources are also used in checking the quality of welds, testing the integrity of oil pipelines, and measuring the thickness of asphalt on roadways. Many sources are weakly radioactive and pose no danger, but many others—surely numbering in the *tens of thousands*—are strongly radioactive and pose a danger if misused.[18]

One of the most dangerous materials is radioactive cobalt, which is used to irradiate food and to sterilize medical devices and other products. If eighteen-inch cobalt bars were turned into fine particulate and dispersed into the atmosphere, the radioactive contamination could force immediate evacuations of large areas. Of course, terrorists would have to protect themselves during the cutting, grinding, and dispersion operations lest they, too, become victims.[19]

Another type of source of special concern, particularly in the former Soviet Union, is used in the radioisotope thermoelectric generator. RTGs deliver small amounts of power to remote sites. They provide electricity for lighthouses in the Arctic and runway lights at isolated airfields. Powered by strontium or cesium, they contain the ingredients of trouble when dismantled, and their innards can be incorporated into RDDs. While snowshoed terrorists in search of unguarded radioactive material may seem like an unlikely scenario, the possibility should not be completely discounted.

The tracking of many dangerous sources is shockingly poor worldwide. According to the International Atomic Energy Agency in Vienna: "*Orphan radioactive source* is a term utilized by nuclear regulators to denote radioactive sources that are outside official regulatory control. . . . Even the United States Nuclear Regulatory Commission reports that companies have lost track of nearly 1,200 sources within the country since 1996, and more than half were never recovered."[20]

Eventually, some orphan sources show up in waste dumps and in abandoned warehouses. Many are never found, as the owners are eager to dispose of them and to relinquish the responsibility for guarding them. It is often difficult to track down former managers of bankrupt companies who may have left orphan sources unattended as their companies disbanded.

Orphan sources are not the only worry. Many other types of radioactive wastes are in dumps throughout the world. These wastes may not be as dangerous as the unprotected ionizing radiation sources described above. To much of the public, however, radiation is radiation, regardless of the level of danger. Simply scattering contaminated linen from hospitals or contaminated equipment from industry, while creating little health hazard, can be enough to cause public outcry for more responsible handling of such material.

It will take decades to find some of the most dangerous orphan sources and to safeguard all dump sites that house radioactive wastes, even if both the necessary political will and the financial resources are in place. Some terrorist groups are surely well-informed about uncontrolled material. Also, they likely know how to obtain and use high explosives to scatter radioactivity in densely populated areas.

What can be done to prevent terrorist attacks through dirty bombs? Tighter controls on ionizing radiation sources and better tracking of those sources that are in use or have been cast aside are obviously essential.

Unfortunately, the development of such tracking programs is low on the scale of priorities in developing countries where both sources and terrorists are located. Assistance programs from the United States and other donor countries are therefore critical. Also, greater efforts to interdict international trafficking in nuclear materials—including both materials that could be used in dirty bombs and those that could be used in nuclear weapons—are crucial.

At the same time, the United States and other countries must be prepared to respond to deliberate contamination by radioactive material. As of late 2005 there had not been a publicly reported serious terrorist-inspired incident that involved radioactive material. In this regard the following 1987 incident in Golania, Brazil, is worth noting.

> Authorities believe that scavengers dismantled a metal canister from a radiotherapy machine at an abandoned cancer clinic and left it in a junkyard. During the dismantling procedure the metal capsule that contained the cesium-137 was ruptured. Over the next week, several hundred people were exposed to the cesium-137 but did not know it. Some children and adults, thinking the cesium powder was pretty, even rubbed it over their bodies. Others inadvertently ate food that had been contaminated with the radioactive powder. . . . After a victim was diagnosed correctly at a clinic, a medical team began an investigation and discovered that over 240 persons were contaminated, four of whom died. The accident also contaminated homes and businesses, and this required a major clean up operation.[21]

Tens of thousands of urban dwellers were evacuated from their homes and offices. The health effects were significant but limited. The incident suggests how easily radioactivity could become a tool even of terrorists-in-training.

In sum, neither the United States nor any other country is adequately prepared to prevent or respond to a well-planned attack with a dirty bomb. The global dimensions of this problem provide an unusual opportunity for the United States to demonstrate its commitment to international approaches, in contrast to recent tendencies to take unilateral actions when security is at stake. The International Atomic Energy Agency is ideally positioned to play the lead role in this field, but the agency needs strong political, economic, and technical support to take on this challenge. And the United States is the logical partner to give the agency the clout to move forward.[22]

As to nuclear sabotage, since 9/11 the United States has greatly improved security of its more than one hundred atomic power reactors. Many other countries have followed suit. Defending power plants against air attacks is at the top of the list of security priorities. As controls are tightened over flight patterns and over access to commercial and private aircraft on the ground, the likelihood of air attacks declines. Also, all power reactors in the United States and many of those abroad are housed within sturdy containment shells that have been designed to withstand impacts.

However, even upgraded defenses are far from foolproof. Once a hijacked plane is within range of a nuclear power plant, the feasibility of defensive action to prevent an attack is close to zero. At the same time, the likelihood of a major release of radioactive material on the order of the Chernobyl accident seems low given the sturdiness of most atomic stations.

Concerns over the storming of a power plant by terrorists also remain on nuclear security screens around the globe. Again, the notorious Semtex or C-4 in the hands of saboteurs is a major worry. The possibility of dissident workers inside a power plant manipulating reactor-control systems in ways that could cause a meltdown continues to be a concern. In addition, in countries where armaments are poorly controlled, special attention must be directed to preventing the possibility of mortar attacks on nuclear facilities from nearby vantage points.

Will there be a terrorist attack on a nuclear power plant somewhere in the world in the near future? Yes. Even a failed attack will undermine international enthusiasm for further investments in nuclear power.

That said, the poor security at many of the 350 research reactors around the world is of even greater concern. Research facilities, often located on university campuses and at research institutions, are best described as *soft* targets. Some may be on hit lists of terrorist groups. The contamination from scattering the remnants of the nuclear fuel could be widespread indeed. The public reaction would be intense.

A variety of international programs have been put in place to help prevent nuclear terrorism. Here are several examples:

- All Soviet nuclear weapons that had been deployed in Soviet states outside Russia, where political and economic turmoil dominated the scene during the 1990s, have been returned to Russia, reducing the likelihood of theft or sale of the devices.
- For more than a decade, the US and Russian governments have worked together to upgrade security procedures at Russian nuclear facilities that during the 1990s fell victim to hard economic times.
- The International Atomic Energy Agency has become a stronger focal point than ever before in encouraging safety and security at civilian nuclear facilities—promoting international standards, providing advice, and conducting inspections.
- The heads of the leading Western countries, Japan, and Russia (making up the G8) have repeatedly adopted policies and programs to enhance nuclear security, which is at the top of their priority list each time they meet.[23]

As the nation that led the world in harnessing the power of the atom, the United States will inevitably be singled out by its foes as responsible for adverse side effects of nuclear programs when they threaten civilian populations—whatever American intentions may be. American leadership in reducing the likelihood of nuclear disasters can help blunt such criticism. For America, nuclear catastrophes, wherever they occur, will be no-win and probably high-loss events.

THE NUCLEAR CAULDRON IN THE MIDDLE EAST

For decades, Israel has relied on its cache of nuclear weapons to ensure the survival of the state. "Never again" has been the understandable reaction to the Holocaust, and nuclear weapons are the ultimate insurance policy. Tel Aviv reasons that the international agreement requiring states to forswear their opposition to obtaining nuclear weapons is not relevant to Israel, at least at this time, since the country has a unique history, it faces unique threats, and it has an internal commitment to use nuclear weapons only as a last resort.

From the vantage point of Tel Aviv, the best way to resist international pressure to cleanse Israel of nuclear weapons is to curtail sharply any discussion of the nuclear issue and to punish harshly anyone who reveals details of Israel's program. For example, only in 2004 was Israeli whistle-blower Mordechai Vanunu released after an eighteen-year jail term for transferring sixty photos of the Dimona nuclear reactor center to the British *Sunday Times* in 1986.[24] Since that time Israeli security lapses seem to have been nonexistent.

On several occasions I have been approached by Israeli scholars to engage in discussions of the roots of "superterrorism." This is the theme of our 1998 book that warned of the intersections of international terrorism and the proliferation of weapons of mass destruction.[25] However, as soon as I have mentioned the importance of considering all dimensions of the problem, including the nuclear dimensions, Israeli contacts have immediately lost interest in a dialogue.

Meanwhile, the pressure for Israel to join the growing international effort to rid the Middle East of nuclear weapons increased following 9/11. As long as Israel maintains a nuclear stockpile, its adversaries in the region have an incentive to respond with their own nuclear weapons programs. Such responses have repercussions far beyond the Middle East. The perception of an Israeli nuclear threat was probably a major motivator for Iraq to seek nuclear weapons, initially during the 1970s and then starting over in the 1980s. In Tehran the Israeli nuclear program has been a primary driver among some Iranian officials to achieve nuclear parity. Of recent concern in Tehran and other Middle East capitals has been Israel's acquisition of five submarines capable of launching nuclear-tipped cruise missiles.[26]

When pressed at intergovernmental forums to address the issue, the Israeli government responds that the elimination of nuclear weapons throughout the Middle East is desirable. However, Israel will consider steps that might be taken only during the "second phase" of implementation of the road map that should guide the Middle East peace process (discussed in chapter 9). At the United Nations and elsewhere, Israeli diplomats endorse the idea of eventually creating a Middle East that is free of all weapons of mass destruction. Israel insists, however, that peace must precede disarmament. The Israeli population supports this view.

As would be expected, for many years there have been private US-Israel discussions on the nuclear issue under the rubric of "bilateral discussions of strategic issues." The substance of these discussions is well guarded and unknown to the outside world.

Under what scenario does Israel need between two hundred and three hundred nuclear weapons—the commonly reported size of its arsenal—and where are the targets for so many weapons located? Surely not in neighboring countries with relatively few large cities. Under what circumstances could the use of nuclear weapons enhance the security of Israel? Surely Israel would not be the first country to launch a nuclear attack and stimulate the ire of the entire world. The Israeli answer is quite simple. Israel has more options with a large nuclear force.

As previously noted, another Middle East country where nuclear weapons have become a lightning rod for international condemnation is Iran. For more than a decade, Western governments have chastised Iran for its intention to obtain nuclear weapons. The primary Western concerns have been the construction of a nuclear power complex at Bushehr on the Persian Gulf and, more recently, the construction of uranium enrichment facilities near Isfahan.

In the view of the US government, the Bushehr project is little more than a front for a clandestine effort to obtain nuclear weapons. Does nuclear power make sense in a country awash with oil and gas reserves? With the Russians involved in the construction of Bushehr, the Iranians will surely have access to technologies with relevance to nuclear weapons, and American officials.

The Iranians have responded to these assertions along the following lines. Dating back to the days of the shah, the Americans, the Germans, and the French supported development of the Iranian nuclear complex. It is now too late to accommodate changes in Western views, given the Iranian investment in nuclear energy. Meanwhile, the Americans offered to help North Korea construct a power plant with a design that is even more closely linked to weapon concerns than the design of the Bushehr plant. Besides, international inspectors make dozens of visits to Bushehr each year and they are free to visit the facility at any time in accordance with Iran's international commitments. As to the Iranian need for nuclear power, the more nuclear electricity that is available, the more opportunities there are to export crude oil and natural gas, conclude Iranian spokesmen.

Iran has consistently concealed important aspects of its nuclear program despite its international commitments to be forthcoming, and the pressure by the United States and European countries for Iran to abandon its nuclear program has been intense. On several occasions, this pressure has actually encouraged Iranians from all walks of life to rally around a belief that Iran needs nuclear energy despite its oil and gas riches and that the world should not deprive Iran of nuclear technology. In one well-publicized show of solidarity, liberals in Iran—who had long protested the government's failure to establish a truly representative government—joined hands with conservatives in protesting before Iran's Department of Atomic Energy the American position on a nuclear Iran.[27]

By 2002 it had become clear that the United States had ample reason to doubt the sincerity of the Iranian claims that their nuclear efforts did not extend beyond interests in generating power. Publicly available satellite photographs revealed that the Iranian nuclear complex had many undisclosed dimensions.[28] International inspectors were then able to confirm that a complex of centrifuges, which can enrich natural uranium to a level that could be used either for power or for weapons, had been established and was operating.

Then in 2004, much to the chagrin of the US government, Iraqi officials revealed to the Iranians that the Americans had cracked Iranian secret codes and were far-better informed on the inner workings of the Iranian security agencies than had been previously appreciated.[29] With both public and secret documentation in the hands of the West, the Iranian contention of innocuous activities began to fall apart. Slowly Tehran agreed to greater international access to its programs.

The Iranians continue to claim that their program is only for peaceful purposes. The West argues that they clearly have the intention to develop weapons. The situation can probably be best described as a program for power generation that has the surge capacity to build nuclear weapons if and when the Iranians feel they need them.[30] One leading American scholar suggests that the only way that the Iran problem can be solved is to "treat them as equals and cut a deal that addresses their concerns."[31] Of course, others argue that their facilities should be destroyed by air attacks.

The Europeans (France, England, and Germany) attempted to cut a deal. By the middle of 2005, it appeared that Iran would suspend uranium enrichment and other activities with clear weapons implications. In return the Europeans would consider supporting the Iranian peaceful nuclear activities and take a liberal position on trading with Iran.[32] With the advent of a new Iranian government in 2005, however, hopes for political rapprochement on this issue faded. Then the Russian government took the initiative to convince Iranian colleagues that nuclear stalemate was not in Iran's interest. Moscow, with the endorsement of Washington, proposed that if Iran abandoned its enrichment capability, Russia would provide fuel for the country's atomic power program. Whether this effort has potential to help resolve key issues remains uncertain.

Why does the Iranian government believe that it may need nuclear weapons in the future? Of course, the government points to Israel's nuclear capability. On Iran's other flank, Pakistan already has nuclear weapons. Why should Iran, as the strongest resident in a dangerous neighborhood, not also want to be able to defend its interests? This was the logic I heard at several international meetings of diplomats and scholars in Tehran between 2001 and 2005.

The third dimension of the Middle East nuclear equation is the possible nuclear ambitions of other countries in the region. At least four countries will be on the fence concerning the development of nuclear capabilities should significant changes in the international environment affect their security calculations—particularly changes related to activities of Israel, Iran, or the United States.

- Egypt flirted with the nuclear option in the 1960s, but as tensions with Israel eased, internal pressures for nuclear weapons also subsided. In the wake of Chernobyl, the government decided to dismantle the country's nuclear infrastructure. However, should Israel conduct a test of a nuclear device or should the currently calm Egypt-Israel relationship come unraveled, the nuclear option would be back on the table.

- Syria is high on the watch list for chemical and biological weapons development. But there has been little evidence of movement toward nuclear weapons. Nevertheless, Syria remains an uncertain wild card in the Middle East.
- Saudi Arabia has a nuclear research institute, but near-term interest in nuclear weapons seems unlikely. Should the US-Saudi relationship deteriorate, however, Saudi money might well be redirected to the nurturing of a nuclear capability that would be worrisome. Heavy reliance on imported technologies would be required.
- Finally, Turkey's commitment to the West and lack of interest in nuclear technology should not be taken for granted. A key issue is whether NATO will continue to provide a safe harbor for Turkey in the years ahead. [33]

Nuclear security in the Middle East deserves a higher priority from Western governments. Progress in persuading both Israel and Iran that nuclear weapons are not the solution to tension in the Middle East is essential. New weight, beyond simple UN resolutions, should be given to promoting a regional approach to denuclearize the Middle East.

A new international mechanism, championed by the US and European governments, should seek commitments by Israel that it will not be the first to use nuclear weapons in the Middle East and that it will discontinue production of weapon-usable plutonium and enriched uranium. As a symbolic gesture of great political significance but with no military consequences, Israel should promptly reduce its nuclear weapon stockpile by 50 percent as a clear statement of a desire to avoid nuclear war at all costs. Finally, Israel should commit to becoming a nonnuclear-weapon state when arrangements are established to permanently rid the Middle East of nuclear weapons.[34]

In return, all Middle East states would take steps to reduce the possibility of biological and chemical weapon programs as well as nuclear weapon programs in the region, with appropriate international oversight. The issues of chemical and biological disarmament have long been of concern to Israel, and supervision throughout the region in this area would be of significant importance to Tel Aviv. Equally important, all parties would pledge to refrain from armed attacks on Israel with appropriate sanctions for states that failed to fulfill this commitment. Meanwhile, the Israel-Palestine peace process must be accelerated.

Iran's nuclear capabilities need to be rolled back. Additional forms of oversight as to activities that are under way also need to be developed. In exchange for concrete actions by Iran to forgo nuclear weapon ambitions, the United States should ease economic sanctions and become directly engaged in cooperative nuclear research programs in Iran designed to promote agricultural, medical, and industrial activities. Cooperation could also include evaluations of the safety aspects of new Iranian power reactors, since Iran's isolation from the extensive international experience in this field could result in unnecessary safety risks in its nuclear power program.[35] Such cooperation would provide much-needed transparency in order to confirm that Iran is moving in an internationally acceptable direction.

A regional mechanism would, as a first step, need to provide a forum for designing the verification procedures and practices to make sure that the Middle East is free of nuclear, chemical, and biological weapons. An intergovernmental effort to begin designing such verification procedures would in and of itself help build much-needed confidence among historic enemies. At the same time, the mechanism would need to commission detailed studies to identify key obstacles to be overcome in transforming the concept of a weapons-free region into a reality.[36]

An effort along the foregoing lines would not only enhance international security, but would also have enormous impact in restoring respect in the Muslim world and, indeed, in Europe and other regions, as well for the "objectivity" of the United States. The initiative would not be a sell-out of Israel, as the United States would continue to be the de facto guarantor of Israeli security. In this regard, a statement by leading nuclear disarmament experts signals the need for much more flexibility in Washington and Tel Aviv. "The United States, as chief cop on the block and Israel's main protector, must demonstrate fairness. The Iranian and Arab polities crave fairness as they perceive it has been denied to them. Their perceptions may be debatable, and Israel's existential security cannot be traded away; but some Israeli contribution to regional disarmament is imperative."[37]

RESTRAINT FOR US NUCLEAR AMBITIONS

Several aspects of US policy concerning its nuclear forces and stockpiles raise worldwide doubts about the sincerity of the United States to work with the international community in search of a world less reliant on nuclear weapons. Indeed, in the views of some governments, American policies heighten rather than reduce the likelihood that nuclear war will break out in the future. Other governments have complained many times about the following nuclear policies:

- **Continuation of hair-trigger alert status for nuclear weapons**: The United States, as well as Russia, continues to keep a substantial but undisclosed number of nuclear weapons on hair-trigger alert status. Such a posture provides the capability to launch nuclear-tipped missiles within minutes of a warning signal. However, this Cold War mentality creates unacceptable risks of accidental or unauthorized launch.[38]
- **Development of the bunker buster**: For several years, the US Department of Energy has pressed for development of the Robust Nuclear Earth Penetrator, usually referred to as the nuclear *bunker buster*. The idea is that existing warheads would be adapted to destroy buried facilities, particularly caches of chemical or biological weapons.[39] However, it is difficult to believe that the United States would detonate an atomic weapon for this purpose. The underground nuclear explosion would vent through the surface, killing many people, probably in the tens of thousands, should it occur near a populated area. Congress has repeatedly rejected the administration's request for funding of a study of the concept, but the proposal keeps reappearing.[40]
- **Potential development of new small warheads**: Congress regularly changes its mind on whether there should be a prohibition on research that could lead to designs of new warheads with explosive power of five kilotons or less. Given the large inventory of many types of warheads, the need for yet another class of weapons seems unnecessary.
- **Threat of preemptive strike**: The US government's National Security Strategy has reaffirmed that in rare circumstances the

United States would not necessarily wait to be attacked with weapons of mass destruction before it could respond with a nuclear strike to serious threats.[41] In the absence of a US policy of no-nuclear first-use, without caveats, it seems duplicitous to argue for other countries to adopt a no-first-use policy.

- **Failure to ratify the nuclear test ban treaty**: Finally, both the executive branch and Congress have shied away from pressing the issue of US ratification of the Comprehensive Test Ban Treaty that has been ready for signature for a number of years. The clear perception abroad is that the United States intends to resume testing on short notice without any legal constraints.

Overarching these policy areas are four principles that were elaborated in the US Nuclear Posture Review of 2002: (1) We must assure our allies that do not already have nuclear weapons that they don't need them, since we are prepared to defend them if necessary. (2) We must dissuade adversaries from developing nuclear weapons. (3) We must deter nuclear threats that emerge. (4) We must destroy threats that are not deterred. It is this last principle that opens Pandora's box. The rationale is similar in a number of respects to the approach for preventing nuclear terrorism initially set forth during the Clinton administration, which also retained the option of a first strike.[42] It is difficult, if not impossible, to predict a realistic scenario for using such an option.

The United States spends six billion dollars annually to maintain and improve its nuclear weapon capabilities. To populations in many corners of the world, this expenditure seems like an enormous sum for a country that claims no nuclear ambitions. They ask, couldn't some of the funds be redirected to supporting international programs of peace that reduce the danger of nuclear war?

Even for those of us in the United States, the sum seems large indeed. In the words of the chairman of the House of Representatives Committee on Water and Energy, which is responsible for the relevant budget, "The U.S. nuclear weapons program is the ultimate in white-collar welfare." Yet the chairman is unable to significantly reduce the budget due to pressures from all sides.[43]

AVOIDING AN ARMAGEDDON

The policy of the US government must be to avoid a nuclear attack anywhere in the world at all cost. How best to achieve that goal without further alienating already angry parties around the world is a central issue.[44]

For decades the United States has promised to work toward eliminating nuclear weapons, including its own. It has also promised to help all countries derive the benefits of nuclear power[45] and of other nuclear applications in agriculture, medicine, and industry.[46] Now America's zeal to prevent nuclear proliferation should not divert attention from achievement of these objectives as well.

Total nuclear disarmament is far beyond the reach of the global community for the foreseeable future. Civilian nuclear power may never reach its full potential. And dangerous nuclear material may ultimately turn up in the hands of dangerous people.

If America makes its best effort to simultaneously reach for the brass rings in all of these arenas, it will win the admiration of both friends and foes. If US policies are seen as simply efforts to deny others access to the most powerful technology on earth, America surely will be considered the nuclear bully. Nuclear bullies don't win friends in the search for international peace and security. Indeed, they incite new efforts by basement terrorists who are determined to use the most powerful weapons ever known in their quest for retribution.

President Dwight Eisenhower had it right in his famous Atoms for Peace speech at the United Nations: "The United States pledges before the world its determination to help solve the fearful atomic dilemma, to devote its entire heart and mind to find the way by which the miraculous inventiveness of man shall not be dedicated to his death, but consecrated to his life."[47]

Now, a half century later, restraint in expanding America's nuclear arsenal is crucial.

CHAPTER 7

MEDICAL DIPLOMACY

★ ★ ★ ★ ★ *Saving Lives and Winning Friends*

The midnight trek from Dar es Salaam, Tanzania, to a field research site of the World Health Organization (WHO) thirty miles outside the city was difficult. The grass-covered dirt road was barely visible in this undeveloped section of the eastern coast of Africa. Finally, my African guide and I arrived at a cluster of tents on the edge of a small village. Walking into the only lighted tent, I was taken aback to see four nearly naked teenage African boys sitting on stools. Each boy was perched under a lightbulb. Each was armed with a small glass bottle. On tables nearby were dozens of additional bottles and plastic bottle caps with tiny air holes.

Their task was to place an open bottle over every live mosquito that landed on an arm, a leg, or other exposed body parts and then to cap the bottle in order to preserve the captured insect. A British scientist who had been sent to Africa by the WHO supervised the activity. He contended that since the boys had learned to react very swiftly when a flying insect landed on their skins, seldom did the mosquitoes have a chance to bite. I could only assume that the boys' payment was tied to the number of mosquitoes that they trapped, since they certainly seemed happy when they made a capture. According to the scientist, the boys were recruited through posters distributed in the city, and there was never a shortage of applicants for the jobs.

The live mosquitoes were taken to a nearby laboratory to determine which of the two hundred strains of mosquitoes found in Africa visited this lighted tent most frequently. The insect of principal interest was the *Anopheles* mosquito, which carries the malaria vector. A key question was the frequency of capture of *Anopheles* mosquitoes during different seasons. The answer would guide the DDT-spraying program to reduce the malaria infection rate. As a bonus, the European virologists in Tanzania obtained live mosquitoes on which to test the effectiveness of chemical controls.

At the time of this visit in 1971, I was an official of the US Agency for International Development (USAID). My primary interest in traveling to East Africa was to demonstrate how recent scientific advances could help stop the spread of malaria. The United States has long enjoyed unparalleled capabilities in many aspects of medical science and technology. In this case, American virologists had discovered how to change the genetic makeup of mosquitoes through irradiation, a change that could impair their ability to reproduce.

Finding research scientists living and working in the region who could support my efforts in using and assessing a new American technology was a challenge. I finally discovered small groups of researchers at two field stations established long ago in the highlands of Tanzania by the British government. At each station, several researchers from Europe, together with a few local scientists-in-training, were investigating the spread of mosquito-borne diseases. They were clearly focused on malaria as a major problem in Africa, but they had given up on any type of control other than heavy doses of DDT, which, at that time, was considered the most practical control method. Environmental side effects were of little concern when lives were at stake.

Thus it was not surprising that they belittled the approach I was exploring—the control of the *Anopheles* mosquito through genetic manipulation. "This is a long-term effort," I stressed. I pointed out that, if successful, the new approach would replace the need for spraying large amounts of DDT into the environment and for developing a never-ending stream of new drugs to ward off malaria, since the drug resistance of the disease vectors constantly kept ahead of the latest pharmaceutical formulations.

What really confused the skeptical researchers I encountered was our idea of beginning the project with experiments on the *Aedes aegypti* mosquito—the mosquito that carries the vector for yellow fever, which at that time had almost been eliminated from the planet. But our logic seemed sound to us. The *Anopheles* mosquito—the carrier of the malaria virus—was difficult to manipulate in the laboratory. The *Aedes aegypti* was an easier research subject. Therefore, the initial experiments would be with the *Aedes aegypti*. Only if these experiments were successful would later experiments target the *Anopheles*. What were the experiments?

American virologists advised us as follows: Female mosquitoes usually mate only once during their lifetimes and they mate only with male mosquitoes of the same strain—*Aedes aegypti* females with *Aedes aegypti* males, *Anopholes* females with *Anopholes* males, and so on. If the female mates with a sterilized male, the female obviously will not reproduce.

Male mosquitoes mate many times. The release of sterilized males into swarms of mosquitoes should provide unlimited opportunities for the males to mate repeatedly, each time negating the reproductive capability of a female mate. Wouldn't these impotent males eventually destroy the reproductive capabilities of the entire female population? Thus, the original idea was to sterilize male mosquitoes in the laboratory and then release them into the environment for nonreproductive mating. With no offspring, the strain of mosquitoes would presumably disappear. That was the logic.

Then reality took hold. There are too many healthy male mosquitoes already in mosquito swarms. Even if thousands of sterilized males were released, they would not be enough to have an impact. They would be overmatched by much larger numbers of sexually potent males that would continue to be present.

Therefore, the virologists decided to sexually cripple, rather than totally sterilize, each male mosquito by irradiating it in the laboratory—altering the male mosquito in a way that would lead to reproduction of even more seriously crippled male offspring. Each time a single genetically crippled male mosquito was taken from the laboratory and released into the environment, thousands of completely sterile male mosquitoes would be born several generations later, since each crippled male offspring would have many mating sessions. The multiplier effect would eventually wipe out the troublesome strain. This was the theory we were attempting to prove in East Africa.

Our initial effort was to demonstrate on an uninhabited island off the coast of Kenya how this experiment would play out. The island was narrow and two miles long. While no humans lived there, it was certainly full of mosquitoes. We planned to monitor how genetically modified *Aedes aegypti* mosquitoes would eventually eliminate the resident population.

After lengthy discussions with local officials who were somewhat bewildered by the proposition, I obtained authorization for preliminary mosquito releases on the island. Skeptical Kenyan officials relented when they learned that there would be new employment opportunities for a few local technicians and workers. They were uncertain as to whether the new breed of mosquitoes could really be controlled and kept away from the mainland, but they were willing to take a chance. And Kenyan scientists were interested in the laboratory techniques to genetically cripple the mosquitoes prior to the releases.

Back in the United States, the next task was to locate a breeding facility that could generate large numbers of mosquitoes ready to absorb the prescribed doses of radiation and thereby change their genetic characteristics. The American virologists uncovered a low-cost mosquito breeding facility in Pine Bluff, Arkansas. There the US Army had constructed such a unit following World War II—an array of high-quality cages with appropriate feeding and handling dimensions.

The army's idea was part of biological warfare efforts. The concept was to breed swarms of mosquitoes and then infect them with dangerous viruses. The infected mosquitoes were to be packed into artillery shells and fired in the direction of an enemy. The shells would split apart as they hit their targets, releasing their swarms of biological bullets aimed at hostile troops.

When word of such a scheme leaked to the press in the 1960s, the army pledged to abandon the program. However, the army still retained the cages. In short order after our overture, the officials in Pine Bluff became eager to dispose of their contraptions, and, without delay, the mosquito factory was on its way to East Africa.

Then the project collapsed before it really started. The USAID officials controlling program expenditures suddenly decided that this type of slow-moving project was no longer of interest. They would retire from their positions well before malaria was eradicated even if the project was highly successful. Why should they be associated with a project that might not work? Therefore, they slashed the budget. With inadequate funds, the American investigators had no choice: they donated their mosquito factory to the WHO, dismissed their local employees, and returned to the United States.

In retrospect, it was certainly a high-risk project. But if successful, the potential payoff would have been very large, for the approach could have revolutionized control of disease-laden mosquitoes. Eliminating only one of the two hundred existing strains of mosquitoes would have had little effect on the ecological balance of target areas.

Thirty-five years later, malaria remains a vicious enemy of populations throughout central and southern Africa, in Asia, and in Latin America. One estimate is that 40 percent of the world's population is at risk from malaria. The increasing resistance of the malaria vector to drugs, the breakdowns in public health systems, and the expanded ranges of mosquitoes are complicating control efforts.[1] While development of more effective drugs is under way, the costs are out of reach in most areas of the world.[2]

Meanwhile, the interest of virologists in genetic manipulation of mosquitoes remains high. Recent research findings suggest a modification of the initial approach, but the overall concept of destroying the reproductive capacity of mosquito populations remains unchanged. Instead of irradiating the male mosquitoes, which might weaken their sexual prowess in addition to reducing their reproductive potency, scientists now suggest introducing specific mutations into the insect genome through chemical injections into the eggs. This technique, they claim, has a comparable genetic effect. This sterile insect technique (known as SIT) is being used in combating agricultural pests.[3]

Meanwhile, in 2003, the Gates Foundation announced that the control of insects that transmit diseases would be one of its fourteen grand challenges in global health, with funds to address each challenge.[4] Developing genetic and chemical strategies to destroy or incapacitate diseases are at the heart of these challenges. Isn't it time to return to Africa?

CONTAINING INFECTIOUS DISEASES

Malaria is but one of a number of infectious diseases plaguing the world. As we witness the spread of HIV/AIDS, tuberculosis, hepatitis, and other diseases in dozens of countries, the death tolls mount. Each year fifteen million deaths are officially attributed to infectious diseases. A much higher number would include unreported deaths and deaths attributable to the indirect effects of flu viruses. Also, when considering death rates of people under forty-five years of age, the percentage attributable to diseases in some regions is alarmingly high, on occasion as high as 50 percent. The reasons for the emergence of new diseases and the staying power of endemic ones include the following:

- **ecological changes** that result in the spread of parasites and viruses into new areas
- **diseases in animal populations** that cross into human populations, particularly as humans move into new ecological zones
- **concentration of people in conditions where diseases thrive** (e.g., slums, refugee camps), due to poverty, uncontrolled urbanization, and population displacements
- **weak public health infrastructures**, buffeted by political changes, natural disasters, and outbreaks of violence
- **globalization of travel and trade** that markedly increases disease transmission
- **overuse of antibiotics**, which causes disease microbes to mutate to new forms that resist available drugs, making once-curable diseases incurable[5]

What do the doctors of the world prescribe to prevent and control infectious diseases at the beginning of the twenty-first century? Not unexpectedly, WHO recommendations include using proven and affordable strategies, such as bed nets to help prevent malaria; improving health delivery systems in developing countries; expanding systems to detect outbreaks; and developing affordable diagnostic tools, drugs, and vaccines.[6]

The United States has for decades deployed medical personnel to combat dangerous diseases around the globe. Given today's ever-rising infection rates, a doubling of the efforts of the United States would have large payoffs both in reducing suffering and winning friends too numerous to count. A vast array of unrealized opportunities are available to use America's medical achievements for saving and extending tens of millions of lives throughout the world, including large clusters of sick people in countries where hatred toward America is intense.

However, caution is needed. While it would seem that even America's staunchest antagonists should welcome the helping hands of US medical personnel, victims of diseases often ask, "Who is to blame for the diseases in the first place? Is America sending medical doctors in search of redemption for its evil acts?" As an example, rumors in the developing world contend that the upsurge in polio resulted from ineffective American vaccines that were really designed to sterilize populations. For years, stories have circulated that the AIDS epidemic began when a virus escaped from experiments at US military research facilities.

Such nonsensical rumors notwithstanding, the international reach of US government and nongovernment health organizations has been extensive. The Centers for Disease Control and Prevention (CDC) in Atlanta have outposts in dozens of countries. The Department of State and USAID have developed impressive programs to combat HIV/AIDS and other diseases. As noted earlier, the Gates Foundation has become a major contributor in attacking global health problems. At the WHO, which must be at the center of global efforts, the United States is a major player, contributing about 15 percent of the total WHO budget.[7]

Unfortunately, this effort is no longer adequate. The United States can and should lead a greatly expanded effort both to protect the American population at home and abroad and to extend lifetimes in the poverty pockets of the world. The US financial commitment of several billion dollars annually to eradication of diseases worldwide pales in comparison with the current commitment of hundreds of billions of dollars to support US military occupations in Iraq, Afghanistan, the Balkans, and other countries.

The United States has long received loud applause for its global health initiatives, while squelching wild rumors as to who is to blame for disease outbreaks. Now the urgency and opportunities to expand its role within a multilateral context are unprecedented. In addition to improving lives, such an initiative would help repair America's reputation, as the United States becomes a team player and a force for wellness.

THE SCOURGE OF HIV/AIDS

More than 20 years and 20 million deaths since the first AIDS diagnosis in 1981, almost 38 million people are living with HIV. . . . In 2003, almost five million people became newly infected with HIV, the greatest number in any one year since the beginning of the epidemic. In the same year almost three million were killed by AIDS. . . . Funding has greatly increased but is still only half of what is needed and is not always effectively utilized. Many national leaders remain in denial about the impact of AIDS on their people and societies.[8]

Such authoritative UN pronouncements clearly underscore that HIV/AIDS represents both an emergency crisis and an international development problem that will plague the world for many decades. By all measures, the epidemic continues to outpace the global response. This situation prevails despite the many clarion calls to action by political leaders around the world and the sharp drop in the costs of HIV/AIDS treatment.

The impacts of HIV/AIDS are devastating, not only for sick and dying individuals but also for societies as a whole. On all continents, HIV/AIDS takes away the income and production capacity of family members who are stricken with the disease, while placing new financial burdens on the families. The disease drains the resources of health systems, with an attendant neglect of other health burdens on the population. The loss of productive workers affects the agricultural base of large regions where the disease is rampant. In industrialized areas, absenteeism leads to organizational disruptions and lost business opportunities.

Now concern over some international peacekeepers as carriers of HIV/AIDS is growing. Reports suggest that they are bringing HIV/AIDS into areas where they are deployed. Other reports indicate that some are being infected in war-torn countries and are taking the virus home when they finish their overseas service.

Women are particularly hard hit. Not only do they constitute about half of the cases, they also are called upon to be caregivers for sick relatives, a task with few rewards. Women may also become targets of ridicule for contracting HIV/AIDS or for living in AIDS-infected households.

The international community is taking many steps to reduce the impact of HIV/AIDS, but much remains to be done. Some countries in southern Africa with infection rates at the epidemic level have yet to evaluate the extent and consequences of the disease. The inadequate coping capacities of individual households are seldom of concern to health authorities, or if they are, few resources are available to them. These households need financial assistance, home visits from health services, and food and nutritional supplements, for a start. Better-trained health staffs are in short supply almost everywhere, as the best-qualified providers often become disenchanted with low salaries and seek other professions.

Comprehensive HIV/AIDS prevention programs are essential. Key components of such programs include

- launching education and awareness campaigns, particularly among the youth
- promoting male and female condoms as a protective option along with abstinence, fidelity, and reduction in the number of sexual partners
- treating sexually transmitted infections of all types
- preventing mother-to-child transmission
- protecting blood supplies
- establishing "harm reduction" programs among drug users that encourage treatment as an alternative to punishment
- changing laws and policies to counter stigmas and discrimination[9]

Access to antiretroviral drugs and other types of HIV/AIDS treatment remains low. The WHO estimates that nine of ten people who urgently need treatment are not being reached. In 2003 the WHO warned that five million to six million deaths could result unnecessarily during 2004–2005 due to lack of access to antiretroviral treatment.[10]

At the same time, the costs of antiretroviral medicine have fallen dramatically. In 2000 the cost of a first-line WHO-recommended drug regimen to treat one patient for one year was between $10,000 and $12,000.

By 2004 the estimated price had dropped to $300. Still, this price remains out of reach for many who need the treatment, and the mechanisms for providing treatment on a sustainable basis, even when the drugs are subsidized, are complicated in most countries of concern. Nevertheless, hope for the future is on the rise, since cost has always been a major barrier to widespread use of available drugs.

Political voices continue to call loudly for more action at meetings of leaders throughout the world. In September 2003 the WHO launched the "3 by 5" initiative. The initial WHO target was to provide antiretroviral drugs to three million people in developing countries by the end of 2005.

Meanwhile, the financial commitments of governments to global HIV/AIDS efforts continue to increase. In 2003 an estimated $5 billion was available from donors, the UN system, international nongovernmental organizations, governments, and out-of-pocket spending by people living with HIV/AIDS and by their families. Yet this is only a small portion of the amount required to begin to turn the corner in stopping the spread of HIV/AIDS.[11]

HIV/AIDS infections increased threefold from 2000 to 2004 in North Africa and the Middle East, areas of large Muslim populations. While the infection rate of 0.3 percent of the population remains lower than in many other regions where it has soared to greater than 1 percent, the trend is indeed worrisome. Injection of drugs is the principal problem in most Muslim countries. In Iran, for example, drug users make up more than two-thirds of the reported thirty thousand HIV/AIDS cases. Condom use is rare throughout the Muslim world, increasing the potential for infection to spread to sex partners.[12]

A number of successful pilot projects have been reported for the region.

- A prevention program in Morocco integrates into the government's literacy programs awareness about HIV/AIDS, sexual health, and gender issues.
- Behavior interventions for drug users in Iran, together with a policy environment that cultivates support networks of infected people, has reduced drug use, needle sharing, and unsafe sex.
- In Algeria, Mauritania, and Tunisia, nongovernmental organiza-

tions have pioneered the establishment of self-help peer education and the support of health service programs for workers in the sex trade and for men who are infected with HIV/AIDS.[13]

As to the US response to the crisis, both the Bush administration and Congress have repeatedly commended each other for the large sums of money being directed to counter the HIV/AIDS epidemic. In 2003 President George W. Bush committed $15 billion across a five-year period to address the problem.

The President's Emergency Plan For AIDS Relief (PEPFAR) is the flagship American program. This initiative has been designed to quickly provide antiretroviral drugs to fifty thousand people in the most highly infected countries. Abstinence messages target five hundred thousand young people in these countries. New programs for sixty thousand orphans include social services, safe water, and HIV/AIDS prevention education. In addition, PEPFAR calls for expansion of safe-blood-transfusion and safe-medical-injection programs.

While governments around the world welcomed this new infusion of funding from Washington, the international enthusiasm for the details of the program is not high. At the Fifteenth International AIDS Conference in Bangkok in 2004, posters read "Bush tells lies. Condoms save lives." Protesters were referring to President Bush's efforts to minimize the importance of measures other than abstinence and fidelity to control the spread of HIV/AIDS. Indeed, the US position, which was perceived as "my way or the highway," became a flash point for an international split in the approach for attacking the epidemic. The specific complaints of many HIV/AIDS activists in Bangkok are noted below, with most of the anger focused on the PEPFAR initiative:

- One-third of the funds are to be directed to encouraging sexual abstinence even though studies show that the appeal for saintly conduct seldom has a significant impact in the absence of much larger complementary programs.
- Condom use is being played down rather than played up, presumably for religious reasons.
- Only those antiretroviral drugs approved by the US Food and Drug

Administration, which means primarily drugs produced in the United States, can be used in the program. The WHO has already approved competitive drugs that reportedly can be combined in a single pill and popped only twice daily in comparison with the six-daily pills required when using the American drugs.

- The public health systems in some of the target countries are being overwhelmed with the sudden influx of new resources in order to achieve immediate "measurable results" demanded by American officials.[14]

Perhaps the most discouraging aspect of the PEPFAR initiative is that, while it may provide important near-term relief, HIV/AIDS patients must receive drugs for lifetimes—that is, until there is a cure.

Nevertheless, the initial reports on the program have been positive. In 2005 the program was on track to support by 2008 treatment for two million people living with HIV/AIDS, to prevent seven million new HIV infections, and to support care for ten million people infected and affected by HIV/AIDS, including orphans and vulnerable children. The fifteen focus countries are among the world's most severely affected. There, one-half of the world's thirty-nine million HIV-positive people reside together with eight million children orphaned or made vulnerable by HIV/AIDS.[15]

The US government, along with most governments around the world, recognizes the need to stop the HIV/AIDS epidemic. They have seen in Uganda, for example, that strong government support and an infusion of well-targeted foreign assistance can reverse threatening trends. With strong political support in Washington and throughout the United States, the US government has a wonderful opportunity to show the best of American intentions in tackling the HIV/AIDS program in a responsible way. But the issue of the use of condoms will not go away.

HALTING THE SARS EPIDEMIC

Severe acute respiratory syndrome, or SARS, is caused by a corona virus known as SCoV. It is unknown whether it is a respiratory virus or a pneumoenteric virus. The incubation period is from two to ten days. Patients typically have influenza-like symptoms such as fever, myalgia, headache, and diarrhea. The fatality rate is high.[16] According to the WHO:

> The SARS epidemic starkly outlined the benefits and dangers of the impact of globalization on infectious disease. The ease and frequency of international travel facilitated the quick spread of infections to five countries within 24 hours and to more than 30 countries on six continents within six months. Likewise the increased migration of workers from rural to urban areas within their home countries or into different countries and continents has increased the risk that new and previously unrecognized viruses will become established in worldwide human populations.[17]

The epidemic began in late 2002 in southern China. Farmers took small, wild mammals from their native environments to local markets. They sold both slaughtered and live animals, side-by-side, for human consumption. Some of these animals carried the SARS virus. The likelihood of the virus spreading from animal to animal was very high in the crowded and unsanitary conditions of the markets. An outbreak of SARS was soon detected in several cities, as the virus spread to humans.

Unfortunately, the outbreak coincided with the Chinese New Year holiday. Many health officials were on vacation, and the additional mingling of the population during holiday celebrations increased the opportunities for spreading of the disease. Further compounding the problem, a spokesman for the Chinese authorities who was available during this period initially misidentified the virus as another bacterial agent that did not warrant heightened concern.[18]

The SARS virus was carried into Hong Kong when a sixty-four-year-old medical doctor, who had treated patients in the infected area of China and had become infected himself, checked into the Metropol Hotel in that city. He thereupon transmitted the disease to sixteen other guests who spent time on the same floor of the hotel. These guests then carried the disease to the general populations in Toronto, Singapore, and Hanoi, as well as to hospitals in Hong Kong, where several victims sought immediate treatment. The Chinese doctor soon fell seriously ill and died, but he had seeded a global outbreak from a single floor of the hotel.[19]

Eventually nine hundred people died, primarily in China, and eight thousand became seriously ill. While the number of deaths was not large in comparison with other health pandemics, the worldwide economic damage was enormous, estimated to be more than $40 billion. The broad publicity of the initial fatalities, the speed of the global spread, and public uncertainty as to control measures contributed to a public alarm on every continent. The travel and tourism industries were particularly hard hit. Hong Kong and Toronto, in particular, only slowly recovered after devastating economic losses.[20]

I happened to be traveling in southern France when the epidemic was being brought under control and heard a firsthand report from an American Express official from Toronto. While her business in Nice was booming, she described a ghost-town business environment in Toronto. She planned to linger as long as possible in France.

The international response to the epidemic was remarkably effective. The WHO already had in place a Global Outbreak Alert and Response Network involving 115 national health services, academic institutions, technical organizations, and individuals. While originally established to manage outbreaks of influenza, the network demonstrated that it could handle the SARS epidemic and, potentially, other crises of even greater magnitude. Worldwide telecommunication networks facilitated collaborative research among eleven geographically dispersed laboratories and helped to identify the infectious agent within one month. The news media and public health organizations disseminated important SARS information in a very timely manner, and they undoubtedly influenced the Chinese government and the Chinese public to take aggressive containment action while actively engaging the international community in the response.[21]

The CDC played a critical role in the international effort to contain SARS. Of course, concern was high over the possibility of the SARS virus reaching the United States through international travelers, and, indeed, one case of SARS was reported in the United States. The CDC's efforts extended around the globe. Eventually more than eight hundred CDC specialists were involved in the response, and eighty-four were deployed to SARS-infected areas in eleven countries. The largest contingents went to Taiwan and China. Medical officers and epidemiologists were dispatched most often.

Several factors contributed to the successful international response to the SARS outbreak, in addition to the readiness of the international community to respond to any disease outbreak:

- **Sense of urgency**: Fear and uncertainty that SARS could go anywhere and hit anyone increased daily.
- **Past experience with HIV/AIDS**: The earlier worldwide focus on the devastation of AIDS spurred health officials to serious action lest another comparable epidemic emerge.
- **Leadership from the WHO**: The WHO took a public, activist stance in mobilizing the global response.
- **New scientific tools**: They enabled researchers to study many aspects of the epidemic from patterns of lung damage to genetic sequencing of the virus.
- **Preparations for bioterrorism already in place**: Preparations to counter bioterrorism attacks enhanced the ability and speed of some countries in identifying new infections.[22]

A good example of the rapid response in many countries comes from Russia. This country has a very long border with China. Daily train and plane service between the two countries raised immediate alerts. Also, Russian students studying in China were of concern.

Upon learning of the outbreak, Russian public health officials alerted border control personnel, train and plane crews, and public health specialists at train stations and airports to take special precautions in observing the health conditions of travelers. Dating back to the Soviet era, the personnel had routinely been trained to be on alert for travelers with symptoms of health problems and they were quickly updated as to special manifestations of SARS. Travelers with suspicious symptoms simply were not permitted to cross the Russian border. Those that were not spotted before they left China were likely detected on arrival in Russia. As a result of this clampdown, only one reported case of SARS in Russia materialized, and controversy remains as to whether that sick person really was a victim of SARS.[23]

Looking ahead, the real lurking killer for the international community is influenza. When a new type of flu emerges from a reassortment of animal and human viruses to which humans have no immunity, a pandemic may ensue. In 2005 avian flu originating in Asia emerged as a major international crisis. Of particular concern are viruses traceable to birds and swine that live in close proximity to large populations. Still fresh in the memory of the medical community is the Spanish flu epidemic of 1918–19, which caused twenty million to fifty million deaths worldwide. Less devastating were the Asian flu epidemic of 1957–58 and the Hong Kong flu epidemic of 1968–69, epidemics that each killed *only* tens of thousands.[24]

ENSURING THE SAFETY OF FOOD

In another alert, the WHO warns, "Each year, at least two billion people, or about one-third of the global population, become ill from unsafe food. Simple prevention techniques could significantly reduce the burden of disease, which can cause serious illness or death."[25]

In the United States alone, seventy-six million people suffer from food-related illnesses of various kinds each year. Several thousand die. More than three hundred thousand end up in hospitals.[26] What is the undocumented death toll in poor countries?

The WHO advocates simple actions to reduce such incidents, particularly cooking food thoroughly and keeping hands clean. This formula seems simple enough, and a focus on the preparers and servers of food is long overdue. Still, it will take much more to reduce the widespread problem of unsafe food to a tolerable level. Too many dangerous chemicals and bacteria find their way into food supplies to rely solely on improved behavior at home and in restaurants. Food-safety practices must be greatly improved all the way from the farm to the fork to cope with the following trends:

- Larger-scale production designed to serve growing global markets means that a single oversight early in the food chain can affect very large numbers of consumers.
- As the demand for year-round access to many types of food increases, countries are importing foods from new producers who may be inexperienced in good agricultural practices, good manufacturing practices, and safe hygiene practices.

- Interest in exotic foods produced at home and abroad is increasing, thereby exposing consumers to new types of relatively unknown hazards.

Well-known harmful bacteria remain at the top of the list of the triggers of food-borne illnesses. For example, *Clostridium botulinum* is usually associated with improperly canned foods or vacuum-packed food. *Escherichia coli* 0157:H7 (commonly known as "E coli") comes from contaminated water, raw milk, raw or rare ground beef, unpasteurized apple juice or cider, and uncooked fruits and vegetables. *Salmonella* is associated with raw or undercooked eggs, poultry, and meat; raw milk and dairy products; and handlers of food, particularly seafood. Most *Shigella* outbreaks result from salads prepared and handled by workers using poor personal hygiene.[27]

Many of the effects of contaminated food are short term and simply uncomfortable. But food diseases can also lead to kidney failure in young children, reactive arthritis, and meningitis. Contaminated water can become a carrier of the hepatitis virus, a truly dangerous vector.

The United States prides itself on having the world's safest food supply. In many ways it does. However, as noted above, tens of millions of Americans are still stricken with disorders attributable to food-borne diseases each year. One can only imagine the agony of living in other countries that are nearer the bottom of the list ranking food safety practices around the globe.

US government authorities, and particularly the Food and Drug Administration, the Department of Agriculture, and state regulatory agencies, have excellent capabilities to help strengthen food safety programs, not only in the United States but in other countries as well. From time to time, they are called upon to do just that, usually with financial support from USAID. They have organized excellent programs to help microbiologists more effectively adapt their basic laboratory training to practical work in assessing food contamination problems. They have shared their extensive experience in disease surveillance and disease record keeping. They have helped other nations develop the capacity to respond to the types of outbreaks of food-borne diseases that have plagued countries the world over.

With the ever-growing international trade in agricultural products, the capability to identify contaminated foods and to verify the shelf life of food is critically important. Particularly in developing countries, only primitive capabilities exist to check on the quality of food imports and exports. It is not surprising that the illnesses associated with consumption of imported foods from these countries are often very severe.

The World Trade Organization and other international institutions have taken on food as a high-priority safety issue. To support such efforts, years ago the international scientific community banded together to recommend safety standards for food in international commerce. Operating within a scientific framework called the Codex Alimentarius Commission, scientists established contamination limits that are to be observed when exporting or importing food.

The key to enhancing food safety, nonetheless, lies not only with establishment and enforcement of international conventions and agreements but, more important, also with local capacity and local determination to ensure the safety of products. All countries should be able to confirm the quality of raw food ingredients; the quality of processing operations and of processing equipment; the integrity of packaging; and the health, hygiene, and education of food workers.[28] Bilateral assistance programs can be meaningful in strengthening the food safety infrastructures to carry out these responsibilities in developing countries.

A recent example demonstrates how international cooperation can serve US political interests. In 2003 private US foundations launched modest efforts to upgrade food safety programs in the Middle East, focusing on cross-border trade in this region. One project involved cooperation among Jordan, Israel, and the Palestine Authority. While Israel has long had a reasonably well-developed system for monitoring and enforcing food safety procedures, both Jordan and Palestine have a much longer row to hoe. This trilateral effort was a beginning to focus attention on food safety in an area under stress. Similar efforts are clearly in order throughout the Middle East and elsewhere. If the United States plays a useful role in reducing food contamination problems, the number of grateful people will be large indeed, while food safety goals are advanced.

BIOTERRORISM: THE LAST FRONTIER

A final reminder of lurking biological dangers comes from the US Institute for Peace: "Bioterrorism became a harsh reality in the fall of 2001 when letters containing a fine powder of dried anthrax spores were sent through the U.S. mail infecting twenty-four people and killing five . . . the ripple effects temporarily disrupted all three branches of government, closed down congressional offices and mail-processing stations, and frightened millions of Americans."[29]

Subsequent mailings of powder, from the deadly biotoxin ricin to the White House in 2003 and to the US Senate in 2004, further underscored the reality of the bioterrorism threat. Fortunately, these latter incidents did not result in deaths or serious illnesses. More ominous scenarios that have been described but not carried out suggest that well-executed terrorist plots could release dangerous biological agents in crowded subways or sports arenas. Also, skilled adversaries could spread them from crop-duster aircraft diverted over metropolitan areas. Such attacks could easily result in tens of thousands of deaths.[30]

Such scenarios are not far-fetched. Documents and computer drives seized during the March 1, 2003, capture of Khalid Shaikh Mohammed—a key operational planner for al Qaeda—revealed that the organization had recruited a Pakistani microbiologist, acquired materials to manufacture botulinum toxin, and developed a workable plan for anthrax production.[31]

These possibilities should not come as a surprise. Warfare using microbes and viruses has a long history. During the fourteenth-century siege of Kaffa, attacking Tatar forces catapulted plague-infected cadavers into the city. In 1763 the British gave Native Americans blankets that had been used in a smallpox treatment hospital. To disrupt exports or damage local economies during World War I, German covert agents spread infection to sheep in Romania, mules in Mesopotamia, horses in France, livestock in Argentina, and animal feed in the United States. In the 1960s the Viet Cong smeared pungi sticks with excrement to infect American soldiers as they stumbled through the jungle.[32]

More recently in the United States, the fascist group Order of the Rising Sun was apprehended in 1972 with thirty to forty kilograms of typhoid bacteria cultures that they had planned to disseminate in water supplies in Chicago and St. Louis. In 1981 an Oregon cult contaminated restaurant salad bars with salmonella, resulting in 750 illnesses. In 1995 an American attempted to smuggle ricin from Alaska into Canada with the intent of using the toxin as a weapon.[33]

About twenty-five infectious microorganisms that are suitable for bioterrorist attacks can be obtained from natural sources, such as infected animals, sick patients, or, in the case of anthrax, contaminated soil. However, many strains of microorganisms that are nested in such environments have relatively low virulence and would cause minimal harm. Since terrorists would have difficulty in separating out the virulent strains, they would more likely steal the dangerous variants from research laboratories or even purchase them under the guise of legitimate research activities from the many commercial vendors of dangerous pathogen strains.

The nascent biological weapons program in Iraq during the 1980s and early 1990s was designed to disperse biological agents on the battlefield. This effort greatly increased the awareness of the US and other governments of the danger of bioweapons in the hands of irresponsible governments or terrorist groups. Now all types of biological research activities in countries with questionable political ambitions have become targets of international scrutiny, even in the absence of evidence of such activities stretching beyond peaceful scientific endeavors. The mere fact that researchers are dealing with pathogens that conceivably could be misused by terrorists triggers tense confrontations. The disciplines of the life sciences and biotechnology have indeed become battlegrounds for clashes between security and scientific interests.

International agreements to reduce the possibility of misuse of dangerous pathogens have long been on the books. The Biological Weapons Convention outlaws programs that are designed to serve offensive military purposes. The Australia Group, an organization that includes most industrialized countries, is an effort to limit exports of dangerous biological and chemical material and of related production equipment to countries and institutions of questionable reliability. Now concerned scientists are calling for new international strictures on biological research that could curb the use of microbial formulations with military applications.

Enforcement of such international agreements is difficult. Seldom can inspections of civilian biological laboratories or manufacturing facilities clearly confirm that militarily relevant activities under the guise of civilian activities are or are not under way. Biology is biology, and applications of biological research results are manyfold. Of course, if an international inspector were to discover a bomb casing stuffed with anthrax, it would be a smoking gun indeed. But the time required for an underground organization to assemble or destroy incriminating evidence is so short that the likelihood of such a discovery seems remote.

Since the late 1990s the response in the United States to the threat of bioterrorism can only be described as massive, with investments in defensive measures skyrocketing into the billions of dollars. Given the potential consequences of a terrorist-implanted contagion that infects millions of Americans, this reaction is understandable and indeed essential.

In 2001 the *New York Times* reported three initiatives by the US government that, if accurately described, clearly were misguided and could be erroneously interpreted as intentions by the United States to use biological weapons:

1. **Project Jefferson** was an attempt by the Defense Intelligence Agency to reproduce a genetically modified strain of anthrax developed by Russian scientists in order to determine whether the strain was resistant to a US vaccine.
2. **Project Clear Vision**, financed by the CIA, called for the construction in the United States of a Soviet-designed bomblet in order to assess its dissemination characteristics.
3. **Project Bacchus**, initiated by the Defense Threat Reduction Agency, led to the construction of a production facility to assess the feasibility of mass-producing anthrax from off-the-shelf equipment.[34]

When surprised by this leak of secrets, the White House contended that the activities were all defensive in character and therefore were permissible under the international agreement banning offensive-oriented activities. Some legal scholars in the United States and abroad disagreed, although there was no adjudication mechanism to resolve the controversy. Also of concern, the United States did not report these activities in its required annual declarations to the United Nations on biological activities. The United States has always prided itself in setting the international standard for proper use of biological assets. But these formerly secret activities quickly shattered that illusion. What would be Washington's reaction if North Korea or Syria were found secretly formulating new strains of anthrax or constructing biological weapons using off-the-shelf equipment?

Setting aside these American missteps will be difficult since other governments have long memories. Nevertheless, the most effective way to provide assurance that illicit activity is not under way is through a broad international program of bioengagement on peaceful biology endeavors. As scientists from different countries work together in search of important solutions to shared health and agriculture problems, they usually develop respect and understanding for one another. They gain many insights not only as to activities currently under way but also as to the long-term intentions of collaborators. And understanding intentions is essential when the United States is considering whether or not to take pre-emptive military action to prevent a bioterrorism nightmare.

THE FUTURE AGENDA

Checking the spread of HIV/AIDS, providing early warning of and preparing for the next outbreak of a flu virus, reducing the number of incidents of food poisoning, and providing reassurances that countries around the world are not misusing the fruits of the biotechnology revolution make up an agenda that will resonate well at home and abroad. In each area the United States has repeatedly demonstrated its commitment to the common good. Now is the time to deepen and broaden that commitment. Vigorous US leadership that is sensitive to the concerns of other nations in these four areas will be welcomed by all, and the United States will be just as much a beneficiary of expanded efforts as any of the other partners in the global effort.

If Americans are identified as the crusaders in warding off diseases— a crusade carried out on behalf of hundreds of millions of at-risk people— the United States will have gone a long way in restoring global confidence in the humanitarian dimension of American policies. For example, America can take the lead in closing the global vaccination gap—in increasing the vaccination rate for diphtheria, tetanus, and pertussis (DPT) for the children of Africa—and in developing new generations of vaccines to prevent pandemic flu, pneumonia, and diarrhea worldwide, to cite but a few of several pressing needs. And there is even increasing optimism that in time a new malaria vaccine will become available for administration to children before or after they become infected.[35]

No one could challenge American motivations for more aggressively leading the international struggle with diseases. But hesitating in order to protect the products of American medical technology for reasons of finance and proprietary rights raises serious questions. Are we determined that only Americans and their well-endowed foreign partners who can pay the price will have access to *our* achievements, while others are simply to admire and covet them? Such a perception raises great suspicions as to America's real interests abroad, and our programs should promptly discredit such questions concerning America's intentions.

Infectious diseases continue to be a serious burden on every continent. In the global village of the twenty-first century, one nation's problem soon becomes every nation's problem. Despite progress in meeting the health challenges of today, the present reality is that the public health, veterinary, and medical care communities of many countries are inadequately prepared to prevent, detect, and control microbial threats to health. As an example of the extent of the problem, in India, a country of almost one billion people, there is not a single first-class school of public health.[36]

Dramatic advances in science, technology, and medicine enable the United States to move forward with dispatch. Yet the problems are large and the solutions are elusive. The most important antidotes to both naturally occurring and intentionally inflicted diseases are strengthened global, national, and local public health systems—including clinics, diagnostic laboratories, surveillance systems, and trained specialists. While certain types of activities that could enhance biological mischief should be banned and international ground rules for carrying out other types of activities are also important, the local healthcare providers will carry the principal burden in protecting the health of populations everywhere.

The United States, with its unparalleled scientific and financial assets, can provide the foundation that supports such efforts of nations throughout the world. We have done a good job in responding to the "disease of the month" time and again. Now we must augment these externally applied Band-Aids with programs to establish self-reliant local capabilities that can cope with both unexpected diseases and endemic contagions. Medical diplomacy should be the order of the day.

CHAPTER 8

WHITHER THE UNITED NATIONS

★ ★ ★ ★ *Uncritical Lovers and Unloving Critics*

"Why are you staying at the Holiday Inn? World Bank teams stay only at the Hilton Hotel." This sharp rebuke in 1988 from the leader of the World Bank's higher-education assessment team took me aback. I had arrived in Kuala Lumpur, Malaysia, one day earlier than the other members of the team. I had opted for the Holiday Inn, four blocks from the Hilton Hotel and $75 per day cheaper. If the costs of meals were considered, I would save the World Bank well over $100 per day. However, I quickly learned that when World Bank teams work abroad, they travel first class and stay in "appropriate" hotels. Arguably, such perks are essential to attract top talent. In any event, while such practices do not convey frugality and instead invite criticism, more profound issues face the developing world than bloated expense accounts.

THE WORLD BANK:
A BASTION OF ECONOMIC POWER

The trip to Malaysia was not the first time I had traveled abroad as a member of a World Bank team, nor would it be the last. Each time I have had reservations about foreign experts providing advice on the ways in which other governments should change their policies—in this case, educational policies—if they wanted to qualify for loans from the World Bank. But forcing changes in policy was the name of the game for almost all World Bank loans.

To some countries in desperate straits, transforming old policies in exchange for new money—a practice sometimes referred to as "loan conditionality"—may be attractive. To the World Bank, such conditionality is often considered essential to ensure that money made available to developing countries through loans is spent wisely. Unfortunately, such efforts by an outside entity to change internal policies of countries can resurrect images of Western colonialists, at least until the new policies demonstrate their effectiveness in strengthening the independent courses of the recipient countries. Then with the appointment of former US deputy secretary of defense Paul Wolfowitz as the World Bank president in 2005, policies that in time could lead to "regime change" suddenly assumed a more prominent role—particularly in lending to countries that have not fully embraced Western concepts of democracy.

What does the World Bank have to do with the future of the United Nations? The World Bank, or, more accurately, the World Bank Group, consists of five financial organizations. It is one of the twenty fiefdoms that make up the UN system, although insiders consider the World Bank as the most independent of the UN institutions. To outsiders, the World Bank may not even appear to be related to the United Nations. It is, and there are good reasons for highlighting the World Bank in discussions of the intertwining of US policies, UN programs, and criticisms of America that are linked to UN actions or inactions.

The World Bank is seen by some governments as a tool of American foreign policy. It is located in Washington, DC. It is always led by an American. The United States is the largest financial contributor. America's representative on the board of governors effectively blocks any activities deemed beneficial to countries on the US "blacklist." This list changes from year to year when diplomacy fails to bring governments in line with policies that are not acceptable to Washington. Its historical entrants have ranged from Chile to China.

The growing number of highly visible protest demonstrations surrounding meetings of the World Bank are testaments to the broad perception of what many consider to be misguided US dominance. These out-bursts are aimed in large measure at policies that are perceived to be US-inspired, or at least US-endorsed. Demonstrators attack the bank's financial support of regimes that have poor human rights records, the bank's failure to react to very low pay for impoverished workers in client countries, a lack of sensitivity within the World Bank concerning environmental disruptions that may accompany economic development, and controversial policies on other hot-button topics.

The World Bank is the economic powerhouse of the UN system, with financial clout in many developing countries unmatched by any other institution. In 2004 the bank provided $20 billion in loan financing.[1] Also, its staff of ten thousand, buttressed by an annual administrative budget of $1.7 billion, is the greatest concentration of development experts anywhere.[2]

Quite often the bank is the primary agent to carry out programs at the country level that are embraced by the UN General Assembly in New York or by other UN forums around the world. The global response to the AIDS crisis, achievement of the UN's Millennium Development Goals, and worldwide efforts to raise educational opportunities are among the many examples of the World Bank taking a leadership role in transforming priorities of the United Nations, which often encompass US priorities, into meaningful programs. Unfortunately, the negative signals sent by demonstrators at major World Bank meetings divert attention from the many positive accomplishments of the organization, such as the following: "After the peso collapse of 1994, the World Bank pumped $1 billion into Mexico's financial system to help resuscitate the country. After Bosnia's Dayton Accords in 1995, the World Bank led the charge for reconstruction. During the emerging market crisis of 1997 and 1998, the bank provided billions of dollars to the submerging Asian, Russian, and Brazilian economies. After the United States toppled the Taliban regime in Afghanistan, the bank proved its usefulness again. . . . In the wake of Asia's tsunami, the bank immediately pledged a quarter of a billion dollars."[3]

Returning to my trip to Malaysia, our task was to develop the details for a loan to strengthen the scientific research capabilities of Malaysian universities. Previously I had worked closely with the leading research institutions in Malaysia on other projects, and my role was to propose ways to link these institutions to the universities through joint projects within the framework of a major loan. However, I did not expect to encounter a high wall of ethnicity-based stipulations within the Ministry of Education for a project to modernize the universities. These conditions were destined to terminate the World Bank project during its initial stage of development.

This background helps explain why. The Malays make up the largest ethnic group in Malaysia. They are Muslims and they provide the political leadership of the country. At the time of my visit, most of the economic assets of the country were under the control of the Chinese minority, while the Indian minority also provided a strong and profitable entrepreneurial dimension to the society. The Malays were determined to obtain a bigger slice of the economic pie and had passed a series of equal-opportunity laws requiring, for example, that every company in the country must hire much larger numbers of Malays than in the past.

The government's attention had also turned to ensuring domination of the universities by faculty and students who were Malays. Most of the faculty members in the science departments of the country's several strong universities had been ethnic Chinese or Indian, and many of the students were also of Chinese or Indian descent. But change was in the air by the time our team arrived: all courses were to be taught in Malay, not English as had been the practice; all faculty members were to pass a Malay language test; and new faculty members would be hired not only on the basis of competence in their academic fields, but of their mastery of the Malay language as well.

Our group quickly concluded that teaching science in Malay, with no textbooks available in the Malay language, made little sense. Indeed, the Malay language had clung to its ancient roots: it simply was not sufficiently well developed to include the scientific terms necessary for instruction even at the secondary level.

Also, the exclusion of a major portion of the intellectual elite of the country from university careers did not seem to be an appropriate policy, even if the government had a major commitment to elevating the status of Malays. Therefore, the team recommended that the World Bank put the concept of a higher-education loan to Malaysia on the shelf. The political leadership of the country was taken aback. "Why have you wasted our time?" they asked. I also wondered why the staff of the World Bank had not been aware of the impending changes prior to mounting our pre-loan assessment effort.

However, Malaysia is not a poor country. It has thrived on exports of cocoa, rubber, oil, palm oil, and tin. When it came to ethnic issues, the government was determined to stay the course with or without the assistance of the World Bank.

Our group decided that it could not be a party to an approach justified on the questionable premise that the social benefits of diversifying the scientific leadership of the university outweighed the losses in the educational experience that would result. Indeed, over the course of the following decade, the logic of retaining the English language as the medium of instruction for university-level science courses in Malaysia won out. This has also been the case in other countries torn between preserving their cultural heritages and entering the modern technological world.

My experiences in other countries with World Bank higher-education loans have been more rewarding. I participated in successful efforts to improve the education systems in Nigeria, Romania, and Hungary. One critical finding from these experiences is that, while the preservation of local languages is an important goal, it cannot push aside the development of national capacity in science and engineering, which are major forces determining the future of the world. Most countries recognize that mastery of the English language in these fields is essential to participate effectively in this future, a future that is being shaped in significant measure by technological achievements emanating from the United States.

In Malaysia, parents of both Chinese and Malay students quickly sensed the inappropriateness of the use of the Malay language in teaching science. Many sent their children to schools in Australia. Others took advantage of programs at American universities, which rapidly established branch campuses in Malaysia.

The international approach to education and other aspects of development is, of course, linked to the US government's zeal for spreading democracy. In 2005 the G8 countries decided to support forgiveness of World Bank debts for a limited number of countries. An important criterion established in Washington was the commitment to democracy of the countries eligible for debt relief. This tactic, if accepted by the World

Bank—which would lose much income from debt repayments—may work for a while, since relief from abject poverty is often more important in poor countries than adopting a particular form of governance. In the long run, however, a US-inspired policy of "buying" democracy could provide fodder for political campaigns of anti-American forces.

What can be offered as a step toward improving the image of the World Bank in the near future, particularly within countries where anti-Americanism is strong? In general, the overall operation of the World Bank is very professional. The loans are highly sought after, and the bank does a good job in telling its story through its programs, its reports, and its Web site, www.worldbank.org.

In early 2005, an important symbolic step would have been for the United States to advocate for the appointment of an official from a developing country to serve as the president of the World Bank. But that was not to be the case. Nevertheless, election of a developing-country candidate should be the goal for 2010. The reasons for the US government to continue to insist that the president be an American are no longer compelling, even if the Europeans are comfortable with casting their votes of support in exchange for an American green light for European presidents of the International Monetary Fund and the World Trade Organization. Election of a carefully chosen developing-country leader could send a highly significant signal that the industrialized countries, particularly the United States, are truly prepared to respond to the needs and priorities of poor populations throughout the world and to increase the size of the sliver of the rich world's wealth that is directed to programs that combat poverty.

ACHIEVEMENTS AND AMBITIONS OF THE UNITED NATIONS

Now on to other aspects of the United Nations. Over the years, I have witnessed the blue flag of the United Nations fluttering in difficult locations throughout the world—from food-laden relief trucks in Bosnia, to a human rights center in Tehran, to a peacekeeping outpost on the Golan Heights, to a center for distributing medical supplies in Nigeria. Tens of millions of people who feel abandoned welcome the blue flags. They look to the United Nations as their only chance to gain recognition as citizens of the world.

Unfortunately, controversies in New York over "dysfunctional" characteristics of the United Nations have obscured many achievements of the UN system since its founding at the end of World War II. A few accomplishments follow:

- UN contributions to peacekeeping in several dozen countries, contributions of sustainable development strategies for countries with limited resource bases, and contributions to economic advancement in the poorest countries
- UNICEF's successes in mobilizing millions of individual contributors to save the lives of tens of millions of children
- internationally accepted UN documents on human rights, which are the gold standard that defines acceptable behavior of states in many areas of governance
- UN mega-meetings that have galvanized international action to promote environmental preservation, encourage a slowdown in population growth, and champion the role of women
- the attainment of an international consensus on Millennium Development Goals that are influencing distributions of hundreds of billions of dollars for foreign assistance (as discussed in chapter 4)

In addition, important programs in areas of core interest to the United States are under way in many UN agencies. They include the programs of the World Health Organization to address malaria, tuberculosis, and HIV/AIDS, and the programs of the International Atomic Energy Agency to contain the spread of nuclear materials. Such significant activities should be loudly trumpeted by UN supporters, for they protect the lives of individuals and prevent global catastrophes.

Looking ahead, UN secretary-general Kofi Annan in early 2005 laid out an ambitious UN agenda that included

- **antiterrorism**: adoption of a convention against terrorism in 2006 and subsequent global treaties to counter nuclear terrorism and to prevent proliferation of weapon-usable nuclear material

- **human rights**: establishment of a Human Rights Council to replace the controversial and ineffective Human Rights Commission—and authorization for countries to intervene with force to prevent genocide and ethnic cleansing
- **emerging democracies**: creation of a fund to support political processes in emerging democracies
- **antipoverty**: a timetable for rich countries to increase their contributions to development assistance and adoption of programs to cut the number of victims of extreme poverty by half
- **environmental**: steps to stabilize greenhouse-gas emissions when the Kyoto Protocol expires in 2012[4]

UNILATERALISTS AND MULTILATERALISTS WITH THE UNITED NATIONS IN THE MIDDLE

The Security Council and other UN bodies have long been caught in a cross fire between unilateralists, who believe these bodies simply complicate resolution of international problems, and multilateralists, who believe that the participation of many governments is essential to resolve global issues. Never before have the ideological arguments been more intense, more polarized, and more dangerous. These sharpened positions are due in large measure to a perception by both allies and adversaries that the US government is determined to impose its will on other countries, and particularly those that have different visions of the future of the world.

The controversies are deepening divisions around the globe. They adversely affect the work of dozens of international organizations within and outside the UN system, and they engender new bitterness toward the dominator of UN policies and programs, the United States.

Clearly, the US government is ambivalent in its UN policies. Washington wants to control the system such that it serves US foreign policy objectives, and US policy is often directed to marginalize the role of UN bodies when this is advantageous and possible. At the same time, international events have compelled the United States to work with the United

Nations in addressing crises in many areas of the world. In such cases, reliance solely on inadequate and short-term American resources would not have achieved much, such as resolving the conflict that arose during the late 1990s in East Timor, at the easternmost reach of Indonesia.

It is an uncomfortable but pragmatic relationship. In short, the United Nations needs the United States in order to be credible and financially solvent. The United States needs the United Nations to legitimize its actions in the eyes of distant populations and of segments of the American public. Also, on a practical front, the United States needs the United Nations' help in sidestepping no-win, prohibitively expensive overseas excursions, particularly in the poorest countries of the world, such as those in central and southern Africa.

Ideological differences concerning the role of the United Nations are stark within the United States, let alone abroad. American multilateralists are wedded to the view that the United States must be a respected member of the international community. To that end, they argue, it is in America's interest to act cooperatively with other nations, always demonstrating respect for others' opinions and interests.[5]

The unilateralists have a different orientation. They believe that the United States should not be constrained by others in using its monopoly of power to pursue national interests. They contend that the United States should embrace multilateral approaches only when they are fully consistent with American policies and can be implemented with dispatch.[6]

Both positions have merit. However, the multilateral approach seems essential in the long term in a world where a critical mass of governments is needed to hold rogue nations in check and also to coordinate the fight with disease and poverty. America must be a constructive partner within a community of nations that in time will no longer easily bend to America's military domination. Even today, collective action is often an imperative if US interests are to be served.

As clearly articulated by many UN advocates, a threat against one nation is a threat against all nations. A failure to deal with one threat can undermine defenses against other threats. For example, a major terrorist attack in an industrialized country can devastate the world economy and threaten the survival of millions of people. One estimate is that eleven million people worldwide were pushed into poverty as the result of the economic chaos that followed 9/11. At the same time, the collapse of one poor state—be it Afghanistan or Rwanda—can punch a hole in the common defenses against not only terrorism but also against diseases and famines.[7]

In the immediate future, however, the United States simply cannot await the outcome of each never-ending UN debate as to how to deal with the crisis of the month. Developing and carrying out American courses of action that appropriately balance international concerns, US interests, and long-term consequences are challenges that are being played out every day on the screens of the United Nations and of the US government— scenes from the Middle East, the Balkans, and Central Africa.

The war in Iraq has clearly been a tipping point in the debate, with unilateralism on the ascendancy. The military power of the United States ensures that when real security is at stake, no one will interfere with the implementation of American policies. Thus, determination of whether the United Nations should play significant roles in important security-related crises around the world has in many ways become largely the prerogative of Washington.

Neither unilateralists nor multilateralists should feel good about Iraq, a disaster zone for the United Nations. The Security Council repeatedly failed in its attempts to enforce sanctions. The UN weapons inspectors did not receive sufficient political support when the going became difficult. The oil-for-food program turned out to be rife with corruption. The views of most UN countries and all UN bodies regarding the invasion of Iraq were ignored by the United States. Insurgents destroyed the UN headquarters in Baghdad and killed one of the UN's most talented and effective representatives. Finally, the United Nations has been forced into an uncertain role with an undefined strategy to extract the United States from the quagmire of a devastated country.

Multilateralists want to use reconstruction efforts in Iraq as an opportunity to help restore eroded American relations with a number of pivotal countries. These include key Muslim countries that have resented their exclusion from meaningful roles in determining the fate of a society in the heartland of Islam. The countries of the Middle East realize that the United States will try to retain a powerful presence in their region. Therefore, they seek a central role for the United Nations in reconstruction activities, which would enable them to become, at the very least, respected participants in the process.

In contrast, the unilateralists envisage nothing but obstacles should the United Nations become a major player in the region. They are adamant in their refusal to pass decision-making power over the use of American funds to international civil servants with their own agendas. In their view, the words of Secretary Colin Powell—when he was asked to comment on long-term US prospects in the Middle East—"if you break it, you own it" come close to describing America's seemingly never-ending role in Iraq.

Kofi Annan, the ultimate multilateralist, claims to appreciate the position of the unilateralists on the need for and right to use preemptive military action and related activities when dangers to international security arise. As would be expected, however, he is overly optimistic in the following statement that new directions of the United Nations will be able to meet the concerns of the unilateralists, at least in the near term:

> According to the argument [of the unilateralists], states are not obliged to wait until there is agreement in the Security Council. Instead they reserve the right to act unilaterally, or in ad hoc coalitions. This logic represents a fundamental challenge to the principles on which, however imperfectly, world peace and stability have rested for the last 59 years. . . . But it is not enough to denounce unilateralism, unless we also face up squarely to the concerns that make some states feel uniquely vulnerable, since it is those concerns that drive them to take unilateral action. We must show that those concerns can, and will, be addressed effectively through collective action.[8]

If an important US foreign policy objective is to restore global respect for America, then certainly some degree of power sharing must be a central element of American policy despite apprehensions in Washington that others will abuse such power sharing and diminish the role of the United States. There are mechanisms other than the United Nations for power sharing—power sharing that is more certain in its outcome (e.g., NATO and ad hoc coalitions). However, the United Nations has unique legitimacy in the eyes of the world, since there is no other forum where so many countries have a voice.

Finally, unilateralists argue that it really doesn't matter whether the countries of the Middle East see only American disdain for the United Nations and adamant rejection of the concept of power sharing. Since US military and economic power cannot be effectively challenged, these countries eventually will give up their efforts to thwart American policies and fall in line with the American viewpoint, they think. However, the multilateralists are quick to point out that extremists are obtaining capabilities to respond to American unilateralism in unconventional ways—from mounting future 9/11 attacks to placing crimps in America's international lifelines of oil and other natural resources. Only the foolhardy can ignore such realities.

REFORMING THE UNREFORMABLE

Intertwined with the debates over the role of the United Nations in peace-keeping, reconstruction, and other activities are the continuing calls for reform of the organization. Indeed, outcries over inequities in UN decision making and in the status of member states, as well as complaints about bureaucratic inefficiencies, began as soon as the signatures on the Charter of the United Nations were dry. They have continued ever since.[9] As evidenced by the list below, members' ideas about specific reforms for the UN are inconsistent at best:

- Reduce excessively ponderous staffs or, conversely, increase staffs in critical areas.
- Create new UN bodies to address neglected areas or, conversely, abolish dormant organizations.
- Strengthen agency accountability to UN political bodies or, conversely, insulate the agencies from political influence.
- Safeguard state sovereignty or, conversely, facilitate invasion of misbehaving nations.
- Increase financial flows for UN activities or, conversely, impose greater fiscal restraint and reduce payments of member states to the United Nations.

- Circumvent political blockages by recalcitrant governments or, conversely, block political decisions by runaway majorities.[10]

Clearly, opinions on needed reform measures depend on the eyes of the viewer. Thus, UN reform agendas routinely bundle widely divergent views from the community of nations. More often than not, such efforts lead to dead ends. This was particularly true in late 2005: A wide-ranging set of proposed reforms—including areas such as management and oversight, use of UN force, humanitarian intervention, and the definition of terrorism—put before member nations' heads of state resulted in little actual change. This outcome resulted, despite recommendations from such bodies as the High-Level Panel on Threats, Challenges, and Change, established by Kofi Annan, and the Task Force on the United Nations, a bipartisan congressional group.

Reform of the United Nations will always be a loud theme of critics. Since the United States is the largest financial contributor to the organization, reform advocates in Washington will continue to link their criticisms with threats to withhold the annual US financial contribution. While the US Congress has placed frequent holds on US funding, defaults on US contributions may become less of a problem. A slowly changing attitude on financial obligations reflects a growing recognition within Congress that despite the many problems plaguing the United Nations, the United States needs UN cooperation on an ever-increasing scale, and a defaulting nation is not in a strong position to garner such cooperation.

However, each time Congress perceives yet another problem with the United Nations, the limited support in Washington to stay the financial course erodes. For example, UN supporters had great difficulty withstanding the shocks from the 2002 financial scandals associated with the food-for-oil program in Iraq, which included the involvement of Kofi Annan's son. And the hypocrisy of Libya obtaining the chairmanship of the Commission on Human Rights in 2003 raised deafening outcries throughout Washington and in other capitals.

Complicating objective public assessments of the United Nations is the widespread misconception that the United Nations is an independent entity. On the contrary, it is simply a meeting venue for about 190 member states and is charged with carrying out the decisions of its members within agreed-upon procedural ground rules. However, the powerful secretariats, which are responsible for implementing UN directives, often add their own interpretations to the intentions of the members. Since these secretariats are filled with citizens of many countries who have dim views of the increasing domination of world affairs by the United States, their actions and statements can raise the ire of American officials and provide grist for harsh criticisms from respected American politicians.

THE SECURITY COUNCIL: THE TYRANNY OF CONSENSUS

The thorny problems invariably end up in the Security Council, which is made up of five permanent members who have veto power and ten rotating members with two-year terms. The Charter of the United Nations gives the council the power to consider issues that are truly determining the fate of the world. Thus, it is in this forum where the entire world sees many of America's most significant foreign policies on display.

At the same time, the charter ensures that decisions of the Security Council will not go beyond the limits of tolerance of any one of the permanent member countries—the five victors of World War II, which not incidentally have all become custodians of nuclear weapons. With the veto at their disposal, the United States, the United Kingdom, China, Russia, and France actively participate in all Security Council deliberations. They have the assurance that while their reputations and influence may be at risk in this forum, their core security concerns will not be compromised by decisions of the body.

The representatives of these five countries have a number of advantages in addition to the veto over other council members when issues are on the table in New York. As permanent members of the Security Council, they are experts in the intricate procedures that govern the work of the council and in its history. As debates unfold, they have the precedents and other historical arguments at their fingertips. Also, they have substantial staffs in New York who have persuasive documentation at the ready to help derail initiatives not to their liking.

The five permanent members have the ability to influence positions of other members of the Security Council, both in New York and through their diplomatic missions around the world. When an important agenda item is to be taken up, US envoys abroad, in particular, often execute an all-court press to persuade other governments represented on the council to go along with the views of Washington. During such consultations, American diplomats may indicate that recalcitrance in following Washington's lead could trigger a reassessment of an overall bilateral relationship—including a review of trade and aid policies that are important for the other country. Of course other countries may threaten to respond in kind, for example, applying tariffs on imports of American products.

Should the five favored countries continue to dominate the Security Council as the world undergoes demographic, military, and economic changes? After all, India has nearly one billion people and a cache of nuclear weapons yet does not have permanent member status. How about Germany and Japan with their enormous economic stakes abroad? For years they have lobbied for permanent membership in the Security Council. The more than one hundred developing countries seem rightly peeved that they are all relegated to second-class status without a single exception. Geographically, why should Africa and Latin America be left out of permanent membership?

In June 2005 foreign ministers of the Organization of the Islamic Conference (OIC) called for a Muslim permanent seat on the Security Council. They proclaimed, "The Islamic world, which represents one fifth of total mankind, cannot remain excluded from the activities of the Security Council, which assumes a fundamental role in keeping security and peace in the world."[11] But little international attention has been directed to this proclamation.

The United States clearly favors the status quo rather than opening new doors for power sharing, although the Bush administration has rhetorically supported the bids of Japan and India for permanent-member status. Kofi Annan calls for "democratizing" the United Nations through expansion of the Security Council. In the fall of 2005 a proposal to add four new permanent members (Brazil, Germany, India, and Japan) gained little traction in New York, with the United States apparently an influential opponent.

Discussions of potential reconfigurations of the Security Council are always under way somewhere. The original composition of eleven members, including the five permanent members and six other members with two-year terms, was changed to a total of fifteen in 1963, with the addition of four more two-year members. Since it is highly unlikely that the veto will be extended to any more members, there has been a clamor for at least permanent status *without the veto* for a few countries. Another frequently raised proposal is to establish a new category of four-year members, possibly in addition to the ten two-year members. Whatever the structure, the five veto-wielding members will continue to control the outcomes of debates at the Security Council for the foreseeable future.

Do Security Council debates and decisions matter? From an American perspective, they surely should. The debates provide opportunities for fifteen countries to discuss issues that are dividing the world, to propose initiatives that can help unite the world, and to support or challenge American policies.

The debates provide international television audiences with meaningful glimpses into American policies and the rationale behind each policy. Do they promote a favorable image of America or are they policies that antagonize others? It depends on both the policy and the observer. Americans should be vitally concerned as to how US policies are viewed, whether or not they are adopted by the council.

Sometimes the US government uses the forum to set the record straight. However, after the debacle in New York in 2003 when Secretary Colin Powell presented his now-discredited case that weapons of mass destruction were hidden in Iraq, the likelihood that viewers of council proceedings will give much credence to American diplomats presenting the *facts*, even with photographs, has been severely compromised. If weapons of mass destruction are the issue, the audience will truly be skeptical.

The Security Council has the authority to initiate many types of important actions, including the following:

- **Public statements**. Consensus views of the five powerful countries joined by some or all of the ten others may prompt the less powerful that are following different tacks to reconsider their actions.
- **Diplomatic actions**. Consultations by the president of the Security

Council with parties in conflict, third-party negotiations with the disputants, overseas missions by council members to persuade parties to resolve their differences amicably, and personal diplomacy by the UN secretary-general can sometimes extinguish flames of hatred before they burn too brightly.

- **Peacekeeping operations**. (These are discussed later in this chapter.)
- **Postconflict peace building**. Many UN institutions are playing major roles in such activities around the globe, and strong Security Council support helps sustain the commitment of these institutions to peace-building missions.
- **Sanctions**. These may include arms embargoes, limitations on financial dealings that could lead to arms purchases, trade restrictions, and other steps to isolate nations that are considered to be misbehaving. But their effectiveness is nearly always questionable.
- **Administration of territories on a transitional or temporary basis**. Such administration responsibilities have been successful, although once undertaken they may never end.
- **Monitoring of weapons of mass destruction**. The experience in Iraq alone has demonstrated many of the problems that can be anticipated in this type of activity.
- **Authorization of the use of force**. Once the Security Council gives a green light in this arena, it may be difficult to keep activities within reasonable bounds.[12]

Notwithstanding the foregoing list of actions that have been initiated by the Security Council many times over, the inability of the United States to obtain Security Council support for the intervention in Iraq and the subsequent decision to go ahead anyway has been characterized by some officials and scholars as the death knell of the council. As stated by one expert in the influential journal *Foreign Affairs*: "One thing the Iraq crisis has made clear is that a grand experiment of the twentieth century— the attempt to impose binding international law on the use of force—has failed. As Washington showed, nations need consider not whether armed intervention abroad is legal, merely whether it is preferable to the alternatives. The structure and rules of the UN Security Council really reflected the hopes of its founders rather than the realities of the way states work. And these hopes were no match for American hyperpower."[13]

This opinion is challenged by others who are not ready to write off the Security Council. They point out that the Security Council was not intended as a mechanism for imposing international law on the use of force. Rather, it provides a legal framework for political bargaining, they argue. Also, they add that while the United States is indeed a hyperpower, its disrespect for the Security Council in the case of Iraq should not and does not signal a total abandonment of multilateral approaches in other areas of the world where the United States simply can't afford to take a unilateral approach.[14]

Just because the views of influential Security Council members didn't conform with US intentions to march to Baghdad, proposals by some for the United States to abandon the Security Council are not helpful. The difficulties for the United States in dealing with the Security Council may be manyfold. But in the long run, a mechanism for addressing global security challenges is essential, and the chaos in attempting to invent another mechanism that the United States could manage more effectively would surely throw the entire world into turmoil.

PEACEKEEPERS AT WORK

"How can you expect troops from Bangladesh, troops who have never seen snow, to be effective as peacekeepers during the winter in the mountains of Bosnia?" The UN secretary-general was explaining some of the difficulties in deploying peacekeepers in the early days of UN involvement in the Balkans. He was quick to add that once the contingents contributed by UN members had been properly trained and assigned appropriate missions, they became an effective force.[15]

Setting forth a related theme, a report in 2000 by a special commission examining the role of the United Nations in peace operations underscored the following:

> Without renewed commitment on the part of member states, significant
> institutional change, and increased financial support, the United Nations

will not be capable of executing the critical peacekeeping and peace-building tasks that the member states assign to it in coming months and years. There are many tasks which United Nations peacekeeping forces should not be asked to undertake and many places they should not go. But when the United Nations does send its forces to uphold the peace, they must be prepared to confront the lingering forces of war and violence with the ability and determination to defeat them.[16]

The United Nations undertakes three types of peace operations as directed by the Security Council.

1. **Peacemaking** that endeavors to bring an end to conflicts in progress, using diplomacy and mediation.
2. **Peacekeeping** that supports both civilian and military activities to build peace in the aftermath of civil war.
3. **Peace building** following cessation of hostilities that strives to reassemble the foundations of peace and build a society characterized by elements more permanent than simply the absence of war.[17]

These activities raise a host of operational issues as they are carried out. At the top of the list are the rules of engagement—when, and to what extent, are peacekeepers expected to engage in combat activities? They surely should protect peace builders, but beyond warding off attacks on UN personnel, what are their ground rules and how much firepower should peacekeepers have at their disposal?

Even when force is necessary, peacekeepers should not be transformed into war-fighting machines. There is a difference between deployment of armed peacekeepers with the consent of all of the parties involved and deployment when one or more parties are less than enthusiastic about the deployment. Appropriate use of different levels of firepower obviously depends on the context of deployment.

A second area of concern is the "rule of law" framework for peace activities. How should UN peacekeeping be reconciled with human rights concerns? They should complement and not contradict one another. How does peacekeeping relate to criminal proceedings? Peacekeeping should reinforce prevention of crime. Should UN teams of military personnel be supplemented with international police and judicial experts? Yes.

Another topic of great interest in the area of peace building is the implementation of "Quick Impact Projects"—a phrase now in popular usage. This thrust is designed to demonstrate to local populations that UN contingents are quickly making a difference in improving lives. Whether these projects involve sewage disposal, sanitation measures, reconstruction of schools, or establishment of medical centers, they are intended to demonstrate concern for the well-being of local populations. Blue helmets should be deliberately linked to such visible humanitarian endeavors.[18]

After a lull in activities during the late 1990s, UN peace operations have increased in scope and size. As of the end of 2004, more than $4 billion was being spent annually on peace operations and the deployment of seventy-five thousand blue helmets. The expenditures are more than three times the size of the regular UN budget. Most of the funds have been provided through special assessments of UN member states, with the five permanent members of the Security Council giving about one-half of the necessary funds.

Peacekeeping activities were under way in many countries in 2005, for example, in Burundi, Ivory Coast, Liberia, Congo, Ethiopia, Eritrea, Sierra Leone, Western Sahara, Haiti, East Timor, India, Pakistan, Cyprus, Georgia, Kosovo, Golan Heights, and Lebanon.[19] Most of the troops are traditionally from developing countries, with Pakistan and Bangladesh leading the way, pleased to benefit from this employment outlet for their otherwise poorly paid military contingents. Conspicuous by their absence are troops from highly developed countries such as France, the United Kingdom, Germany, Spain, and Italy, which are reluctant to place their forces under UN control.[20]

Of special significance are arrangements with regional organizations to work closely with blue helmets in volatile battle zones. In Bosnia, NATO forces were deployed along with UN forces in a very messy situation that demonstrated many of the weaknesses in the UN capabilities to respond decisively to confrontations. Finally, after NATO had restored a semblance of order to the region, UN forces were able to take over the burden of peacekeeping. Many other examples of cooperation between UN and regional organizations have emerged, particularly in Africa, and such cooperation should be encouraged.

The role of UN peacekeepers can be very difficult. In the Ivory Coast in 2004, for example, the peacekeepers considered their mission to be providing stability so that elections could take place. But many local residents wanted them to take sides. "The U.N. is here for one thing and one thing only: to disarm the rebels." With these fiery words, the leader of a menacing pro-government group warned that there would be trouble if the blue helmets did not start disarming the rebels immediately. Within several months violence did indeed erupt. Many French peacekeepers operating in parallel with UN peacekeepers were killed in the effort to quell violence emanating from the discrimination against Muslims and other populations in the northern part of the country, provocations that subsequently led to a civil war.[21]

A different report came from Afghanistan, where the United Nations employed a "peacekeeping light" mode. The United Nations limited its involvement to encourage Afghans to assume responsibility for their own political reconciliation and reconstruction. The blue helmets did not move outside Kabul or employ a foreign police mission. The presence of military forces from a variety of countries surely enhanced the image of the UN presence. The UN's light footprint helped protect the United Nations from criticism but contributed little to real security.[22]

There is a trend, however, of the UN using more force in its peacekeeping activities. A distinguished group of international experts reports as follows: "The United Nations, burdened by its inability to stave off the mass killings in Rwanda in 1994 and by failed missions in Bosnia and Somalia, is allowing its peacekeepers to mount some of the most aggressive operations in its history. The change has been evolving over the last decade, as the Security Council has adopted the notion of 'robust peacekeeping.' They reject the idea that the mere presence of blue-helmeted soldiers on the ground helps quell combat."[23]

In the end, we should be prepared to see a patchwork of UN successes and failures in reducing violence throughout the world. In some situations, the blue helmets will continue to intercede in security messes and in humanitarian crises in a satisfactory manner. At the same time, there will also be many instances when the UN missions are having little impact.

The United States, through political and military support of UN missions, can play an important role in improving the success-failure ratio, and that role will be visible to all interested parties. In the field, American military forces should make every effort to ensure the success of blue helmets, particularly when they are nearby. The United States should also press for a stronger standby constabulary force that will be trained to deal with security situations that are beyond the grasp of hastily recruited personnel. These newly minted specialists may be well schooled in carrying out battlefield instructions set forth in military manuals but usually have little experience in policing urban areas (see chapter 10 for more details on constabulary forces).[24]

GIVING AMERICA'S IMAGE A BOOST

The United Nations has many tentacles that reach into the cores of difficult problems the world over. From promoting economic development activities to hosting sometimes acrimonious debates to bringing order to chaotic situations, the United Nations seems to be everywhere.

The United Nations will never be structured to satisfy everyone. Financial scandals within the system will continue to be uncovered. Poor political judgments will be made, both by the members and by the staffs. Nevertheless, it is the *only* global intergovernmental political institution and it must be supported. America should be patient for the long haul. Small steps by the United States to help smoothly pave the long road will speak volumes to the world. An old African proverb describes the preferred path: "If you want to go fast, go alone. But if you want to go far, go together."

Of course driving the discussions of the future of the United Nations are votes and money. The United States has both—a critical vote in the Security Council and deep pockets to support UN activities. Also, the United States has by far the largest contingent of diplomats and supporting analysts who understand the issues on agendas throughout the UN system. They know UN procedures for gaining either a consensus or a favorable vote. With these three assets, the United States is in an excellent position to advocate constructive partnerships in the search for long-term peace and prosperity.

The United Nations has been described as both "a thinly disguised tool of American global hegemony" and "a cat's paw of redistribution-minded developing-country tyrannies."[25] Both characterizations contain elements of truth. But the United Nations can and should be more than an American puppet and a bank for developing countries.

For decades American officials have sought UN seals of approval for activities that require broad international support. Now, more often than not, they are giving up on their efforts to have the United Nations ratify decisions made in Washington. At the same time, dozens of developing countries on all continents highly value the United Nations as the only place where their views as to the future of the world will be heard. An increased American willingness to listen and to share decision making will indeed be welcomed by all.

Moreover, when the US government loses short-term battles for UN endorsement of US foreign policies, US support for the United Nations must not waver. The longer-term stakes are too great, as suggested in the challenges facing the United Nations noted earlier. Each American pronouncement or action degrading the role of the United Nations will only be interpreted abroad as yet another manifestation of America's intention to ignore the aspirations of other nations that are less powerful, less prosperous, and, in many cases, increasingly hostile to the United States.

US diplomats are on the center stage of the world every day in New York with the international media at the ready to report their views to populations around the globe. The views of these diplomats will often differ from the views of others. But a willingness of the US government to listen and to consider seriously the views of others will go a long way toward regaining global respect for America while facilitating global cooperation on a broad scale.

CHAPTER 9

ROAD MAPS IN PLACE OF ROAD KILLS IN THE MIDDLE EAST

★ ★ ★ ★ ★ *Jerusalem as the Way Station for*
American Credibility

In February 1994 Carole and I landed at Ben Gurion Airport in Tel Aviv for a week of sightseeing. Senior officials of the US Department of State had assured us that despite sporadic outbreaks of violence, the danger was contained and that visitors to Israel should not worry about personal safety. We could travel to the West Bank, the Golan Heights, and other interesting areas, although special arrangements were necessary to go to Gaza.

After quickly passing through highly visible but surprisingly nonintrusive airport security procedures, we boarded our tour bus and headed for Jerusalem. Our local historian-turned-guide presented an upbeat assessment of the stabilization of the security situation. He added as a footnote a gentle warning that the drinking water was heavily mineralized, and occasionally a foreign visitor suffers mild gastrointestinal discomfort.

Early the next morning, Carole and I again boarded the bus and headed for the first visitor destination—a water distribution system developed centuries ago. As we stepped off the bus, the mineralized water made its presence known to both of us. We had each consumed several glasses of tap water. Now we faced the embarrassing consequences.

By sheer luck, we spotted a hand-lettered sign advertising a public toilet about fifty yards up a hill from the bus stop. While the others joined the long line awaiting admission to view huge water storage tanks, we hustled up the hill. No attendant was in sight as we entered the poorly lit facility. Since time was of the essence, we did not delay to search our pockets for the one shekel that should be placed in the admission dish in the entranceway. We simply bolted through appropriate inner doorways in search of immediate relief.

Just as I finished ridding myself of the unwanted minerals, I was startled by a loud bang on the door to the men's room. Then the door to the stall in which I was perched was yanked open by a machine gun–toting youth in camouflage attire. Was I going to be arrested because I failed to deposit my shekel in the dish? In no position to adequately defend myself, I simply reached into my shirt pocket for my passport and mumbled, "American." With a scowl on his face, the uniformed teenager turned around, slammed the door to the stall, and shouted "security" as he left, apparently convinced that I was harmless. Were those Department of State advisory messages to relax and enjoy a visit to the Holy Land really an understatement of the personal danger in traveling in Israel?

As we toured the cities and the countryside during the next few days, one question kept looming before us. Whether passing through security barriers at museums, emptying purses and pockets in foyers of movie houses, or walking through the narrow and crowded streets of Jerusalem, we wondered how Jews and Palestinians, living in such close proximity, could contain their urge to retaliate in the wake of assassinations, suicide bombings, and destruction of homes. The physical space for venting anger was severely limited, and opportunities for either side to seek retribution were numerous.

Still, we were fortunate not to be involved firsthand in the violence. A report of only one incident of a Palestinian bombing within Israel, many kilometers distant from the route of our group, punctuated our visit. Several days after we left Israel, however, the brutal killing of twenty-nine Palestinians at the Tomb of the Patriarch in Hebron on the West Bank during a shooting spree by a reportedly deranged Jewish American medical doctor living in Israel sparked yet another volley of violent acts. Many of the tourist sites we had visited were suddenly off-limits to foreign travelers.

Due to the timing of our trip, we were spared witnessing the horror of wanton death and destruction that the world has repeatedly seen on television screens. In Ramallah and other Palestinian towns, we were shown only quiet streets and rest stops for tourists. Our guide did not hesitate to constantly remind us of the suffering of helpless women and children who were and continue to be victims of rampant violence.

Consequently, discussions with our fellow tourists and with local interlocutors focused on how to ensure the safety of both Israelis and Palestinians by ending the violent conflict that has gone on for decades. Even the first-time visitor's fascination with the ancient lands is constantly distracted by the realization that suicide bombings by Palestinian militants and attacks by Israeli forces routinely take place in this crowded living space, which is the size of the state of New Jersey. Regrettably, the road to peace continues to elude policymakers and leaders throughout the region and the world. In the words of King Abdullah of Jordan, "We cannot talk about growth and stability in my region without addressing a core conflict that threatens our world, the long and hateful cycle of violence between Israelis and Palestinians."[1]

UNSTINTING US SUPPORT OF ISRAEL

The dynamics between the Israeli government and the leadership of the Palestinians reflect the complexity of the situation. The relationship has many dimensions that infuriate politicians and the public on both sides of the divide: disputes over divisions of limited land, controversies over sharing inadequate water resources, struggles for economic opportunities, and clashes everywhere over security arrangements. These volatile confrontations involve personalities that embrace hostility and others that promote moderation. Whatever the approach, lurking in everyone's mind is the policy of the United States that can override any local initiative— even an initiative designed to bring peace to the region—if it does not coincide with Washington's views.

No other issue rivals in importance the situation or "plight" of the Palestinians in shaping attitudes toward the United States. It transfixes the attention of tens of millions of Muslims throughout the Middle East and other regions. American policies on other issues critical to peace and stability in the region also rile governments throughout the Middle East. But perceptions of subjugation of the Palestinians by an American-backed Israel vastly overshadow other irritants rooted in American policies.

When violence intensifies, the Israelis are seen in lockstep with the United States—their source of money and weapons—while the Palestinians are viewed as having nowhere to turn, whatever the situation, except to the Arab states. This perception angers populations in these states and aggravates relations between the governments of the region and the US government. According to leading American scholar Shibley Telhami: "Growing insecurity has pushed Israel to rely more than ever on its close relationship with the United States whereas Arabs and Muslims have rallied around the Palestinian cause. As these alliances are reinforced, the divide between the United States and the Arab and Muslim world is inevitably deepening."[2]

Rightly or wrongly, well-informed and thoughtful Arabs, as well as the general public of Muslim countries, see America as the only country in the world that provides unwavering support for Israeli actions, however harsh—support that they view as unjustified. They are convinced that Israel has been and continues to be a suppressor of human rights, dignity, and economic progress of the Palestinians—all with the backing of Washington. And, indeed, the US Department of State regularly documents many acts of institutional, legal, and societal discrimination against the Arab citizens of Israel, as well as abuses of human rights in the West Bank, in Gaza, and in East Jerusalem. In all fairness, however, the same documents point out many atrocities committed by Palestinians.[3] Despite efforts of the US government to be evenhanded in addressing human rights issues, few Arabs have confidence in the sincerity of the occasional political pronouncements from Washington that condemn Israeli actions.

For example, the common view is that resolutions adopted by the UN Security Council—resolutions that must have American backing—may criticize Israel, but they ultimately have no positive effect on the lives of the Palestinians and are usually ignored by Israel. Indeed, Middle East leaders repeatedly point out that even the American press quickly forgets these resolutions. At the same time, the press—in their view—never hesitates to report violations of UN resolutions by other governments in the region.[4]

Indeed, US financial support for Israel is unprecedented. During the past fifty years, the United States has provided more than $200 billion in foreign assistance to Israel, a nation with a current population of about 6.8 million people.[5] As to recent levels of assistance, in December 2004 the Council for the National Interest, a Palestine support group, correctly reported in a widely circulated newsletter that "pure economic assistance" to Israel had declined to an annual level of $360 million. But they noted that the foreign aid package also included $2.2 billion in military aid, and, in addition, the US Department of Defense was funding an Israeli defense program at an annual level of $300 million. As an example of the significance of this assistance for Israel's security, the US government has provided during the past two decades more than $1.2 billion for support of Israel's Arrow missile defense system with a comparable amount committed for the future.[6]

Meanwhile, Israel has long been the *only* recipient of American economic assistance with a commitment from Congress, set forth year after year in enacted legislation, ensuring that it will receive its annual allocation in cash within thirty days of passage of the Foreign Assistance Act. Other countries must wait many months as they work through well-established administrative processes to ensure that foreign assistance funds earmarked for assistance in their countries will be spent wisely.[7] This reality of perceived favoritism is well known throughout the Middle East.

The United States has provided equipment both through government assistance programs and through commercial sales that makes Israel the most technologically advanced military machine in the region. At the same time, the United States has supported development of a modern defense industry in Israel where talented engineers, replicating technologies imported from the United States, have developed a potent defense complex. In its search for paying customers, this industry has exported advanced military systems to China, South Africa, and other countries. For years some experts have believed that the US government has turned a blind eye to Israeli contravention of US export control laws that limit reexport of sensitive defense technologies. These are limitations that have been enforced on all other nations that have access to US technologies.[8] Most important, by providing large amounts of financial assistance and military support, the United States is widely perceived as the de facto guarantor that Israel will not be overrun by any invader or destroyed from afar by any adversary.

When it comes to Palestine, the White House has repeatedly made pledges of tens of millions of dollars of assistance to the Palestinian Authority. However, there has been great hesitancy within Congress to entrust Palestinian leaders, whose predecessors established a track record of unabashed corruption, with appropriate stewardship of US funds. Therefore, almost all US funds earmarked for Palestinian assistance have followed two routes. First, funds have been given to American non-governmental organizations for support of advisers and service providers that may or may not have responded to the priorities and interests of the Palestinian Authority's leaders. In this regard, these leaders have been charged by the US government with building an infrastructure for improving governance, security, and services. Second, a significant portion of the funds have been transferred to the Israeli government for distribution to projects that were to benefit the Palestinians.

In looking at how the interests of Israel have clashed with the needs of the Palestinians when it comes to use of external funds, consider the following example. US assistance, in the amount of $50 million earmarked for the Palestinians in 2005, was used by Israel to install high-tech processing terminals along the Israeli security wall that intrudes into the West Bank. This was justified on the grounds that Palestinians, as well as Israelis, would be processed through the terminals more rapidly. But the security wall has become anathema to the Palestinians. From their viewpoint, installing security terminals is clearly a stretch of the definition of foreign assistance for the Palestinians.[9]

On the eve of submission of this manuscript for publication, the extremist organization Hamas won an unexpected victory in the election for seats in the Palestinian parliament, a victory with repercussions that jolted Western capitals and inspired extremists throughout the Middle East. Congress and others immediately began the process of terminating all American assistance to the Palestinians. With other Middle Eastern states apparently ready to step in to help sustain the newly configured Palestinian government, however, the economic importance of this withdrawal of aid is questionable. The political and security implications of the Hamas victory seem far more significant, at least in the near future.

THE UNITED STATES AS THE
ONLY BROKER OF PEACE

The US government has long believed that providing substantial financial support to Israel is in the interest of the United States. Washington believes that an economically sound and secure Israel is essential in promoting democratic concepts and values throughout the region—a goal consistent with American ideals, which have received new emphasis under the Bush administration. Also, the Israeli government *does* responsibly manage funds that are provided. However, the contrast between the level of funding that has been provided for the benefit of the Israeli population and the level of funding that has benefited the Palestinian population is striking and has constantly fueled animosities throughout the Middle East toward America.

In recent years, many Arab leaders have publicly branded terrorism as despicable. At the same time, they only grudgingly condemn terrorism where it is most regularly practiced—in Israel.[10] They believe the Palestinians have no recourse but to use any weapons they can obtain to gain their rightful place in an area they consider their own. Many Muslims consider suicide bombers as freedom fighters, even martyrs, but not terrorists. Thus, with such external encouragement of terrorist acts, is it any wonder that Israel has little confidence in arrangements other than sheer military force to hold the Palestinians at bay?

Indeed, for years the Israeli population has been subjected to terrorist attack after attack in markets, on buses, in cafés, in restaurants, and wherever else people gather. By the beginning of the twenty-first century, suicide bombing had become endemic to the country. Israel has tried to limit its strikes to assaults against the perpetrators of such incidents, but collateral damage to innocent bystanders is inevitable. As a result, more than 800 Palestinians were killed in 2004 during Israeli military operations, while 117 Israeli soldiers and civilians were killed in clashes with Palestinian militants. Since 2000 more than three thousand Palestinians and one thousand Israelis have been victims of violence.[11] While most Americans and other Westerners understand that Israel is committed to forceful action to deter still more dastardly acts, Muslim communities around the world often limit their vision to the immediacy of television broadcasts showing Israeli tanks overpowering teenagers armed with stones. This unfairness in armed confrontations, they believe, is attributed directly to the programs of support by the Pentagon.

Predictably, the passing of the Palestinian leader Yasir Arafat was a significant, albeit confusing, event. The *Economist* reported: "When half the world lauds you as a statesman and the other half vilifies you, as a terrorist, you know your passing will be controversial."[12]

In the West, hopes for peace soared. They had soared before, too, only to be brought back to the reality of more attacks and casualties. The violence, while reduced, continued, and political compromise by any party was slow in coming. The Israeli government pointed out a 45 percent reduction in the number of Israelis killed in attacks by Hamas, Hizballah, Islamic Jihad, and the Popular Front for the Liberation of Palestine during 2004. They attributed this drop to the construction of the security wall in the West Bank.[13]

During the summer of 2005 the Israeli government ordered the evacuation of more than five thousand Israeli settlers from Gaza. The stories of Israeli troops forcibly removing distraught Israeli families from land that had provided for their homes and livelihoods for decades were indeed tragic. Many Israeli politicians condemned this action on the grounds that it would only give Hamas and other terrorist groups unfettered access to strategically important territory. Many Palestinians viewed the move as simply an Israeli ploy to garner international support for broader Tel Aviv policies: a focus on Gaza would divert attention from the occupation by Israeli settlers on the West Bank—the heartland of Palestine. All the while, the Israelis pressed Washington to provide more than $2 billion to cover costs of resettlement of the evacuees and costs of installing new security arrangements that will protect Israel in the light of the new geographic divide.

False expectations at every turn will continue to characterize US intervention in Israeli-Palestinian negotiations. As they have for more than half a century, repeated diplomatic efforts to quell political upheaval and end the acts of terrorism have led to dead ends. While the diplomats have talked—from Oslo in 1993 to Camp David in 2000 and dozens of other efforts before and after—innocent civilians have been dying.

Numerous strategies have been developed over the years in Washington, in Europe, and in the Middle East for finally ending the cycle of violence and beginning down a more promising road to peaceful coexistence. Certainly, many of these well-conceived approaches contain useful concepts that should be preserved, even with the elevation of Hamas as a potent political force. In particular, President Bush's commitment in 2004 to the establishment of two independent states by 2009 added considerable impetus to resolving long-standing animosities, although his timetable will probably be delayed, since Hamas has consistently opposed the right of Israel to exist.

Regardless of the formula that leads to permanent peace, the role of the United States in the process is critical. The policies emanating from Washington are the key for bringing about a lasting truce while demonstrating fair and balanced treatment of both Israelis and Palestinians. A perception of fairness by the United States is indeed the linchpin for restoring respect for the United States throughout large segments of the world.

America's potential clout in influencing Israeli policies is enormous and should be more fully activated. As noted earlier, Israel receives billions of dollars in American aid each year, along with access to technology and with assurances that the country will not be overrun by growing populations that have never truly accepted the legitimacy of the Israeli state. In addition, when all other countries of the world line up against Israel at the United Nations, Tel Aviv has always been confident that the United States would use its veto power to prevent action that could jeopardize the security of Israel. While on occasion the United States has voted against the interests of Israel, these votes have seldom been followed by US actions to enforce implementation of the resolutions.

America's influence with the Palestinian Authority has also been significant. First and foremost, Palestinian leaders, including the leaders of Hamas, know that the United States can steer the course of actions of Israel. Indeed, some leaders consider Israel to have the status of America's fifty-first state. Second, there is no other nation with real clout that the Palestinians can turn to. The European and Arab states can speak loudly, but only the United States has the capability to turn rhetoric into action.

When the electoral victory of Hamas became clear, the US government immediately vowed not to deal with a terrorist organization. In time the United States will surely begin to engage Hamas directly or indirectly in diplomatic discussions because there is no realistic alternative for Washington. Also, a modification of Hamas's adamant refusal to accept the reality of the Israeli state will undoubtedly emerge, perhaps within months but more likely within a few years.

While this new drama plays out, long-standing resentment reverberates among the Palestinians each time they have evidence that the Americans are negotiating the fate of the Palestinian homeland with Israel without including Palestinians in the negotiations. And this happens often. For example, in an article titled "Why Did Bush Take My Job?" the chief Palestinian negotiator during 2004, who is generally considered a moderate, expressed outrage that President Bush would announce at a press conference how the president and the Israelis had resolved the issue of Israeli settlements on the West Bank—without input from the Palestinians.[14] This was but one of scores of US "clearance" meetings with Israel before moving forward with policies that have affected the Palestinians as well. According to a negotiator for six American presidents: "We had to run everything by Israel first . . . our departure point was not what was needed to reach an agreement acceptable to both sides but what would pass with only one—Israel. . . . We can still be Israel's close friend and work with Israelis and Palestinians to ensure that the needs of both sides are met."[15]

Still, the Palestinian leadership has long recognized that American intervention is the only possible near-term counterweight to Israeli domination of the situation. Other governments and the United Nations can only be effective in championing the cause of the Palestinians if they work with the US government.

For decades, the American position vis-à-vis the conflict has been driven in large measure by a resolve to let the democratic processes in Israel formulate the country's policies. Indeed, Israel is the most developed democracy in the Middle East. If the United States should interfere in Tel Aviv's established political processes, American credibility in promoting democracy around the world could be in jeopardy, according to the champions of democracy.

Meanwhile, Arab populations believe that the United States stands for democracy, freedom, and human rights everywhere *except* in the Middle East and for everyone *except* the Arabs.[16] They repeatedly point out that years ago, and particularly since 1996, the Palestinians themselves adopted the vital principles of democracy and that Yasir Arafat was elected through a process that was open, at least by their standards. It was the Americans, not the Palestinians, who had a problem with his election and leadership, they add. Now, as the United States refuses to recognize the legitimacy of the Hamas victory in a free and fair election, Washington is losing its credibility as a proponent of democracy by accepting only outcomes that are favorable to the West.

Given the continuing crises in the region, certain elements of democracy must take a backseat—temporarily—to more pragmatic approaches in resolving the situation. A suspension of traditional democratic processes in times of war or during other security crises in the United States or elsewhere has not in the past—nor will it in the future—meant the death knell of democracy. Specifically, endless internal debates within Israel and Palestine must give way to externally imposed solutions that will stop the killings and reduce the suffering that plague the two populations. If no solution is found, the standoff will continue to foment anger that will persist for future generations. As stated by the Global Mothers of Austria, for example: "It is the children who will be traumatized for years to come. They—if they survive—will be the innocent victims of false and brutal policies. The seeds are being sown for vengeance for years to come. And the governments of the world look on."[17]

Such an externally driven approach to reducing violence was generally followed in development of the "road map," unveiled in 2003. It was a strategy constructed by the international community and outlined in a document intended to point the way to peace. It was prepared by a quartet of nations and organizations. The United States was clearly the driver, however, with the European Union, the United Nations, and Russia active participants. Israel and the Palestinian Authority were consulted along the way, but in the end, they were told that they could not veto the road map. This externally developed solution was to be the policy to guide the path toward peace.[18] As of the end of 2005 the road map was still on the table as the basis for negotiations.

With elections in Israel as well as in the Occupied Territories in 2006, the road map as such may slide off the table, but many of its concepts remain key to resolving the conflict. Clearly the road map was too vague in its details, leaving too much to the parties to resolve between themselves, even with help from members of the quartet that designed it.[19] The Palestinians accepted the road map, while the Israelis raised a number of reservations in their formal response. These included many concerns linked to security measures that must be taken by the Palestinians themselves.[20] Would the Israeli reservations be accommodated by the United States? Probably, since without Israeli support and without the threat of external military muscle, the initiative would fail.

An important factor behind the reluctance of Israel to accept the road map without qualification has been Israel's stance never to give in to terrorist tactics of the Palestinians. Many Israelis interpreted the road map as a concession to the terrorists. How could the government appear to be giving in to a band of unruly and ill-equipped militants, while setting themselves up for still further concessions? Such concessions would compromise the strategy that Israel has long embraced—deterring attacks by projecting an image of strength. These are core concerns of Israelis.

Consequently, one clear benefit of an even more forceful plan imposed by the United States and its allies would be that the Israeli government could hardly be blamed for compromises in its position. In other words, when Washington is adamant, Tel Aviv has no choice but to comply. At the same time, by applying appropriate pressure on Israel to achieve a lasting peace that is in the interests of all concerned parties, the United States certainly would gain respect and enhance its broader security interests in the region.

The multinational dimension of the quartet enhanced the legitimacy of the road map in the eyes of some Middle East politicians. But couldn't governments of the region also have played a useful role if they had been asked to participate in the process? They are close to the scene of the violence and they have considerable self-interest in securing the future for *their* children while providing a bridge for enlisting broadly based Arab support.

To that end, Senator Richard Lugar (R-IN), chairman of the Foreign Relations Committee of the US Senate, suggested expanding the group to a sextet by adding Egypt and Saudi Arabia. Involving these Arab nations might make it easier for the Palestinian leaders to accept conditions that required retreating from earlier positions.[21] However, is it appropriate to add governments that seem to have deeply rooted biases against Israel?

Finally, if strong and sustained intervention by the United States was ever warranted anywhere, it certainly is warranted in this area of the world. America's inaction when violence erupts continues to raise the danger of terrorist strikes in America by extremist groups that are only too happy to carry out their personal retaliations. Some extremists have sought and will continue to seek retribution for what they perceive as American promotion of Israeli aggression against Palestinians.[22]

In sum, the US government has the capability to impose its will on the actions of both Israel and the Palestinians. The capability will remain regardless of the course promoted by Hamas. Time is long past to impose that will in an impartial but forceful manner.

A NEW COURSE FOR A BETTER FUTURE

Can a course be found that in time replaces suicide bombings with negotiation and achieves a fair compromise in the West Bank? As already discussed, America is the gatekeeper to the answer of this question.

Of course, the views of the leadership within Israel, and of the Israeli population as a whole, are also central to whether a successful formula for peace can be achieved. The leaders in 2005 were all longtime warriors in dealing with the Palestinian issue—Shimon Peres, Ehud Barak, and Benjamin Netanyahu, in addition to Ariel Sharon. They and their successors will ensure that any arrangements to which they agree will put Israel's security above all other considerations. Perhaps a new face with new perspectives will emerge and become the next prime minister. While the leaders of Israel may disagree on tactics, their visions for the future of Israel will undoubtedly remain focused on the safety of their citizens.

In Ramallah will there simply be a pause in the relentless efforts of the Palestinians to eventually remove what Arafat considered the illegitimate Israeli presence? Or will the right for Israel to exist finally be embraced by Arabs and, most important, by Hamas? As Hamas takes on the awesome responsibility of shared governance of the desperate Palestinian people, pragmatism in addressing the status of Israel may eventually emerge.

As repeatedly noted, the history of the confrontation is long and contentious.[23] Thirty years ago, a highly respected American diplomat advocated the following formula for resolving the conflict:

- Israel must withdraw from the West Bank and Gaza to the Green Line (the Armistice line from the 1949 conflict). Any territory retained by Israel should be balanced by territory of equal areas and value transferred to the Palestinians.
- Palestine should become a demilitarized state. A major international reconstruction program that gives Palestinians a stake in a reordered Middle East should be initiated. The Israeli financial contribution to reconstruction should be considered partial compensation for its confiscation of property of Palestinians who were expelled or who fled the conflict in 1948 and thereafter.
- Jerusalem must be a shared capital.
- Water resources should be equitably shared, and Palestine should control its own aquifers.
- The Palestinian refugees' right of return should be limited to no more than a reasonably small number of refugees (e.g., fifty thousand) based on family reunification considerations.
- An international peacekeeping force should be installed as a buffer on the borders until both sides agree that its presence is no longer necessary or desirable.
- The settlement and the security of each party should be guaranteed by the United Nations and the sponsoring powers should include the United States and major Arab neighbors.[24]

These suggestions of thirty years ago continue to have salience. Of particular importance is the proposal to have an international force with clout on the ground.

Perhaps the most realistic proposal that has recently been put forth is to turn the job over to NATO.[25] A robust mandate for NATO commanders—empowering them to use force when necessary to maintain order, coupled with strong diplomatic pressures to encourage compliance by both sides—would offer a real chance of ending the conflict once and for all. While there may be NATO casualties, the killings would pale in comparison with the death tolls in Afghanistan and Iraq. When queried about such a proposal in February 2005, the NATO secretary-general responded, "If there is a peace agreement, an invitation from both sides, and a UN mandate, then NATO is ready and willing to act."[26]

To be effective, an international force must have American troops in the ranks. Then the conflicting parties will know that the stakes are at the highest level. Also, the force must be dispatched under the umbrella of the United Nations to avoid charges of a new form of Western colonialism. While the process of dispatching troops may seem complicated and fraught with danger, the risks of not taking such decisive action far outweigh the risks of deploying armed forces to replace a wall as the keeper of the peace.

A formula that could set the stage for a separation of the adversaries has been proposed by former secretary of state Henry Kissinger. The United States and Israel looked favorably toward his proposal, but the Palestinians had considerable difficulty with ceding 8 percent of the West Bank to Israel as Kissinger suggests. His proposal is as follows:

> A more precise and specific roadmap should guide the peace process. The existing *quartet*, should define the principles and outlines of a possible settlement, seek support of regional powers, and take a leadership role in its implementation. . . . The territorial dividing line should be defined by a security fence paralleling the 1967 borders along principles discussed at Camp David and Taba. This would return all of the West Bank to Palestinian rule except the five to eight percent needed for the strategic defense of Israel. In compensation, Israel would transfer some of its territory elsewhere to the Palestinian state. Such a plan should set forth provisions for the establishment and support of an interim government in Gaza for the time between the withdrawal of Israeli forces and the conclusion of negotiations. The Palestinian contribution to peace must be a genuine recognition of Israel, transparent institutions, and a dismantling of the terrorist apparatus on Palestinian territory or aimed at Israel from other neighboring states.[27]

As suggested earlier, an essential component must be international peacekeepers, an aspect that Kissinger rejects. He argues that foreign peacekeepers could be taken hostage or could become protective shields for insurgents plotting terrorist acts. However, these dangers are acceptable when compared to the muscle they would add in making separation real and in setting the stage for a genuine two-state solution.[28]

Returning to political developments, at the beginning of 2005 a cease-fire was declared. Such pauses in violence have come and gone in the past. If they are reflected in more secure and better lives throughout Israel and the Occupied Territories, then movement toward permanent peace and an acceptable final status should be swift and convincing to all concerned.

First and foremost, the issue of land ownership must be resolved. This issue has long been recognized in Washington to be the key to resolution of the conflict as indicated in the following statement by James Baker during his term as secretary of state more than a decade ago: "Every time I have gone to Israel in connection with the peace process I have been met with the announcement of new settlement activity. This does violate United States policy. It is the first thing that Arabs—Arab governments—and the first thing that Palestinians in the territories, whose situation is really quite desperate, raise when we talk to them. I don't think there is any greater obstacle to peace than settlement activity that continues not only unabated but at an advanced pace."[29]

Central to the controversy over land ownership is Israeli construction of the security wall on the West Bank. Most Palestinians do not seem to object to a security wall. They simply object to its penetration into the West Bank. They claim they would live peacefully with a wall or any other type of barrier along the Green Line. But they violently object to the trace of the wall developed in early 2005, which separates the homes of tens of thousands of Palestinians from the rest of the West Bank. They certainly will not accept a wall that separates East Jerusalem from the West Bank.[30]

Nevertheless, it seems clear that some Israeli settlements will remain permanently on the West Bank beyond the Green Line. The inhabitants will undoubtedly retain Israeli citizenship even though they live on Palestinian land, while Palestinians in Israel will continue to become Israeli citizens. The trace of the wall established in 2005, although less intrusive than earlier concepts, certainly complicates the task of determining eligibility for citizenship. Many Palestinians have been separated by the wall from their lands and will permanently lose these lands. A new path that gives greater recognition to the daily challenges faced by both Palestinians and Israelis on the ground should be developed and imposed by the United States and Western allies.

The other two issues that are keys to resolution of the dispute and the associated violence are the right of return to Israel of Palestinian refugees scattered in camps in several countries of the Middle East and the status of East Jerusalem as the capital of a new Palestinian state. It seems clear that most displaced Palestinian refugees will remain where they are. At the same time, they should have the right to become citizens of other countries. The Jordanians have effectively integrated most refugees into their country, but the government is now reversing this policy of granting citizenship lest the country become too strong a magnet for stateless Palestinians. International pressure should be placed on other states of the region such as Lebanon to also grant citizenship to *longtime* residents of the countries. As to the status of East Jerusalem, past negotiations have demonstrated that this issue can be resolved, perhaps by enlarging the boundaries of Jerusalem and redefining the limits of East Jerusalem.

Turning to foreign assistance for the Palestinians, an expanded assistance effort will have to be part of a settlement package. The living conditions in Gaza and the West Bank are poor by any standard, and the United States should set the example for a truly multilateral effort to provide sufficient support to enable the people to begin to function like a population with a future. Israel must turn in its gatekeeper keys for Palestinian access to Western financial assistance. Only then will the Arab nations believe that America is sincere in its desire to help the Palestinian people and, by extension, to treat Muslim and non-Muslim populations equitably.

Finally, and most important, suicide bombings in Israel will continue for the foreseeable future. It will take many years until all militants are brought under control. We can only hope that these incidents will be at a much-reduced frequency compared to the early years of this century—a possibility should some of the actions recommended here begin to take effect in improving the lives and circumstances of those who might otherwise be tempted to sacrifice their lives in protest.

The Israeli government also must change its policy of responding through targeted assassinations or other means each time there is a killing in Israel. The adverse long-term consequences for both Israel and the United States of never-ending attacks against the Palestinians greatly outweigh the near-term deterrent effect. Indeed, there is little evidence to show that retaliation does more than swell the ranks of militant organizations and provide photo opportunities for the international press corps.[31] British prime minister Tony Blair has repeatedly urged such restraint, and now it is time for Washington also to weigh in on this issue.

Patience has long ago faded as a virtue in addressing the conflicts in Israel and Palestine. The future is now. Osama bin Laden and other terrorists of his ilk must be denied the use of the banner of downtrodden Palestinians in arousing sympathy for their terrorist schemes aimed at the United States.

As repeatedly noted, a rapidly increasing number of Muslims—while shocked and awed by the military might of the United States—deplore those American approaches they see as callously dealing with issues that directly affect the lives of millions of people, and particularly the lives of Palestinians. Their litmus test of American intentions toward the Muslim world is centered in Jerusalem and the West Bank. Events in Baghdad and elsewhere are important. But in the eyes of tens of millions of people, measurement of the true attitude of the United States toward Muslims begins with the American position on the West Bank and Jerusalem.

At the same time, while US support for Israel remains a priority, certain requirements must be made and met. As underscored in 2005 by former secretary of state James Baker, Israel will never enjoy security as long as it occupies the territories, and the Palestinians will never achieve their dream of living in peace in their own state as long as Israel lacks security.[32] Regrettably, temporary deployment of American forces in Israel and the Occupied Territories now seems essential in order to bring security and peaceful side-by-side living to the two states and the people of the region.

AFTERTHOUGHT

Several newly elected Hamas leaders quickly advocated a "long-term" truce with Israel while not compromising their position on the illegal status of the Israeli state. Clearly, a termination of the fighting is more important than legal niceties. Indeed, ensuring peace can provide a positive political environment for working out deeply rooted legal disputes. If the Hamas pronouncements turn out to be serious proposals, they should be promptly embraced by all parties.

At the same time, Israelis simply do not trust Hamas, and for good reasons. That said, what better way to ensure the permanence of a voluntary or imposed truce than by deployment in the region of a substantial number of international peacekeepers, including American troops? Only such peacekeepers could help ensure that fighting does not break out and quell the fighting if it does erupt.

On a broader regional basis, the United States was clearly a loser at the ballot box in the Occupied Territories. Washington can no longer assume that democracy will automatically lead to pro-American policies. As has been seen recently in Egypt, Turkey, Lebanon, Iran, and Iraq, elections will not necessary result in votes for factions kindly disposed toward the West. Of course, democracy must remain a long-term objective throughout the world, but the US government must be prepared to absorb short-term setbacks and adjust its policies accordingly. There is no better place to begin such adjustments than with the Israelis and Palestinians.

CHAPTER 10

MILITARIZATION OF
THE WORLD

★   ★   ★   *American Troops Stationed in 120 Countries*

Each time I invite foreign visitors to dinner at the Army-Navy Club on Farragut Square in Washington, DC, I take considerable pride in having served in the US Army at home and abroad. The historic club is but two blocks from the White House where the US commander in chief holds forth. Club members do not hesitate to dust off their medals for formal events.

Several paintings adorning the club depict US naval vessels near Manila and Santiago de Cuba a century ago. Another recounts the victory ceremony at Versailles. Others pay homage to American heroes of World War II. In sum they reflect wise and appropriate use of the military power of the United States in distant lands. America's armed forces have repeatedly changed the course of history around the world, benefiting the United States, its allies, and the countries it has assisted. Americans should be thankful that the armed services have been at the ready and that they have performed so well. So should our allies.

My overseas military stint was limited to a single tour of duty along the Iron Curtain in the aftermath of World War II. Nevertheless, for several decades I have worked closely in other capacities with American generals, admirals, junior officers, and enlisted personnel serving abroad. For example, army and navy officers, well schooled in Kremlinology, supported my efforts in Moscow to build US-Soviet scientific partnerships during the height of the Cold War. In the waning days of the war in

Vietnam, air force pilots ensured my safe passage to the battle zone to inspect a nuclear research reactor that had to be dismantled. In the 1990s technically trained and highly experienced captains and sergeants stationed in Bosnia helped in my search for new ways to safely remove land mines from agricultural lands. Then in 2005 military commanders stationed in Hawaii, who regularly visited nations throughout the Pacific region, helped me devise new strategies for responding to tsunamis, earthquakes, and floods in the region.

I have also witnessed in my travels the many contributions of our military personnel serving abroad to projecting a positive image of America—improving communication systems in Ethiopia, leading tropical medicine research efforts in Malaysia, and rebuilding collapsed bridges in Bosnia. But do we really need more than 300,000 military personnel stationed at more than 5,000 facilities, both large and small, in 120 countries? Of course, many of our troops are based in current hot spots in Iraq, Kuwait, Afghanistan, South Korea, and the Balkans. However, tens of thousands are also deployed in dozens of countries where the need for their presence is highly questionable.[1] It is my contention that we can enhance our country's image by reducing our military presence while not eroding our national security interests.

An examination is called for of several important issues concerning the basis for introducing and maintaining American military and paramilitary forces around the globe. I challenge the notion that the United States must have prompt military access to every corner of the world to demonstrate its commitment to world peace. I encourage the American military establishment to reevaluate the importance of large deployments of American armed forces abroad and, moreover, to think through the long-term implications of so many permanent outposts in so many countries. In the words of the commandant of the US Marine Corps, "Even our very best friends in the Asia-Pacific region do not want the Stars and Stripes flying at US bases in their lands."[2]

As to the role of the military in countries where its presence is crucial, note the following warning of General William Nash, former regional UN administrator in Afghanistan. "I am deeply concerned that the United States is seen as being represented by a military force rather than by its identity as a democratic, free-market, rule of law nation."[3]

The Pentagon recognizes that the military strategies of the last century—to counter other powerful nations that were expanding the reach of their military forces—are simply not appropriate for the security landscape of today. Still, by characterizing the new challenge facing the United States as a *war on terror* with a *Muslim* enemy who can be defined simply as *extremist*, the US government has given the Pentagon a broad and dangerous mandate. The US armed forces are now directed to be prepared to attack extremist groups abroad. They are authorized to engage in information operations that explain America's intentions to the moderates, an unfortunate term that for some connotes weakness in responsible Muslim leaders. The armed forces are to play a key role in humanitarian relief missions. They are not only to help counter illicit trafficking in weapons but also to help destroy the ideological basis that holds together terrorist networks. These are, of course, important missions, but should the Department of Defense be a leader in these areas?[4]

The need is clear for a balance between a military presence abroad that is designed to prevent attacks on American assets today, and one that also contributes to long-term national security goals that are dependent on widespread goodwill toward America. A critically important goal is to foster attitudes that promote other countries' policies that are advantageous to the United States. The extent and manner of American troop deployments abroad will have a significant impact on achieving that goal, by either quelling or fanning resentment toward the United States.

BRINGING HOME THE TROOPS

President Bush has vowed that by 2010 we will reduce America's overseas military footprint by seventy thousand personnel (about 23 percent). At the same time, the Pentagon has its eyes on new deployments as it adjusts its vision to a changing global security environment—a vision that calls for aggressive forward strategies to cut off dangers in distant places and to provide protection for those civilian groups engaged in building democracies.[5] If such strategies are adopted without constraints, reaching the president's goal will be not only difficult but likely impossible.

The challenges in bringing home soldiers, sailors, pilots, and marines who are already in place overseas are manyfold. How many troops can be moved out of Europe without causing major political and economic disruptions among our allies? Can the American presence in Asia be decreased in light of the bellicose attitude in Pyongyang and uncertainties surrounding an ever-stronger China? As global terrorists seek sanctuary in remote areas, will on-the-ground personnel be needed in even more countries? In considering such questions, a thorough analysis is required of not only the need for deployed military capabilities but also of the political ramifications of such actions.

More than 170 countries were hosts to permanent and temporary American troop deployments in 2003, and the number has increased since that time. Of course, in capitals of still other countries, military personnel are assigned diplomatic responsibilities at American embassies—a routine function well accepted internationally. The less-than-routine operations of military personnel have ranged from training police in Mongolia who are responsible for protecting the nation's borders, to writing the constitution in Paraguay, to providing health services in villages of South Africa, to treating sick cattle in the Horn of Africa.

When a new American ambassador arrives in a distant land, the greeter is usually an official of the Ministry of Foreign Affairs of the host country. Sometimes even the foreign minister is on hand. In contrast, when the commanding general of Central Command from Tampa, Florida, visits many countries of the Middle East, he may be greeted by entire cabinets. These reception committees reflect the extent and weight of the US military presence that is orchestrated from Tampa.[6]

When military personnel are stationed near trouble spots, the temptations in Washington to move them quickly into the centers of bubbling turmoil are great. "Why are we spending so much money on building a powerful overseas military machine if we hesitate to use it?" some argue. Unfortunately, such logic too often distorts rational decision making as we witnessed in the abortive attempt to check the warlords in Somalia who were interfering with humanitarian relief efforts.[7]

Making any changes in overseas deployments, even on a very limited scale, attracts enormous global attention. Troop movements raise endless questions and stimulate the wildest conspiracy theories imaginable about

American intentions. In the past, the US government has repeatedly been able to defend quite extensive deployments on the basis of their contributions to regional stability—a vague but fine-sounding concept. Garnering support for the new rationale for stationing forces in distant lands—the rationale of preventing terrorism—is more difficult and often proves highly controversial.

In particular, the US focus on "regime change" as an antiterrorism prophylactic is constantly on the screens of leaders of other governments. It adds to their anxieties about the movements of American military forces. The obvious question they ask themselves is: Will they or their friends be among the regimes that America has determined need to be changed?

While adjustments in the global coverage of US military forces are needed, an increase in foreign suspicions of troop movements will inevitably continue—particularly if the overall force levels do not decline. Even the most skillful American diplomacy cannot satisfactorily answer all questions about America's agenda as changes in force deployments are undertaken. Unfortunately, both foreign governments and people on the streets increasingly see the United States as the world's best-armed cop—a cop that does not need a court order to gain entry into the lives of people anywhere.

As noted, many American service personnel stationed abroad trigger local admiration for America through their individual and collective deeds. In a particularly important example, the hard work of American military forces after the tsunami disaster in South Asia at the end of 2004 won the genuine gratitude of thousands of people in the region. Victims were treated in hastily assembled military hospitals, transported to safety, or received packages of food dropped from helicopters.

Despite such well-publicized heroic acts in times of humanitarian crises, the stationing of American troops on foreign soil increasingly creates new resentments toward the United States even when their deportment is beyond reproach. While some military units are hailed by local residents as welcome saviors who have brought stability to lands in trouble, others are condemned as occupiers. The benefits of the American presence to local economies are usually substantial. However, those residents who are not direct beneficiaries are not impressed by increased incomes for a favored few, who are often accused of corruptive practices in handling inflows of American money.

For the foreseeable future, the United States will not face large armadas of warships or tanks bent on waging conventional warfare. Rather, troublesome developments are energizing as a few renegade nations seek weapons of mass destruction. Also, pockets of insurgents are expanding across North Africa, through the Middle East, and into South Asia. These new realities call for new military deployment strategies. But reliance in the first instance on raw military power to prevent or quell outbursts of violence is unlikely to be effective in enhancing international peace and stability.

In addressing what he considered to be the excessive overseas deployment of US military forces, Admiral Jack Shanahan and his coauthor have observed:

> Afghanistan and Iraq should have taught us that people and ideas fight wars, not weapon systems. The United States needs forces built around speed, maneuverability, and agility, trained in urban and guerilla warfare and in nation building and humanitarian assistance. These forces should be based in the United States, ready to be deployed in appropriate strength on short notice when it is in our vital interest to do so. . . .
>
> In developing his military strategy for this century, the President should relegate military force to its support role and forget preemptive unilateral use of the US military as the principal tool of statecraft. It's a matter of priorities, and needlessly spreading brave soldiers around the world should be at the bottom of America's priority list.[8]

Perhaps these authors have simplified the complexities of necessary interventions. Perhaps they have not given adequate weight to the importance of deterrence through a military presence. Yet their underlying theme is sound. We simply have too many military personnel in too many places too much of the time. Let us hope that President Bush will fulfill his pledge to significantly reduce the number of troops abroad.

THE DOCTRINE OF PREEMPTION

As the war in Iraq very slowly winds down and the clamor for American troops to return to the United States increases, a "never-again" attitude seems to be building in the United States despite government warnings that the "war on terror" will last for many years. This withdrawal mentality is similar to stay-at-home attitudes that developed following the war in Vietnam. Thus, historians, politicians, and the American public are examining how we became embroiled in such a mess, and how we can avoid such involvement in the future. Was there simply no other way to rid the world of the tyrant Saddam Hussein? Clearly, if ridding the world of tyrants has become a US goal, the list of targets is an extensive one.[9]

US intervention in Iraq was initially justified on the basis of flawed intelligence. The opposition to that action by many of America's historical allies was intense. Early concerns over the presence of weapons of mass destruction eventually gave way to allegations of strong linkages between Saddam's brutality and the activities of al Qaeda, claims that could not be documented. Thus, the US rationale for the preemptive military strike evolved into the need for regime change: to remove a threat to the entire region and to demonstrate to all the importance of democratic governance.

Of course, Saddam was not the first dictator to be removed by American military power. In recent years, the United States has sent its armed forces into a number of countries where military intervention was judged to be essential to protect America's interests. Those "interests" that were threatened have been very broadly defined. For example, in 1989 twenty-five hundred American troops entered Panama to protect American lives, safeguard the canal, apprehend President Manuel Noriega, and seat Panama's elected government. In the early 1990s the United States dispatched twenty-five thousand troops to Somalia on a humanitarian mission, as previously mentioned, but this intervention became a disaster. Also, in the 1990s US troops became involved when riots broke out in Haiti; troops have since moved in and out of Haiti in a series of confused missions.[10]

In short, for decades American political and military leaders have considered preemptive deployment of American forces into trouble spots. Buoyed by the ending of the Cold War but still sensitive to the miscalculations in Vietnam, they have increasingly turned to unchallenged US military power to achieve what diplomacy could not accomplish when difficulties arose. If US interests were at stake, the political judgment was that the United States should play its trump card.

Following Desert Storm in the early 1990s, Colin Powell, then chairman of the Joint Chiefs of Staff, counseled that six questions should be addressed before a decision to intervene militarily in the affairs of another country is reached.

1. Is the political objective clearly defined and understood?
2. Have all other nonviolent policy means failed?
3. Will military force achieve the objective?
4. What will the cost be?
5. Have the gains and risks been analyzed?
6. Once the situation is altered by force, how will it develop further and what will the consequences be?[11]

A decade later, the same Colin Powell was busy defending the preemption policy that the Bush administration set forth in its National Security Strategy of 2002. He vigorously denied that the administration was obsessed by terrorism and hence biased toward preemptive war on a global scale. He defended the threat of preemptive war by the United States for two reasons: (1) When you recognize that a threat is evolving, you do not allow future attacks to happen before taking action. (2) It is necessary to convey to America's adversaries bent on violence that they will be in big trouble if they attack innocent populations anywhere; instilling a certain amount of anxiety in terrorist groups will increase the likelihood that they will cease activity or make mistakes and be caught.[12]

Powell then went on to explain that preemption applies to threats that come from nonstate actors such as terrorist groups, which cannot be deterred through a counterthreat of retaliation. The concept was never intended to displace deterrents. Rather, it supplements deterrents, he added. How this explanation applies to the invasion of Iraq, however, escapes even the most perceptive analyst of foreign affairs.[13]

Much of the confusion over the justification for preemptive war is rooted in the many terms that are being used to characterize military interventions. For example, there are preventive attacks and punitive attacks. Forces are deployed to deter aggression or to interdict the buildup toward aggression. Invasions may be launched to rescue populations under siege or to facilitate the provision of humanitarian aid in times of natural or human-made crises. Also, the boundaries between peacemaking, peace-keeping, and nation building are far from clear.[14] But when well-armed American troops are seen on foreign soil, the local residents do not take time to analyze the terminology used for their deployment.

The most dangerous aspect of an aggressive policy of military pre-emption by the United States is the signal its sends to the rest of the world. If the United States can intervene whenever it considers that its national interests are at stake, then other countries surely have a right to invade the sovereignty of their adversaries to protect their interests as well. Do Americans really want this type of world, where all decisions on intervention are left to those nations with military power sufficient such that they can ignore the principle of sovereignty and take matters into their own hands?

For centuries, a military attack on another state in the absence of an "imminent" threat has been considered aggression. "Imminent" is a useful, albeit vague, standard in justifying preemptive action. New international rules and norms are needed to define the circumstances in which nations can initiate the legitimate use of force in responding to challenges resulting from the internal behavior of others. Some basis for quantifying and categorizing distant threats would surely be helpful. Indeed, a user's manual is needed.

Is the United Nations up to the task of defining such rules and norms? Can the United Nations elaborate on the very general principle in Article 51 of the UN Charter that permits nations to defend themselves? The like-lihood of international agreement on the basis for initiating "just" wars seems low, nevertheless the diplomats should try their best to help reduce the chaos that ensues as countries with military might flex their muscles at the expense of weaker countries.

Another concern with the interventionist policy of the United States is the possibility that such a doctrine may provoke a troubled country to push its own button of aggression, internally or against a neighbor, before the United States strikes. "There is nothing to lose," might well be the reasoning.

The preemptive option will not disappear from the national security lexicon of the United States. Nor should it disappear, particularly as weapons of mass destruction come closer to the grasp of states and terrorist groups set on killing Americans or destroying American assets in the United States or abroad. At the same time, the decision-making process for using preemptive force should include consideration of not only the planned activities of an adversary but also a clear calculation of the worldwide ripple effects of any preemptive act.

NATO'S PREEMPTION AND EXPANSION POLICIES

Widely perceived as an instrument of American power, the North Atlantic Treaty Organization plays an important role in shaping international views on the security objectives of the United States. While many member states participate in NATO deliberations, the United States has the loudest voice and, in fact, mainly leads NATO actions. This reality comes through clearly to countries around the globe.

During recent years, NATO has given increasing attention to political intervention and military preemption as strategies for dealing with hostile states. This is not surprising, since its most prominent member has initiated preemptive strikes. Some NATO planners believe that NATO should pursue military preemption or at least more subtle intervention, not only in the name of self-defense, but also in cases of gross violations of human rights, grave threats to regional stability, or serious threats to global security. Two issues that face NATO in this realm are: (1) the criteria to be used in taking action, and (2) the type of action that is appropriate in specific situations—diplomatic, economic, or military. Of course, it is the criteria for preemptive military strikes that pose the most uncertainty within the organization.[15]

NATO planners appear more inclined than American officials to call for prior international endorsement of proposed preemption or even intervention, be it through NATO, the United Nations, or other appropriate bodies. Most NATO governments bristled at former secretary of state Madeleine Albright's notion of America's "virtuous power" and at current secretary of state Donald Rumsfeld's principle that "the mission determines the coalition." The differing views of European and American strategists concerning the need for international consensus when security is at stake are clear and cause turmoil both within and outside NATO.[16]

Despite different opinions within NATO of how and when to intervene in the internal affairs of troubled countries, the organization has reached a consensus on actively expanding its reach into several states of the former Soviet Union. Limited intervention that begins with technical contacts and exchanges, and eventually proceeds to stationing troops in countries of interest, seems to have become the approach advocated in Brussels. In the long run, the expansion of activities of this regional military organization will also increase the prominence of military authorities in its member states. Such a militarization trend does not bode well for a peaceful world over the long term. As noted earlier, why should a country increase its military strength unless it is prepared to use it?

Three states of the former Soviet Union—Estonia, Latvia, and Lithuania—are now members of NATO. This eastward march of NATO did not involve military invasions; rather, it was a response to the desires of the countries themselves to come into the protective security shield of stronger Western nations. In addition, the United States has bilateral military ties with the three Baltic countries.

As to other former Soviet republics, the United States established military bases in the Central Asian countries of Uzbekistan and Kyrgyzstan to provide logistical support for the military campaign in Afghanistan, although, as previously discussed, the base in Uzbekistan is closing due to issues concerning political governance of the country. Finally, the United States has developed ambitious programs of military training and of establishment of electronic communication facilities in the former Soviet republic of Azerbaijan. With the United States in the lead, the strategic importance of Central Asia has not been lost on NATO. Some commentators believe that an "Asianization" of the European-based NATO has begun.[17]

All the while, the NATO Partnership for Peace programs, which promote technical exchanges, workshops, and training programs in countries on the eastern borders of the NATO countries, are expanding throughout the former Soviet Union. Of special interest are developments in the Southern Caucasus—in the countries of Armenia, Georgia, and Azer-

baijan, where the United States and other NATO members have had foreign-assistance and related programs for a number of years. These countries had been the southwest flank of the USSR, geographically positioned near Turkey and Iran.

Much of the momentum to expand NATO's influence in these three
countries of the Caucasus region is rooted in the West's mistrust of
Russia's imperial ambitions. Even though such ambitions may currently
be in abeyance, historical realities remain fresh in the minds of NATO
leaders. Indeed, Russia can do little to convince Brussels and Washington
that it is not planning in the long run to annex independent countries of
the former Soviet Union. Cold War memories in the West are strong. To
the north in Russia, resentment over Western efforts to dominate the policies of countries within its traditional sphere of influence is also strong.

Some politicians in these new states look to NATO as their protective
shield in the long run. In addition, the financial benefits of dealing with
the West seem far greater than doing business with a financially weak
Russia. At the same time, other local politicians have long-standing personal and professional ties with their Russian counterparts, and they are
not pleased with the ever-increasing Western military presence in the
region. They are particularly disappointed that the United States is in the
forefront in such efforts.

The three countries of the Caucasus have differing views of their relationship with NATO. The Georgian government has never hidden its
ambitions to join NATO. Azerbaijan has been involved in an armed confrontation since the early 1990s with Armenia over disputed territory, and
it realizes that NATO is not prepared to become engaged in resolving the
conflict to the benefit of Azerbaijan. Also, Baku is economically linked to
Russia in a number of ways and is hesitant to add difficulties to this relationship through flirtation with NATO. Armenia is geographically isolated, blocked by trade embargoes on its western front with Turkey and
on its northeastern front with Azerbaijan. At the same time, Armenia is a
member of a collective security arrangement sponsored by Russia, and
therefore it sees little point in seeking NATO membership, at least at this
time.[18]

While it will be many years before Georgia or any of its neighbors
become NATO members, the increasing presence of the organization in

the region raises both hopes and anxieties. When local newspapers report new NATO interest in the region, much of the population imagines military personnel on the ground with welcome dollars finding their way into the local economies. To some this is reassuring, while to others it is disturbing. In any event, the NATO presence surely adds to a belief that the future of the region increasingly will be determined by military prowess of the countries themselves and of their link to Western powers. It is indeed unfortunate that discussions of the region's future are not more about food, health, and education, and less about tanks, rifles, and bombers.

A MILITARY PRESENCE IN CIVILIAN GARB

For decades many governments around the world have relied on civilian mercenaries to carry out military tasks, from flying supply planes into violence-infested areas, to providing guard services at beleaguered military compounds, to conducting combat operations on the battlefield. However, civilians working for the US armed forces have historically been restricted largely to noncombatant roles—in mess tents, supply stations, and motor pools. The war in Iraq dramatically expanded these behind-the-scenes roles and alerted the American public to the greatly increased use of civilians in combat situations. In 2004 thirty thousand civilian contract personnel were paid to perform both military and civilian tasks in Iraq. According to one press report:

> Contractors in Iraq and elsewhere are doing a lot more than building and maintaining camps, preparing food, and doing laundry for the troops. They support M1 tanks and Apache helicopters on the battlefield; they train American forces, army ROTC units, and even foreign militaries under contract to the United States. And they have flooded into Iraq to provide the military with security and crime prevention services. . . . The government is even outsourcing the interrogation of military prisoners. . . . There are no standard procedures for deploying private security workers, and they are not covered by the Code of Military Justice.[19]

Indeed, photographs of contract employees captured by insurgents in Iraq were shown on television on a number of occasions during 2004, sometimes with swords held threateningly across their necks. While only a small percentage of contract personnel supporting American forces in Iraq, Afghanistan, and elsewhere have been heavily armed security personnel, the number in battle gear continues to grow in these and other combat zones. The distinctions between military and nonmilitary personnel on and close to battlefields are certainly more blurred than ever before.

Many former Navy Seals and Special Forces experts eagerly seek jobs with security contractors in combat zones. The pay frequently ranges from $100,000 to $200,000 per year—greatly exceeding that of senior noncommissioned officers and often even that of senior officers. Among the biggest organizations in the private security market are companies based in France, Great Britain, Israel, and South Africa. Meanwhile, the share of the market captured by American companies has grown dramatically in the aftermath of 9/11.

Personnel employed by contractors to support military operations may undergo some of the most rigorous training that the armed services of their countries have to offer. Also, many have highly specialized skills in fields such as medicine, engineering, communications, intelligence, and linguistics. They are usually older and more experienced than the average soldier. Thus, they are in high demand when combat operations expand quickly.[20]

In a highly publicized incident in Naja, Iraq, in 2004, eight commandos from the North Carolina–based firm Blackwater took three casualties, while withstanding an attack by rocket-propelled grenades and AK-47 fire. They stood their ground for four hours before US Special Forces arrived. Even then, they awaited evacuation by a helicopter operated by their firm. The civilian commandos had done their job and kept insurgents away from the US government's local headquarters.[21]

Activities like this inevitably lead to anxieties among residents of countries where they take place as to who is a soldier and who is a civilian. They increase the likelihood that all Americans near the battle zone will be suspected of having military ties. Such misidentification of affiliations certainly makes interactions among civilian nation builders and local populations difficult. In many cases, residents are not enthusiastic about the US military presence in their countries, and American specialists who have no ties to the military services may have extraordinary difficulty promoting social and economic agendas. Moreover, on occasion the conduct of such contractors has adversely influenced the reputation of the United States due to inappropriate actions in guarding prisoners and disrespect of local customs during off-duty hours.

A more worrisome development than the use of civilian contractors during and immediately following hostilities, however, is the establishment of military espionage units that operate on a global scale. The Pentagon is moving into clandestine operations that had previously been the exclusive purview of the Central Intelligence Agency (CIA). Newly formed covert military units have been dispatched into friendly and unfriendly nations whether or not outbursts of violence are near at hand. Apparently the motivation of the Pentagon is to reduce its dependence on an unreliable CIA in satisfying its intelligence needs.[22]

As more clandestine agents are deployed, more useful intelligence will be collected, argues the Department of Defense. But it has taken the CIA fifty years to master the art of clandestine operations, and foul-ups still abound. As a novice, the Department of Defense will soon add to the list of embarrassing missteps. Also, when a spy who represents a military force armed with missiles and other types of devastating firepower is uncovered abroad, the discovery can be an unsettling experience for peaceful populations. More human-intelligence resources are needed on the ground, but the job should not be turned over to an unbridled Department of Defense.

PEACE AND STABILITY OPERATIONS

Military and civilian roles have frequently become confused in the aftermath of conflict. Yet achieving political goals often involves not only military success on the battlefield but also military muscle to ensure security for stabilization and reconstruction operations.

For many critical assignments, one can find no better-qualified personnel than military specialists. The erection of temporary hospitals, construction of small bridges, and installation of reliable communication systems, for example, are routinely accomplished by armies in dangerous situations.[23] For many tasks, however, and particularly those involving enhancement of the governance and financial accounting capabilities of foreign governments, military personnel may have the required skills but may not be suitable in the eyes of the country to which they are to be deployed. The determination of the appropriate role of US military forces in stabilization and reconstruction efforts will, of course, vary from situation to situation. Unfortunately, past decisions to rely on military personnel for certain tasks have often been driven by on-the-scene necessities for quick action rather than by adequate advanced planning.

In principle, once the fighting is over, US military forces should come home as quickly as possible. However, the pressures from Washington to ensure that military and political gains are not quickly reversed usually result in withdrawal delays. Also, even if civilian units are ready to move in, the problem of maintaining order remains, and this responsibility for security inevitably falls to the military services.[24]

Of course, nation building is far more than constructing hospitals, bridges, and communication systems. It involves the establishment of governance, economic, and social infrastructures as well as physical reconstruction. These are tasks that take years to accomplish. The American specialists recruited to assist in such efforts should be prepared for the long haul, not for short-term military deployments.

An insightful study points out that on more than two hundred occasions since its founding, the United States has sent its armed forces abroad in efforts to quell turbulence and reinforce efforts of other governments. The study distinguishes between "ordinary" military actions and nation-building efforts. For the purposes of the study, it defines "nation building" as having three characteristics: (1) The intervention is designed to effect a regime change or to help ensure the survival of an existing regime under attack. (2) Large numbers of US ground troops are deployed. (3) American military and civilian personnel are involved in the political administration of the country and have decisive influence in the selection of the leaders to head the regime.[25]

Using these criteria, only sixteen of the two hundred interventions can be classified as nation building, although American troops participated in many more. Only four of the efforts can be considered successes:

Japan and Germany after World War II and Grenada and Panama during the 1980s. This disappointing record is attributed in large measure to ill-considered decisions to ally with unsavory elites in Latin American and Southeast Asia. Such alliances of political expediency were ultimately rejected by the people in the target nations as illegitimate.[26]

The record of UN nation building is also mixed, with both successes and failures. The United Nations has launched fifty-six blue-helmet missions since 1948, and, as of the end of 2004, thirteen were still under way. American troops have sometimes been on the ground, but usually American involvement is in the form of sending civilian police units to work under the leadership of the United Nations.[27]

In Afghanistan, American troops have been on the front lines since 9/11. However, both the United Nations and NATO have also played roles. Despite success in providing security for the carrying out of elections, military contingents from different nations have encountered difficulties in providing a cohesive approach to securing the broader activities of the country. Regional garrisons made up of foreign troops that work closely with reconstruction units, known as Provincial Reconstruction Teams (PRTs), are attempting to bring order to the country. One difficulty is that each nation providing troops at a particular PRT has given its soldiers different instructions. For example, the German contingents are prohibited by their government from participating in riot control or intervening to thwart the drug trade. Meanwhile, American forces operating from PRTs have built schools across southern Afghanistan but in areas where they were least needed.[28]

The reports about UN-led activities in East Timor are far more encouraging. Of course, this is a small nation. Nevertheless, the challenge of putting the nation on a course to greater stability and eventual prosperity is formidable.

The US government clearly recognizes the need to strengthen its capabilities to stabilize postconflict situations, while making the transition from military operations to civilian control. Senators Richard Lugar and Joe Biden have led a congressional effort to establish a special office within the Department of State to do just that. As of late 2005 the office had been established, although it has struggled with its vague charter and limited staffing and funding.[29]

Finally, a popular concept is the establishment of international constabulary units that help shift security responsibilities from military to police units. This concept has been described as follows:

> Constabulary forces are composed of personnel who have received both military and police training. They are equipped with armored personnel carriers, armed with automatic and crew-served weapons, and can fight as light infantry, if required. They are also equipped with non-lethal weapons and are specially trained to deal with civil disorder, crowd control, and general lawlessness. As police they can engage in law enforcement and are especially useful in conducting high risk arrests and in dealing with situations that do not require conventional military forces but are beyond the capacity of regular police.[30]

Western experience in this area has increased substantially in recent years. The French National Gendarmerie and the Italian Carabinieri are often cited as examples of constabulary forces that should be emulated. The United States and other countries have gained considerable experience with constabulary-type approaches and they continue to recruit many police officers to serve in US contingents abroad. The US Border Patrol has also been singled out as an American organization that has characteristics akin to those of constabulary forces.[31]

Thus, the military's main role in postconflict situations should be to establish and maintain security so that other groups may carry out their many responsibilities. The military should not provide assistance on an ongoing basis, except in circumstances where the security situation prohibits humanitarian aid workers and other civilians from carrying out their tasks. Of course, civilian workers may request transportation, evacuation, and demining assistance, but the military orientation should be to promote a transformation of the security situation to local civilian control and then to withdraw from the area as quickly as possible. History has too often shown that long-term military involvement breeds resentment, unhealthy dependence, or both.

Finally, a caution is offered concerning the exuberance of the Pentagon in taking on new tasks related to peacekeeping and to nation building. In 1997, as the conflict in Bosnia was stabilizing, the Pentagon announced its new efforts to develop nonlethal weapons to be used in stabilization efforts. US troops would be equipped with sponge grenades designed to knock people down but not cause serious injury and also with balloons filled with latex paint that would mark ringleaders among insurgents. Special devices that covered rioters with glue were being developed, and a new type of gun was to fire sticky nets on top of demonstrators. New chemicals would be released that would glue attackers to the ground. Finally, acoustic weapons would make internal organs vibrate and cause disabling vertigo or diarrhea. Such schemes, whether or not they are carried out, project an image of America trying to ridicule populations that do not have the technological wherewithal or time to consider such antics. Paintball may be for children on holiday, but it certainly is not for soldiers.[32]

EMPHASIZING AN APPROPRIATE ROLE FOR THE ARMED FORCES

When appropriately used overseas, American troops can promote American interests in the broadest sense. But when they usurp responsibilities of civilian authorities, they run the risk of having devastating impacts on America's image.

In considering military preemption, America's leaders must realize that short-term successes will more than likely be outweighed by long-term problems. We may achieve the objective of killing adversaries quickly and efficiently. Indeed, we may think we have a first-round knockout. However, our adversaries will not play by our rules, and their followers will work tirelessly to have a rematch on American soil.[33]

If military forces are to help win hearts and minds around the world, then the planners in Washington and the commanders on the ground must limit military deployments. They must promptly pass the baton of nation building to others, recognizing the aspirations of local populations to govern themselves without the presence of foreign combat boots.

In weighing how American troops can make a positive contribution to bringing stability to a region once the intensive fighting ceases, leaders should take the warning of the Defense Science Board seriously: "Knowledge of a nation's security interests and external relations; armed forces; the local political scene; internal social, cultural, and economic conditions; security; and social and economic well-being are as important to stability operations as the knowledge of the enemy's order of battle is during hostilities. We need to treat the learning of culture and the development of language skills as seriously as we treat learning combat skills. Both are needed for success in achieving US political and military operations."[34]

Reducing the US military presence abroad, using preemption only rarely and very carefully, turning reconstruction activities over to civilian authorities as soon as possible, and limiting the use of civilians to carry out military missions should reduce the likelihood that US military deployments will alienate foreign populations. Yes, inadvertent mistakes will occur. But an occasional misstep that is quickly acknowledged and put into the history books should not have a large negative impact on foreign views of America.

Fortunately, many American generals and colonels recognize the folly of using military power as a first resort. They are rapidly adjusting to the new realities. Wars will no longer be won primarily on battlefields. They will be won only if current and future generations recognize the appropriate role of the military in ensuring peace and security around the world—and that preemptive war is not the path to better lives.

CHAPTER 11

TONE-DEAF TO THE
VIEWS OF OTHERS

★ ★ ★ *Fast Talking by Diplomats or Broadcasters*
Can't Replace Listening

In recent years American embassy complexes throughout the world have been transformed from inviting outposts of civility and friendship into imposing fortresses of power and foreboding. Armed guards are omnipresent. These security forces probe under entering vehicles to check for explosives. They use wands to search each visitor for hidden metallic objects. They scrutinize television screens as cameras scan for impending trouble. All the while, armed US Marines are at the ready to respond quickly to any breach in security.

No longer is a high-flying American flag, together with the history it symbolizes, the emblem of the US presence around the world. Rather, fences and concrete barriers indicate that the US government is ready for business—on its terms. Towering communication antennas are set to send clear messages to Washington about local missteps, whether they are political or economic, let alone military, shenanigans. If necessary, reinforcements will soon be on the way from nearby aircraft carriers or military bases.

These edifices are the offices of American diplomats assigned to spearhead efforts to win the hearts and minds of those who deplore the United States. In decades past American embassy complexes were the showplaces of American culture. Reading rooms bedecked with spectacular photographs of the Lincoln Memorial, the Golden Gate Bridge, and amber fields of waving grain provided unforgettable introductions to

America's achievements for millions of local residents eager to learn about America. But such initiations have now been replaced in many capitals with scowling militias hired by both host governments and the embassies.

During my visit to Bangladesh in January 2005, the transformation of the image of America really hit home. Many important government buildings in this desperately poor and heavily overpopulated country were built with funds provided by the US foreign assistance program. In the capital city of Dhaka, the world-famous Center for Diarrheal Diseases has long been led by American doctors supported by the US government. This single hospital saves the lives each year of ten thousand children on the verge of death. It also provides research findings that help in halting the spread of disease throughout the country and, indeed, throughout all of South Asia and beyond. The United States installed a water-monitoring system in the countryside of Bangladesh that warns of impending floods and thereby provides time for evacuation of hundreds of thousands of people each year. The introduction of rice/wheat rotation in agricultural areas, under the guidance of American experts, has contributed immensely to a dramatic increase in food production. But these transformative contributions of the United States are rapidly being lost on the new generation of Bangladeshis.

Now American diplomats hesitate to leave the embassy compound to talk about these achievements. They cannot travel outside the capital city if the security officer senses impending danger. So how can they realistically be expected to be the outreach ambassadors of peace and friendship, as well as the conduits for assistance? These tasks are more important than ever, as extremists begin to find fertile ground in the country.

The Bangladesh example is far from unique. In a far-ranging assessment of US facilities that support outreach efforts abroad, a government-sponsored advisory group of distinguished Americans reported as follows: "Cost cutting after the end of the Cold War forced the closure of many outreach facilities. Others were transformed into 'Information Resource Centers' open only by appointment. Security concerns, meanwhile, created irresistible pressure to move the remaining facilities into the fortress-like perimeters of our diplomatic and consular establishments, thus rendering them almost inaccessible to the general public. One

Pakistani told us that getting to the American center was 'like going to jail or getting into Fort Knox.'"[1]

In Turkey the new $83 million US consulate outside Istanbul satisfies important security concerns, but it is viewed by many as a remote "crusader castle."[2]

Against such a backdrop, the art of public diplomacy is at a disadvantage as the US government tries to sell America's message abroad. The message has to do with American values, America's vision for the world, and US programs to help others adopt a similar vision. It also has to do with policies of the US government, the very policies we have discussed in this book.

Public diplomacy is obviously important. But sugarcoating unpopular policies and fast-talking to gloss over criticisms of the United States simply will not work. Even though details of many American policies may be misunderstood abroad, the general gist of the approaches advocated in Washington is usually well known throughout the world. Most of the challenge of transforming growing hatred to global respect for America lies not in better communication but in fixing US policies, particularly policies that unnecessarily irritate other governments and their people. As finally recognized by the Department of State in 2004: "Arabs say cosmetics won't change ugly US policies. Sweet words and pictures cannot cover US bad policies and double standards. Skeptics deplore another American propaganda machine."[3]

FIRST A GOOD PRODUCT, THEN GOOD MARKETING

Terrorism expert Walter Laqueur reflects on US policy as follows: "International relations is not a popularity contest. . . . Big powers have been respected and feared but not loved for good reasons—even if benevolent, tactful, and on their best behavior, they were threatening simply because of their very existence. Smaller nations could not feel comfortable, especially if they were located close to them. A moderate and intelligent policy may mitigate some of the perceived threat, but it cannot remove it, because potentially the big power remains dangerous."[4]

While elements of this analysis by a renowned defender of aggressive antiterrorism policies are true, the argument is somewhat misguided in that now even the smallest countries may soon have the capabilities to use weapons that can annihilate large populations with a single blow. Nor is the argument accurate in describing the past history of America—a history adorned with small-country admirers around the globe. In short, the problem is not that the United States is big and powerful. The problem is that many US policies unnecessarily agitate countries both large and small.

Of course, some leaders and their followers are determined not to be influenced by American ideals. They believe that human rights and tolerance are imperialist inventions. They are comfortable with their extremist interpretations of the Koran and other works not rooted in Western civilizations. They may quickly seize on American policies that they know are unpopular in their areas and use them to discredit American values. They have audiences ready to believe the wildest distortions of the facts—that the United States weakens its enemies by poisoning their drinking water and that trafficking in baby parts is a popular moneymaker for American capitalists.

Unfortunately, many highly personalized accounts of unacceptable actions by the US government targeting Muslims provide fodder for these extremists—examples of incarceration of foreigners for minor visa violations, misuse of the USA PATRIOT Act to humiliate law-abiding US citizens, and sending recalcitrant Muslim prisoners to nations where torture is an accepted means of interrogation. Photos of Israeli military operations in Palestinian neighborhoods are constantly shown throughout the Arab world, with underlined reminders of American acceptance of such operations. In addition to the horrendous photographs of American abuse of Iraqi prisoners in Abu Ghraib prison, new reports of misbehavior of American combat troops deployed in Iraq, Afghanistan, and other foreign lands continue to surface. Such stories, sadly often true, are repeated throughout the Middle East—and then throughout the world—like a persistent drumbeat.

Perhaps most disheartening of all, leaders of the Muslim world are convinced that the US government is not interested in two-way discussions on any significant issue. Many believe that the leaders of America have made up their minds as to what is best for *its* world and for the regions and the individual countries that should belong to *its* world. Negotiations are viewed solely as opportunities for America's representatives to lecture other parties on future directions that listeners need to take. Even if another nation is trying its best to install democratic principles, the United States is seen as not hesitating to criticize the slowness of progress in meeting the US timetable.

The first step in winning the respect of other societies is a demonstrated willingness to listen to their points of view—*before* US policies are adopted. The art of public diplomacy must be transformed from the art of lecturing to the art of listening. While it will be cumbersome and sometimes painful for America's leaders to hear the complaints of others while formulating important policies, attentive listening is at the core of winning global respect for America while developing mutually supported international goals.

This imperative has not been made explicit in the charge from the Department of State to officials responsible for public diplomacy. Rather, diplomats are instructed to "influence" attitudes of the audience through "improving understanding," through engaging in "constructive disagreement," and by gaining "active support" for US policies. These are admirable objectives, but they neglect the core concern—two-way dialogue early in the policy formulation process. Also, too often success in public diplomacy is measured by the size of the audience receiving the message. While audience size is important, changing minds, even of one or two individuals at a time, is what public diplomacy should be about.[5] Only by listening will common misperceptions about the Muslim world on the part of many American politicians and officials be changed.

USING RADIO AND TELEVISION TO EXPLAIN AMERICA

For sixty years, the US government has employed radio broadcasting and then television broadcasting to help improve global understanding of American values and policies. The overriding objective now seems to be to convince the world that the United States has found the only path to peace and prosperity and that others should sign up and follow. A degree of such arrogance has always been inherent in broadcasts from Washington, but never before has US policy been so America-centric. The annual broadcasting budget to trumpet the path to the ideal world exceeds half a billion dollars and is growing. No corner of the world is out of reach of the messages originating in Washington. The daily audiences are measured in the tens of millions of listeners, and some popular commentators apparently have as many admirers abroad as do Hollywood stars.[6]

At the same time, US government–sponsored programs face tough competition from commercial broadcasts from the West, programs sponsored by other governments, and independent media in regions around the world. However, the directors of three key news services sponsored by the US government are proud of their achievements, and, indeed, some of their accomplishments are noteworthy, as follows:

- The Voice of America (VOA) broadcasts AM and FM programs via cable through thirteen hundred partner stations around the world, while maintaining twenty-two transmitting stations for shortwave broadcasts. VOA offers news and cultural programs in fifty languages, and at the same time continues its slow-paced delivery of Special English programs to help listeners learn English.[7]
- Radio Free Europe/Radio Liberty (RFE/RL) has shifted much of its focus from central and southeast Europe to regions where the majority of the populations are Muslim, including Farsi-language broadcasts to Iran and Arabic broadcasts throughout the Middle East. In Afghanistan the service sponsors training programs to support the development of local commercial radio stations.[8]
- Radio Free Asia (RFA) broadcasts call-in programs that are targeted at several areas of China, thereby providing an important window into developments of concern to the US government. The service played a significant educational role in the response to the SARS epidemic. Also, a priority is transmission into North Korea where modifying one-channel radios to listen to foreign broadcasts is a popular avocation.[9]

Other US-sponsored broadcasts, some of which rely on support of the aforementioned services, also target important audiences abroad. Radio

Marti has long sent broadcasts to Cuba, and new delivery options are being developed to avoid jamming. The Arabic-language station, Radio Sava, and the Farsi-language broadcast, Radio Farda, command large audiences in the Middle East. Worldnet is a global satellite-based TV service. In these efforts, the mantra in Washington of the media war is to combat disinformation, incitement to violence, hate radio, government censorship, and journalist self-censorship.[10]

A special target for American broadcasts is Iran, with Radio Farda in the lead. Indeed, Radio Farda's and VOA's Persian-language Web sites attract one million visitors per month. Weekly roundtables allow viewers and listeners to call in and speak with prominent figures regarding politics, social issues, and entertainment. Also, a special weekly show provides "cultural fare," including the latest in sports, technology, fashion, Hollywood, and car reviews.[11]

Serious criticism has been leveled at the broadcasting approach toward Iran, an approach that is intended to attract the youth in a country where 70 percent of the population is under thirty years of age. The emphasis on a computer-generated mix of current American and Persian pop music punctuated by the occasional short news features presumed to be of interest to the youth is repeatedly questioned. The service apparently assumes that young Iranians lack sufficient tolerance for serious discussion and information—which they do not. The reaction of one knowledgeable Iranian to the efforts of Radio Farda is as follows: "This radio program has a lot of music and does sort of news bites . . . but has come under some criticism because Iran right now is at a stage in which it is a highly politicized environment, and young people are actually more interested in talking about policies than Britney Spears."[12]

A recently initiated service, Alhurra (Arabic for the free one), went on the air in February 2004. It is a US government–funded satellite television channel—the latest and most ambitious effort in American public diplomacy in the Arab world. Its broadcast beam reaches one hundred and seventy million Arabic-speaking people in twenty-two countries. The fare includes hour-long news broadcasts twice each day and news updates each hour. Daily discussion shows are enhanced by features on fashion and cuisine.

The linkage of the station to the US government is well known—a linkage that in the eyes of many viewers contradicts its repeated claims of objectivity. What did the station do the very first day it went on the air? It broadcast an interview with President Bush. This is the same approach that is used by state-sponsored stations throughout the Middle East so that viewers do not forget that they are listening to important voices of the government.[13]

A businessman from Egypt who has followed the station from its inception offers the following opinion. "It's not all good, not all bad. But I don't believe it is really Hurra. It's what we call 'American freedom.' It's not the kind of freedom you give to your people. We don't need that kind of station. We need freedom."[14]

The first hurdle, now higher than ever for this extensive broadcasting effort to overcome, is the widespread belief that broadcasts financed by the US government are merely propaganda efforts to mask hegemonic policies or otherwise mislead foreign audiences about America's real intentions. In the minds of many, at the top of the list of such intentions are obtaining access to oil and establishing military bases to support pre-emptive actions against unruly states. Such a perception of US intentions was very clear when I met with colleagues in the oil-rich country of Azerbaijan in November 2005. What else should they have thought when a former US ambassador to this strategically located Muslim country nestled between Russia and Iran became vice president of an American oil company determined to gain access to the country's oil resources? Then the US government downplayed its support of *fair* elections in order not to irritate the victors of a less-than-fair election who would determine whether the United States should have a military airfield in the country. Public diplomacy simply cannot gloss over such well-known developments.

At the same time, foreign leaders and opinion makers often rely on news broadcasts from the West to stay abreast of international developments, even events in their own countries. Thus, they turn to CNN. This service is widely known to be independent of the US government and is usually a respected source of information abroad.

The US government takes many steps to help ensure the factual accuracy of its broadcasts and to offer programs that attract large numbers of listeners, particularly young listeners. But the political overlay on the broadcasts is omnipresent. They must be slanted to command congressional support—unashamedly biased in the news reports to be aired, in the guests to be interviewed, in the questions to be debated, and in the aspects of American life to be highlighted.

Certainly, the US government deserves credit for its efforts to spread American viewpoints throughout troubled regions of the world. Undoubtedly, millions of hard-core fans of America cherish the American focus on their regions. Many more listeners, however, want to be convinced that they should line up with the US government as the way to a better life. However, they will only raise supportive voices when they are convinced that the United States is on the right course, which often means a new course.

Even in the slums of the Middle East where minimal plumbing and poor sanitation are the norm, hundreds of households have hand-wired TV dishes. Despite dire economic and social conditions, people are watching broadcasts from around the world. What are they watching? Most are watching Al Jazeera, Al Arabia, and other local stations.[15] Others are watching BBC, CNN, and other foreign stations that feature news over commentary. This is the challenge facing US-sponsored broadcasting.

As in other aspects of public diplomacy, listening is the first key to a successful television and radio presence. Call-in programs, interviews on location with local personalities, and listening to and then rebutting distorted accusations about American intentions are obvious mechanisms. The most important step that must be taken is to respond positively whenever possible to what the voices are saying—a response that will be persuasive if policies are adjusted to take into account local concerns when appropriate. The United States needs to keep close account of the voices, and policymakers at the highest levels must be informed of foreign opinions, however misguided they may be.

Clearly, America must communicate its story. The story that is to be told is the issue. No amount of dialogue will change opinions of tens of millions of people throughout the world about the United States and its intentions absent of tangible changes in policy. But, just as certainly, changes in policy cannot and will not speak for themselves.[16]

THE ADVENT OF THE INTERNET

In addition to television, the Internet is increasingly penetrating the Middle East and other areas of turmoil. Terrorists certainly know how to use the Internet. Does the US government understand how strategic use of blogs, chat rooms, and Web sites can complement traditional means of public diplomacy?

Much of the Western concern about terrorist organizations using the Internet has been directed to cybercrime and plotting of terrorist attacks. Indeed, these aspects are extraordinarily important. At the same time, there is a much broader war of ideas under way, with hundreds of Web sites promoting extremist visions of the future and allegations of the United States trying to take charge everywhere.

Just like savvy politicians in the United States, extremist organizations have mastered the art of persuasion through the Internet. They send messages to current and potential supporters of their causes. They attempt to sway international public opinion. They target citizens of states that deride their philosophies. They attempt to demoralize the populations of these states by threatening attacks and by fostering feelings of guilt about US military interventions abroad.

Several ways that extremist organizations use the Internet in this war of words have been reported in a comprehensive analysis of their messages. Their tactics are not new and they are frequently employed by the US government and its allies as well. When an extremist group resorts to this approach, Washington pays attention. Such groups often concentrate on

- **psychological warfare** to raise fears of future violence or of cyber-attacks within the context of "just" causes and propaganda that advocates peaceful solutions to contentious problems or urges non-violence in order to temper images of their bad behavior of the past
- **spreading information** on available data sources that support their goals and that provide technical information on tools of terrorism
- **fund-raising** targeted at sympathizers for particular issues
- **recruitment** of followers of their causes[17]

The United States attempts to blunt the impact of such communication. For example, VOA and the other US government broadcast services energetically promote their Web sites and regularly e-mail messages to large audiences. VOA's Web site (www.VOANews.com) reports tens of thousands of hits each day, with millions of pages viewed by visitors each month. Technologically, the system is well tuned to foreign audiences. Unlike many news services, it provides free access to both old and new postings. It provides convenient access both to users with broadband connections and to users without such access who must pay per-minute charges both for telephone time and for dial-up Internet service. The low-bandwidth option provides text only, whereas the broadband option includes pictures, graphics, and audio and video links. Wireless applications are also being considered, as handheld devices become a popular Web-surfing method in countries where mobile phones compensate for inadequate landlines.[18]

In a limited sense, bloggers have come to replace governments and established news services as the gatekeepers of news in the United States and abroad. Individual activists seem to reveal inside stories everywhere. Fact-checking bloggers have also challenged the objective reporting of traditional media. They thrive on showing that news reports are not always correct or complete. Of course, filtering authoritative blogger reports from deceptive ones is difficult. As some bloggers acquire credibility, their Web sites become ever more popular. Their role is growing into an ongoing dialogue between bloggers and like-minded users of the Internet.[19]

War blogging, or repeatedly commenting on reports of military operations in the midst of combat, gained popularity among both supporters and opponents of the war in Iraq. While their audiences cannot compare in size with TV viewers, they have helped keep the newsrooms honest. They punched holes in reports from the front lines and encouraged individuals with access to the Internet at home and abroad to step forward with their views.

King Abdullah of Jordan certainly is not ignoring the power of the Internet. By 2004 he had created seventy-five public "knowledge stations" that provide public walk-in access to Internet-linked PCs. He invested his own funds to start this extensive effort to introduce upgraded versions of Internet cafés to the country. A broadband learning and public access network linking all schools, colleges, and universities in the country is scheduled to be in operation by 2006.[20]

ARABS REACHING ARABS

Arab public opinion has been described by author Marc Lynch as a more complex phenomenon than conventional notions of a cynical elite and a passionate, nationalistic state of mind. What matters more than the famed "Arab street," and sometimes even more than the rulers, is the consensus of elite and middle-class public opinion. According to Lynch, opinions are articulate and assertive, and combative and argumentative. This public sphere increasingly sets the course for the street and the palace alike. It is here that the battle of ideas about internal reform and relations with the United States must be won.[21]

A new Arab-media infrastructure based both in the region and abroad, where it is beyond the reach of government control, recognizes the importance of the elite and middle classes. Its creators know the power of the street as it challenges the conservative state-controlled broadcasts of the countries of the region. This growing source of information and commentary projects itself as speaking for Arabs frustrated with their regimes and can claim to be beholden to none of those regimes. The stations thrive on news broadcasts that stimulate widespread debate as this emerging news sector eats into the market share of the state-run broadcast services. From its very beginning in 1996, Al Jazeera, for example, set as a priority its commentary on policies. Its heated debates were ideally suited for television broadcasts that shocked audiences unaccustomed to such fireworks. When asked during an Al Jazeera talk show whether the Arab regimes had become worse than colonialism, one of the guests and 76 percent of the call-in audience answered yes.[22]

This is the competition that US government broadcasters face in the Middle East. Indeed, the competition is so overpowering that the US government has made a number of pleas to the government of Qatar to tone down or shut down Al Jazeera, which Qatar supports. However, such diplomatic initiatives make a mockery of American free-speech rhetoric.

Washington thought that the shock-and-awe military tactics

employed in Iraq would win wide respect. It therefore did not hesitate to report each tactical achievement by military forces in the pursuit of Saddam Hussein. In contrast, the local media reported incessantly on the imbalance of power as the United States rolled over the weak resistance. The audience hardly needed to be reminded of what they considered to be the unfairness of the battle. Osama bin Laden's comment that people flock to the "strong horse" did not mean a horse stabled in America.[23]

These few examples underscore that even the smallest sound bites from officialdom in Washington must be carefully reviewed in advance for their potential impact lest they backfire and further undermine America's reputation.

DIRECT CONTACTS PAY OFF

As discussed earlier, education is an area where American and Muslim populations share common ground. In particular, many American universities are highly respected around the world. These universities take most foreign students away from rote memorization that characterizes traditional methods of learning in many countries and move them toward more critical thinking. Students' overall experiences give them a much more balanced view of the United States. One cannot help but take note of the statistic that in 2004, 80 percent of the members of the Saudi cabinet had American masters' or doctoral degrees.[24]

The US government has long sponsored a variety of international exchange programs as evidenced by the visitor programs highlighted on the Department of State's Web site (http://www.state.gov). Here again the statistics are impressive. Thirty-nine heads of state in 2004 had participated in these programs. Looking further back, more than two hundred current and former heads of state came to the United States at some point as exchange visitors. Of course, simply being exposed to the American way of life does not mean that all visitors buy in to the values and approaches of the United States. But they certainly have experiences that are more significant than listening to US government broadcasts in their home countries.[25]

It is difficult to separate general anti-Americanism from hostility over specific US policies. In general, however, foreign leaders and students alike who have visited the United States should have an easier time in making this distinction. It seems fair to say that they are more likely to be in the camp of opposing specific policies rather than having broad-based hatred for America and all things American. These programs are effective in building cross-cultural understanding, and US government support for these activities must not waver. The costs are incredibly small in comparison to the benefits of having well-informed people with direct understanding of the United States in significant positions around the globe.

Unfortunately there is not a strong history in the Middle East of university-based programs that emphasize studies of American history, culture, economics, and/or foreign policy. The two American universities in Lebanon and the one in Cairo supported by private funds have opened new windows into America for many students—currently numbering about eighteen thousand at the three universities. Unfortunately, they have been small islands amid a vast population. Since 9/11 several other local universities in the region have introduced American studies programs, and the US government is quick to back these with library support and with stipends for visiting professors from the United States.[26]

Of all the steps that could be taken to improve the image of America in the Middle East, expanding educational exchange and establishing American studies programs in the region should be at the top of the list.

PUBLIC DIPLOMACY REVISITED

The United States can no longer assume that public opinion in the Middle East and elsewhere does not really matter, believing that authoritarian states will control any discontent within their own countries. Nor can hostility in those countries toward America be pushed aside as irrelevant or unimportant. The assumptions that anger in homes, in restaurants, and on the street is intrinsic to the Islamic culture and that it represents the envy of the successful by the weak are simply wrong. Such assumptions have too often driven the American approach to public diplomacy, and, not surprisingly, this approach has alienated the very people whose support the United States needs on its side.[27]

A number of suggestions are on the table for increasing funding for public diplomacy efforts, for modifying the content of messages sent over the airwaves, and for restructuring the Washington bureaucracy to give the advocates of public diplomacy more clout. Without becoming entangled in budget priorities and organization of the various departments and offices of government, one suggestion is offered to better frame public diplomacy efforts.

Specifically, the activities of USAID and the Peace Corps should be more fully recognized and lauded as pillars of the American approach to public diplomacy. While the Japanese government revels in its construction of the highly visible Opera House in Cairo, USAID needs to take credit for its little-known construction of the sewer, water, and electrical systems in sections of the city. The Peace Corps has many success stories to report in its person-to-person diplomacy and should be encouraged to publicize its work with accounts of personal experiences.[28]

Whatever the program, direct discussions between Americans and their counterparts in lands in turmoil are vitally important. At the official level, two-way dialogues with Muslim populations *before* American policies are irrevocably in place would go a long away toward easing deep-seated hatred over American arrogance and hypocrisy, as long as the feedback and input are actually taken into account and used to shape policies. Such a consultative approach could change the color of hostile attitudes toward virtually everything the United States does. It could help nurture the very kind of liberalization that is the cornerstone of the American political strategy in troubled regions.

Secretary of State Condoleezza Rice has crisply summarized an essential path for the United States to follow. "Our interactions must be conversations, not monologues. We must reach out and explain, but we must also listen."[29] Let us hope that her colleagues throughout Washington and elsewhere have listened carefully.

In summary, the US government should be promoting a new branding of American foreign policy with an image that emphasizes openness and opportunities for participation by others in the development of US positions. The tag line should be "We welcome your views."

CHAPTER 12

THE ROAD TO SECURITY AND PEACE

★ ★ ★ ★ ★ ★ *Why Not a Common Journey?*

"Today we are all Americans." On September 12, 2001, the editor of *Le Monde* wrote these memorable words. Four years later, photographs of an effigy of Ronald McDonald being dragged through the streets of Paris were displayed on newsstands around the globe.

What went wrong? The primary cause was not Washington's ineptness in dealing with global leaders—although clumsiness had become a trait of intergovernmental discourses of the United States with all nations but Great Britain. It wasn't the inability of America's diplomats to adequately inform others of the intentions of the United States—although American unilateralism constantly caught leaders who were not in NATO's inner circle off guard. It wasn't poor packaging and marketing of US policies, although public diplomacy had been relegated to a backseat in Washington and abroad. It was simply that *too many important policies and programs emanating from Washington were designed simply to deal with immediate problems without adequate thought to the long-term implications of these policies and programs.* The actions to implement these shortsighted efforts inflamed anger around the globe.[1]

Previous chapters have highlighted seven policy areas where America can and must do better. The large US government expenditures for foreign assistance, for international education programs, and for global health initiatives need far stronger and better-oriented foundations.

Nuclear arrogance must give way to nuclear compromise lest the United States inadvertently trigger widespread destruction of heavily populated corners of the world. While the United Nations needs reform, so does Washington's lack of respect for this necessary institution. Also, it is high time to break out of the endless international discussions of the Israeli-Palestine standoff and forcefully bring an end to this Middle East disaster zone. Finally, the US military's leadership of the *war on terror*—a term that has been used to define any action by people passionately opposed to American policies and willing to fight for their beliefs—must be radically transformed. America is involved in a long-term struggle with extremists who seek to restructure their societies, using violence when necessary, and who resent American interventions in what they consider to be their own regions. The US military should be ready to assume a supporting role when needed to resolve such confrontations, but should not be out front in these efforts.

In addressing the global challenges of the next decade, the United States will enjoy an enormous advantage over all other countries. Its military, economic, and technological prowess will not be challenged. At the same time, however, other countries will increasingly make Washington pay a higher and higher price for any military action by the United States that they oppose. If other states or terrorist groups obtain nuclear or biological weapon capabilities, the price could be carnage in America.[2]

On a broader basis, globalization—with its expanded flows of information, technology, capital, goods, services, and people—will increasingly influence international trends. But the benefits will not be global, and those countries that cannot access modern technologies will fall farther behind. China and India are, of course, the emerging powers. Just the sheer size of their populations, which will reach 1.4 billion each within several decades, seems overpowering. They have already racked up many impressive economic and technological achievements. At the same time, Muslim populations will continue to grow, reaching an estimated 1.8 billion people worldwide by 2025. Within this context, the factors that have spawned international terrorism show no signs of abating. In particular, political Islam will have an increasing global impact, rallying disparate ethnic and national groups in many geographical settings through greater international outreaches.[3]

The United States should not assume, as it has in the past, that the best antidote to extremism in the Middle East and other areas heavily populated by Muslims is the imposition of Western-style freedom. Indeed, "freedom" has several historical meanings in the Middle East: free from being a slave; privileged and exceptional; and independent, for example. Many modernists ask, "Free from what? Hunger, disease, poverty, unemployment?" These interpretations are not exactly what Washington has in mind. The skeptics of a US policy based almost entirely on the concept of freedom ask, "Is this a Christian remedy to treat a Christian disease?"[4]

With regard to democracy, to many the concept of citizenship is alien, and representation through voting is an unfamiliar concept among important Muslim populations.[5] At the same time, the impressive turnout of voters for the Iraqi and Afghan elections cannot be ignored. Still, along with Bosnia, Kosovo, and Macedonia, these two nations have become American protectorates, and when American troops depart, the lengths of the roots that tie democracy to the local populations and their strength to withstand ethnic and cultural divisions will be severely tested.[6] The conditions under which elections in Iraq and Afghanistan were held were extraordinary. The positive results should not suggest that similar outcomes can be achieved quickly in other countries. In fair elections in many areas of the Middle East, fundamentalists will have an advantage since they talk the talk of the ordinary people and since they command the mosques. And even Hamas has won in a fair election.[7]

Another debate that will play out during the next decade is the controversy over the relationship between poverty and extremism. As documented throughout this book, the linkages between poverty and specific terrorist acts may be weak, but poverty is a conditioner that can provide a fertile context for the emergence of future terrorists. As reported by the 9/11 Commission and embraced by former secretaries of state James Baker and Warren Christopher, "When people lose hope, when societies break down, when countries fragment, the breeding grounds for terrorism are created."[8]

Of course, at the center of hatred toward America is the perception that the United States obviously favors Israel whatever the circumstances. The extent of the impact of this policy is difficult to exaggerate. When King Abdullah of Jordan, a moderate voice in the region, set forth the following warning, the US government should have reconsidered its policy. "We cannot talk about growth and stability in my region without addressing the core conflict that threatens our world, the long and hateful cycle of violence between Israelis and Palestinians."[9]

Thus, the US government must reverse its distaste for policy adjustments and diplomacy as the way to counter the rise of extremism. It must also modify its penchant for threats and coercion and its tendency to divide the world into simple categories of good and evil. It should recognize that "shock and awe" alienate more people than they persuade and that the United States cannot kill more terrorists than it is creating in its current course.

While sex, Nikes, and rock and roll are on the rise throughout the world, the powerful forces of traditionalism will not let go for decades into the future. The lure of green cards simply will not trump distaste for the crude images of Hollywood throughout many regions. While promotion of American values is important, great care is needed in selecting the values that are to be promoted as well as the approaches in advocating concepts that clash with tradition.

From time to time, the United States will have to continue to flex its muscles of military and economic power, for alienation and hatred have reached a level of intensity that will not be easily extinguished. Eventually, the attractiveness of American institutions and culture can win out if US policies promote rather than undermine their strengths. Soft power can be compelling, but only if hard power is kept in check.[10]

In conclusion, leading American academic John Esposito had it right when he observed the following: "Quick and easy responses to quiet the Arab street through overwhelming force may be emotionally satisfying but will in the long run prove ineffective and contribute to greater radicalization and anti-Americanism . . . the cancer of global terrorism will continue to afflict the international body until we address its political and economic causes, causes that will otherwise continue to provide a breeding ground for hatred and radicalism, the rise of extremist movements, and recruits for the bin Ladens of the world."[11]

We can combat terrorism in two ways: reduce the numbers and motivations of potential terrorists, and destroy the operational capabilities of terrorist organizations. I argue for as much attention to the first course as is being directed to the second. With so many potential targets in the United States—hospitals, schools, sports arenas, power networks, subway systems, and bridges, for example—reducing hatred toward America must be at the top of our nation's agenda for decades into the future.

EPILOGUE

★ ★ ★ ★ ★ ★ ★ ★ ★ ★ ★

A s my driver sped toward the international airport outside Islamabad, Pakistan, at 4:00 AM on November 11, 2005, I reflected on the *sights* and *sounds* of the capital city, which I had encountered during a brief visit. I had been a member of a negotiating team that developed a series of joint US-Pakistan cooperative projects to enhance Pakistan's capabilities to participate more fully in international efforts to address scientific issues of importance for economic and social progress.

Many of the *sights* were depressing. But an equal number of *sounds* were encouraging. I saw the remnants of buildings devastated one month earlier by one of the world's most destructive earthquakes in modern times. But I heard the constant whir of American Chinook helicopters carrying roofing and building material to the highlands, where more than two million people would soon face the bitterness of winter. I gazed at the entrance of the Marriott Hotel, where one year earlier a terrorist's bomb had exploded, injuring more than a dozen visitors. But I heard about US programs of assistance to upgrade the education system that for decades has been producing recruits for extremist groups. I observed the nearly inaccessible US embassy, where two hundred employees were bunkered down as they struggled to reach out to Pakistani populations. But I listened to the optimism of the US ambassador, who was determined to mobilize America's assets in support of Pakistan's efforts to improve the well-being of the population as the nation pursues important democratic principles.

Then in the waiting room of the airport I turned to a book by a Pakistani scholar, Hassan Abbas, who had written the following: "Muslims all around the world perceive America itself as, if not the perpetrator, then at least the instigator of outrages and injustices similar to 9/11. Two years before this event, many in Muslim countries had been asking, 'What compels America to be so unjust?' Except for some intellectuals, journalists, and academics, none in the United States had taken the plaintive cry seriously."

"The new confidence that unchallenged power has given to the United States," wrote Abbas in *Pakistan's Drift into Extremism: Allah, the Army, and America's War on Terrorism* (New Delhi: Pentagon Press, 2005), "has made it prone to unilateralism and to see war as a solution to problems. Sooner or later it must realize that it cannot bomb an idea [extremism] out of existence. If injustice has sparked a fire, it will be justice that will douse it—not injustice. It is certainly within the United States' means to help usher in such an era."

As my plane lifted off the runway, I reflected on the phrase used so often by Pakistanis when responding to the suggestion that we can all play a positive role in making changes that improve the lives of people. That phrase is "Why not?"

And so we ask, "Can the United States promote its self-interest in ways that also promote the interests of all populations?" And we answer, "Why not?"

NOTES

INTRODUCTION

1. Bruce Stokes, "Muslim Diversity: Its Challenges to U.S. Policy," *Great Decisions 2004*, based on Pew Global Attitudes surveys, http://www.greatdecisions.org (accessed June 2004).

2. "American Image Gets Mixed Results, U.S. Image Up Slightly, but Still Negative," Pew Global Attitudes Project (June 23, 2005), http://www.pewglobal.org (accessed September 2005).

3. Ibid., p. 1.

4. Ibid., p. 4.

5. Polls of Globescan and University of Maryland reported in Steven Kull, "It's Lonely at the Top," *Foreign Policy* (July–August 2005): 36.

6. For a commentary on anti-American rage in the world of Islam, see Robin Wright, "Turning Point, Will the Modern Era Come Undone in Iraq?" *Washington Post*, May 16, 2004.

7. Remarks by the vice president at Ronald Reagan Presidential Library and Museum, March 17, 2004, http://www.whitehouse.gov (accessed March 18, 2004).

8. Remarks by National Security Advisor Condoleezza Rice, August 19, 2004.

9. Madeleine Albright, "Bridges, Bombs, or Bluster," *Foreign Affairs* (September–October 2003): 4.

10. The word *jihad* has many meanings: a struggle for a good life; a struggle against evil in one's self; a fight against injustice; a movement to spread and

defend Islam; and a holy war. It is now being used to characterize the struggle of Islam with America. For more on the topic, see John L. Esposito, *Unholy War: Terror in the Name of Islam* (Oxford: Oxford University Press, 2002), pp. 27–28.

11. Akbar S. Ahmed, "America and the Challenge of Islam," *Hedgehog Review* (Spring 2003): 31.

CHAPTER 1

1. Samuel P. Huntington, "The Clash of Civilizations," *Foreign Affairs* 72, no. 3 (Summer 1993): 22–28.

2. Samuel P. Huntington, *The Clash of Civilizations and the Remaking of World Order* (New York: Simon & Schuster, 1996).

3. "Samuel Huntington's *The Clash of Civilizations:* The Debate," *Foreign Affairs*, Council on Foreign Relations (New York: Norton, 1996).

4. Huntington's reference for the author of this fault line was W. Wallace, *The Transformation of Western Europe* (London: Pinter, 1990).

5. Huntington, *The Clash of Civilizations and the Remaking of World Order*, p. 258.

6. Walter Laqueur, introduction to *The New Terrorism and the Arms of Mass Destruction* (Oxford: Oxford University Press, 1999).

7. Samuel Huntington, "America in the World," *Hedgehog Review* (Spring 2003): 14.

8. Akbar S. Ahmed, "America and the Challenge of Islam," *Hedgehog Review* (Spring 2003): 23.

9. Glenn E. Schweitzer with Carole C. Dorsch, *Superterrorism: Assassins, Mobsters, and Weapons of Mass Destruction* (New York: Plenum, 1998).

10. In his remarks on the war on terror, October 6, 2005, President Bush referenced in "Fact Sheet: Plots, Casings, and Infiltrations" ten recent terrorist incidents that had been derailed. For details, see http://www.whitehouse.gov/news/releases/2005/10/20051006-9.html (accessed October 2005).

11. Peter Slevin, "Report Urges Tighter Nuclear Controls," *Washington Post*, March 24, 2004.

12. For further commentary on Iraq, see Martin Abramowitz, "Does Iraq Matter?" *National Interest* 75 (Spring 2004): 39–51.

13. Ron Suskind, *The Price of Loyalty* (New York: Simon & Schuster, 2004).

14. William Raspberry, "Tracking Why We Went to War," *Washington Post*, May 31, 2004.

15. Oscar R. Estrada, "The Military: Losing Hearts and Minds?" *Washington Post*, June 6, 2004.

16. Shibley Telhami, "The Iraq War One Year Later: Arabs See Dangers and Hopes in Iraq," *Los Angeles Times*, March 14, 2004.

17. Congressman Frank Wolf (R-VA), statement at Conference on Public Diplomacy, George Washington University, Washington, DC, May 12, 2004.

18. Max Boot, "Neocons," *Foreign Policy* (January–February 2004): 20–29.

19. Carl W. Ford, "Current and Projected Threats to National Security of the United States," statement before the Senate Select Committee on Intelligence, February 6, 2002.

20. Daniel Brumberg, "Liberalization versus Democracy. Understanding Arab Political Reform" (Washington, DC: Carnegie Endowment for International Peace, 2003); Marina Ottoway, "Promoting Democracy in the Middle East, the Problem of Credibility" (Washington, DC: Carnegie Endowment for International Peace, 2003); and Ronald Spiers, "The Anatomy of Terrorism," *Foreign Service Journal* (September 2004): 49.

21. Henry A. Kissinger, "Intervention with a Vision," *Washington Post*, April 11, 2004.

22. "Democracy Aid Up to $1.2 Billion," *Front Lines*, US Agency for International Development (July–August 2005): 1.

23. Marina Ottoway and Thomas Carothers, "Middle East Democracy," *Foreign Policy* (November–December 2004): 28.

24. See http://www.hrweb.org/legal/undocs.html (accessed February 12, 2004) for details on the UN elaboration on international obligations to protect human rights.

25. "Globalization's Last Hurrah?" *Foreign Policy* (January–February 2002): 38–51.

26. Thomas Friedman, *The World Is Flat: A Brief History of the Twenty-first Century* (New York: Farrar, Straus and Giroux, 2005). For a less optimistic view of globalization, see Richard Florida, "The World Is Spiky," *Atlantic Monthly* (October 2005): 48–51.

27. *The National Security Strategy of the United States of America*, White House, September 17, 2002.

28. Colin Powell, "A Strategy of Partnerships," *Foreign Affairs* 83, no. 1 (January–February, 2004): 23.

29. Ford, "Current and Projected Threats to National Security of the United States."

30. Khurshid Ahmad, *America and Unrest in the Muslim World* (Islamabad, Pakistan: Institute of Policy Studies, 2002).

31. "Global Terrorism after the Iraq War," Special Report 111 (Washington, DC: US Institute of Peace Press, 2003).

32. Powell, "A Strategy of Partnerships," p. 34.

33. James Dobbins, "Iraq: Winning the Unwinnable War," *Foreign Affairs* (January–February 2005): 19.

34. Zbigniew Brzezinski, *The Choice: Global Domination or Global Leadership* (New York: Basic Books, 2004), p. 215.

35. Ibid., p. 217.

CHAPTER 2

1. For a discussion of geographic determinism, see Jared Diamond, *Guns, Germs, and Steel: The Fates of Human Societies* (New York: Norton, 1997).

2. For one view on the correlation between democracy and economic growth, see Joseph T. Siegle, Michael M. Weinstein, and Morton H. Halperin, "Why Democracies Excel," *Foreign Affairs* (September–October 2004): 57–71.

3. For a recent assessment of conditions in and near the Aral Sea, see Anthony Kolb, "An Ominous Flip Side: Population Dynamics in an Environmental Disaster Zone," *PECS News*, Environmental Change and Security Project (Spring 2003).

4. "Radical Islam in Central Asia: Responding to Hizb-ut-Tahrir," International Crisis Group, *Asia Report* 58 (June 30, 2003): 14.

5. "Central Asia: Islam and the State," *Asia Report* 59 (July 10, 2003): 12.

6. "3rd Day of Violence Claims 23 Lives in Uzbekistan," *New York Times International*, March 31, 2004.

7. Ibid.

8. "World: Three Killed in Uzbekistan Blasts," http://www.cnn.com/2004/WORLD/asiapcf/07/30/uzbek.blasts/ (accessed August 2004).

9. "Background Note: Uzbekistan," Department of State, July 2005.

10. C. J. Chivers and Thom Shanker, "Uzbek Ministries in Crackdown Received U.S. Aid," *Washington Post*, June 18, 2005.

11. Among the sources not already noted that were used in developing this section are Alisher Khamidov, "Countering the Call: the U.S., Hizb-ut-Tahrir, and Religious Extremism in Central Asia," analysis paper no. 4 (Washington, DC: Brookings Institution Press, 2003); Fiona Hill, "Reflections on Private and Public Islam: Is There a Threat from Eastern Europe and Eurasia?" (presentation, Georgetown University, April 14, 2004); and *Uzbekistan, The World Fact Book* (Washington, DC: Central Intelligence Agency, December 18, 2003).

12. Khalid Medani, "How Islamic Extremists Are Able to Recruit Followers" (unpublished manuscript, Center for International Security and Cooperation, 2004).

13. "On the Brink: Weak States and U.S. National Security," in *Report of the Commission on Weak States and U.S. National Security* (Washington, DC: Center for Global Development, 2004), p. 6.

14. Princeton N. Lyman and J. Stephen Morrison, "The Terrorist Threat in Africa," *Foreign Affairs* (January–February 2004): 75–86.

15. Anthony H. Cordesman, "The Grand Strategic Meaning of U.S. Intervention in Iraq" (presentation, Woodrow Wilson International Center for Scholars, February 5, 2004).

16. Phillip Longman, "The Global Baby Bust," *Foreign Affairs* (May–June 2004): 64.

17. Nicholas Eberstadt, "The Population Implosion," *Foreign Policy* (March–April, 2001): 44.

18. "Macroeconomics, Poverty, Population, and Development," *UNFPA State of the World Population 2002*, http://www.unfpa.org/swp/2002/english/ch3/index.htm (accessed April 20, 2004).

19. *Global Trends 2015: A Dialogue about the Future with Nongovernmental Experts*, NIC 2000-02 (Washington, DC: Central Intelligence Agency, December 2000).

20. Ibid.

21. "Muslim Europe," *Wilson Quarterly* (Summer 2003): 108.

22. "The United Nations on World Population in 2030," *Population and Development Review* (March 2004); Nicholas Eberstadt, "The Population Implosion," pp. 42–53.

23. See, for example, "Islamic Republic of Iran Caspian Environmental Programme—National Report of the Islamic Republic of Iran" (Tehran, Iran: Department of Environment, 1999).

24. David N. McNelis and Glenn E. Schweitzer, "Environmental Security, an Evolving Concept," *Environmental Science and Technology* (March 2001): 108a–113a.

25. *Global Trends 2015.*

26. Ibid.

27. *Treaty of Peace between the State of Israel and the Hashemite Kingdom of Jordan*, Article 6 "Water" (October 26, 1994); *Israel-Palestine Interim Agreement on the West Bank and Gaza Strip*, Article 40 "Water and Sewage" (September 28, 1995).

28. For background for addressing water shortage problems in the region, see National Academies, Royal Scientific Society of Jordan, Israeli Academy of

Sciences and Humanities, and Palestine Academy for Science and Technology, *Water for the Future: The West Bank and Gaza Strip, Israel, and Jordan* (Washington, DC: National Academies Press, 1999).

29. Cordesman, "The Grand Strategic Meaning of U.S. Intervention in Iraq."

30. John Sewell, "The Realpolitik of Poverty, Environmental Change and Security Project Report," Report 9 (Washington, DC: Woodrow Wilson Center of International Scholars, 2003), pp. 35–39.

31. David B. Sandalow, "A Green Peace Prize," *Washington Post*, October 18, 2004.

32. Geoffrey D. Dabelko, director and environmental change and security program coordinator with the Global Health Initiative, "The Next Steps for Environment, Population, and Security," Environmental Change and Security Project, Report 10 (Washington, DC: Woodrow Wilson International Center for Scholars, 2004), p. 5.

33. Glenn E. Schweitzer with Carole C. Dorsch, *Superterrorism: Assassins, Mobsters, and Weapons of Mass Destruction* (New York: Plenum, 1998).

34. Ibid.

35. *Global Trends 2015*, p. 41.

36. For background, see "Tajikistan Background Notes," Department of State, http://www.state.gov/r/pa/ei/bgn/5775.htm (accessed April 30, 2004).

37. Karl Vick, "Small Arms' Global Reach Uproots Tribal Traditions," *Washington Post*, July 8, 2001.

38. Pervez Musharraf, "A Plea for Enlightened Moderation," *Washington Post*, June 1, 2004.

CHAPTER 3

1. Bob Woodward, "With CIA Push, Movement to War Accelerated," *Washington Post*, April 19, 2004.

2. Colin Powell, "Remarks to the United Nations Security Council," US Department of State, February 5, 2003.

3. For this reference and related assessments of the intelligence community's estimates, see Kenneth M. Pollack, "Spies, Lies, and Weapons: What Went Wrong," *Atlantic Monthly* (January–February 2004), http://www.theatlantic.com (accessed February 2004).

4. Greg Thielmann, "From Intelligence Analyst to Citizen Watchdog," *Foreign Service Journal* (March 2004): 44–49. Also see "Conclusions," *Report on the U.S. Intelligence Community's Prewar Intelligence Assessments on Iraq,*

Conclusion 72, Select Committee on Intelligence, United States Senate, released July 2004.

5. Thielmann, "From Intelligence Analyst to Citizen Watchdog."

6. "Conclusions," *Report on the U.S. Intelligence Community's Prewar Intelligence Assessments on Iraq*, Conclusion 3.

7. Ibid.

8. See, for example, Walter Pincus, "Experts Say U.S. Never Spoke to Source of Tip on Bioweapons," *Washington Post*, March 5, 2004.

9. "The Weapons That Weren't," *Economist* (July 17, 2004): 24.

10. Stefan Halper and Jonathan Clark, *America Alone: The Neoconservatives and the Global Order* (Cambridge: Cambridge University Press, 2004), p. 215.

11. See, for example, Hans Blix, *Disarming Iraq* (New York: Pantheon, 2004). Also, for general background on events leading up to the Iraqi intervention, see Bob Woodward, *Plan of Attack* (New York: Simon & Schuster, 2004). Additional negative findings of Iraqi possession of weapons of mass destruction were then reported after a two-year search by hundreds of American intelligence specialists on the ground. See, for example, David Kay, *Chemical and Engineering News* (October 25, 2004): 15; and Lois R. Ember, "Assessing Iraq's Weapons," *Chemical and Engineering News* (October 25, 2004): 8.

12. Public briefing by CIA representative, George Washington University, Washington, DC, November 22, 1999.

13. George J. Tenet, "The Worldwide Threat 2004: Challenges in a Changing Global Context," Senate Select Committee on Intelligence, February 24, 2004.

14. "Conclusions," *Report on the U.S. Intelligence Community's Prewar Intelligence Assessments on Iraq*, Executive Summary and Full Report, chapters 10 and 13.

15. Reuel Marc Gerecht, "The Counterterrorist Myth," *Atlantic Monthly* (July–August 2001), http://www.theatlantic.com (accessed August 2001).

16. Tenet, "The Worldwide Threat 2004."

17. Ibid.

18. Vice Admiral Lowell E. Jacobs, "Current and Projected National Security Threats to the United States," Senate Select Committee on Intelligence, February 24, 2004.

19. US Department of State Press Conference, June 22, 2004, broadcast on C-SPAN and carried at http://www.state.gov; Alan B. Krueger and David Laitin, "'Misunderestimating' Terrorism, the State Department's Big Mistake," *Foreign Affairs* (September–October 2004): 8–12.

20. Susan B. Glasser, "Global Terrorism Statistics Released," *Washington Post*, April, 28, 2005.

21. Loch K. Johnson, "Spies," *Foreign Policy* (September–October 2000): 18–26.

22. Ibid.

23. For an overview of the prison situation, see, for example, Margot Williams, "The Secret World of U.S. Interrogation," *Wall Street Journal Europe*, May 12, 2004.

24. Seymour M. Hersh, "The Gray Zone," *New Yorker*, May 24, 2004; Sewell Chan and Michael Amon, "Prisoner Abuse Probe Widened," *Washington Post*, May 2, 2004.

25. Ibid.

26. CNN TV broadcast, May 5, 2004. See http://www.cnn.com (accessed May 2004).

27. For advice of prominent Americans as to how the United States should have reacted, see, for example, Jackie Calmes et al., "Images Are Public Relations Nightmare," *Wall Street Journal Europe*, May 14–16, 2004.

28. Hisham Melhem, "Prisoner Abuse Fallout," broadcast on WETA-TV, *Jim Lehrer NewsHour*, May 3, 2004.

29. Johnson, "Spies," pp. 18–26.

30. *Conducting a Conflict Assessment: A Framework for Strategy and Program Development*, US Agency for International Development, January 9, 2004.

31. *Global Trends 2015: A Dialogue about the Future with Nongovernmental Experts*, NIC 2000-02 (Washington, DC: Central Intelligence Agency, December 2000).

32. Seminar on Yemen, Department of State, June 14, 2004.

33. Bernard Lewis, *What Went Wrong: Western Impact and Middle Eastern Response* (Oxford: Oxford University Press, 2002), p. 159.

CHAPTER 4

1. "Special Report: Indonesia's Election," *Economist* (September 25, 2004): 32.

2. "Background Notes: Indonesia," US Department of State, http://www.state.gov/r/pa/ei/bgn/2748.htm (accessed September 2004).

3. Rana Foroohar, "Wary of Aid," *Newsweek*, January 24, 2005, p. 18.

4. *USAID Assistance to Internally Displaced Persons Policy*, US Agency for International Development, August 2004.

5. For commentaries on the relation of poverty to stability and security, see the collection of papers in Environmental Change and Security Project Report, issue 9 (Washington, DC: Woodrow Wilson International Center for Scholars, 2003), pp. 12–39. Also see Carla Koppell with Anita Sharma, "Preventing the Next Wave of Conflict, Understanding Non-Traditional Threats to Global Stability" (Washington, DC: Woodrow Wilson International Center for Scholars, 2003).

6. *On the Brink: Weak States and U.S. National Security* (Washington, DC: Center for Global Development, 2004), p 1.

7. Ibid., pp. 3–5.

8. *Institutional Development,* USAID policy paper (Washington, DC: Agency for International Development, March 1983).

9. Andrew Natsios, untitled speech, National Press Club, Washington, DC, February 25, 2004.

10. "National Security Strategy," National Security Council, 2002.

11. Natsios, untitled speech.

12. *Strategic Plan, Fiscal Years 2004–2009*, US Department of State and US Agency for International Development, August 2003.

13. *Fiscal Year 2005, Budget Justification to the Congress*, US Agency for International Development, February 20, 2004, p. 189.

14. Sources for this section include Colin Powell, "Statement at the February 2, 2004, Inaugural Board Meeting of the MCC," US Department of State; "Testimony by Paul V. Applegarth," chief executive officer, Millennium Challenge Corporation, House Committee on International Relations, May 19, 2004; "Guidance for Developing Proposals for MCC Assistance in FY 2004"; and "Sample Elements of a Proposal for Millennium Challenge Account Assistance." For more information on the MCC, see http://www.mcc.gov.

15. "Foreign Aid in Peril," *Washington Post*, September 16, 2004.

16. *Net Official Development Assistance in 2003*, OECD, April 16, 2004.

17. "Ranking the Rich 2004," *Foreign Policy* (May–June 2004): 46–56.

18. UN Millennium Development Goals, http://www.un.org/millennium goals/ (accessed July 2004).

19. *G8 Action Plan: Applying the Power of Entrepreneurship to Eradication of Poverty*, Sea Island Summit, June 2004, http://www.g8usa.gov/d_060904a .htm (accessed July 5, 2004).

20. Sea Island Summit, June 2004, http://www.g8usa.gov/d_060904b.htm (accessed June 2004).

21. Marina Ottoway and Thomas Caruthers, *The Greater Middle East Initiative: Off to a False Start*, Policy Brief 29 (Washington, DC: Carnegie Endowment for International Peace, March 2004).

22. Andrew S. Natsios, "Foreign Aid for a Changing World," *International Herald Tribune*, April 16, 2004.

23. For a broad perspective of the future of foreign assistance, see Steven Radelet, "Bush and Foreign Aid," *Foreign Affairs* (September–October 2003): 104–17.

CHAPTER 5

1. *Assessment Report. Education in the Chechen Republic: Conditions, Problems, Perspectives of Development, and Restoration*, Ministry of Education of Russian Federation and Ministry of Secondary and Professional Education of Chechen Republic, Moscow-Grozny (2002).

2. The author was in Moscow when the events unfolded, witnessed them on the Russian television channel NTV, and discussed them with dozens of Russian colleagues.

3. Dmitri V. Trenin, *The Forgotten War: Chechnya and Russia's Future*, Policy Brief 28 (Washington, DC: Carnegie Endowment for International Peace, November 2003).

4. David A. Hamburg and Beatrix A. Hamburg, *Learning to Live Together, Preventing Hatred and Violence in Child and Adolescent Development* (Oxford: Oxford University Press, 2004), p. 11.

5. For more information on the Fulbright program, see http://exchanges .state.gov/education/fulbright/ (accessed July 2004).

6. US Department of State Briefing for Nongovernmental Organizations, July 26, 2004.

7. Information provided by USAID Office for Economic Growth, Agriculture, and Trade, May 2004.

8. For more information on USAID's American Schools and Hospitals Abroad program, see http://www.usaid.gov/our_work/cross-cutting_programs /asha/overview.html (accessed July 2004).

9. Author interviews at Carnegie Corporation of New York, August 4, 2004.

10. Hassan Zohoor, "Distance and Open Learning in Iran," *Proceedings of a Workshop on Higher Education*, Academy of Sciences of Iran, Tehran, October 25–26, 2002.

11. Author discussions at Sharif University, Tehran, Iran, October, 27, 2002.

12. Joseph S. DiGregorio, "Distance Learning," *Proceedings of a Workshop*

on Higher Education, Academy of Sciences of Iran, Tehran, October 25–26, 2002.

13. Daniel del Costillo, "Jordan Says It Will Encourage Distance Programs in Public and Private Universities," *Chronicle of Higher Education* (May 6, 2002).

14. Neil Kestner, "The Use of Technology in Teaching," *Proceedings of a Workshop on Higher Education*, Academy of Sciences of Iran, Tehran, October 25–26, 2002.

15. For more information on international business partnerships via USAID efforts, see http://www.usaid.gov/our_work/global_partnerships/gda/ (accessed July 2004). Such collaborations are significant and should be encouraged.

16. 9/11 Commission Report Implementation Act of 2004, 108th Cong., 2004, S. 2774.

17. For these and other budget estimates, see "USAID Education Strategy," US Agency for International Development (August 2004).

18. Hussain Haqqani, "Islam's Medieval Outposts," *Foreign Policy* (November–December 2002): 58–64.

19. Ibid., p. 60.

20. Interview with former Pakistani police inspector, July 2004.

21. US Department of State briefing for invited guests, "Making of Militancy in Pakistan," Meridien International Center, June 2, 2004. Also, Dale F. Eickelman, "Madrassas: Historical Perspectives and Strategies for Today" (unpublished manuscript, June 2004).

22. Ibid.

23. Ibid.

24. "Strengthening Education in the Muslim World, Summary of the Desk Study," Issue Paper Number 2 (Washington, DC: USAID, June 2003).

25. Ibid.

26. Ibid.

27. Christina Rocca and Wendy Chamberlin, "The U.S. and South Asia: Challenges and Opportunities for American Policy," testimony before the Subcommittee on Asia and the Pacific of the House of Representatives Committee on International Relations (March 2003), p. 31. A broader perspective on USAID activities in Pakistan is included in "Aid to Pakistan's Government Schools Gives Poor Parents an Alternative to Madrassas," *Front Lines* (Washington, DC: USAID, September 2004), p. 11.

28. US Department of State Briefing for invited guests (June 14, 2004).

29. Barbara Herz and Gene B. Sterling, "What Works in Girls' Education, Evidence and Policies from the Developing World" (New York: Council on Foreign Relations, 2004).

30 "Aid to Pakistan's Government Schools Gives Poor Parents an Alternative to Madrassas," p. 4.

31. Herz and Sterling, "What Works in Girls' Education."

32. Author interviews at the University of Tehran, December 2003.

CHAPTER 6

1. George Perkovich et al., *Universal Compliance, A Strategy for Nuclear Security* (Washington, DC: Carnegie Endowment for International Peace, June 2004), p. 9.

2. For a discussion of developments in India at the time, see Strobe Talbot, *Engaging India: Diplomacy, Democracy, and the Bomb* (Washington, DC: Brookings Institution Press, August 2004).

3. Michael Krepon, "Kashmir: A Trip Report" (Washington, DC: Stimson Center, December 23, 2004); Christine Fais, "India and Pakistan Engagement, Prospects for Breakthrough or Breakdown?" Special Report 129 (Washington, DC: US Institute of Peace Press, January 2005); and "In from the Cold," *Economist* (May 28, 2005): 44.

4. Wajahat Habibullah, "The Political Economy of the Kashmir Conflict, Opportunities for Economic Peacebuilding and for U.S. Policy," Special Report 121 (Washington, DC: US Institute of Peace Press, June 2004).

5. Perkovich et al., *Universal Compliance*, p. 9.

6. Seymour M. Hersch, "The Deal," *New Yorker*, March 8, 2004, pp. 32–37; "Sold," *Economist* (February 7, 2004): 38; and Alan Sipress and Ellen Nakashima, "Malaysia Arrests Nuclear Network Suspect," *Washington Post*, May 29, 2004.

7. Joseph Cirincione, "Addressing Proliferation through Multilateral Agreement: Success and Failure in the Nonproliferation Regime;" in *Combating Weapons of Mass Destruction, Ultimate Security*, ed. Janne E. Nolan, Bernard I. Finel, and Brian D. Finlay (New York: Century Foundation Press, 2003), p. 67.

8. Andrew K. Semmel, "Universal Compliance with Nuclear Nonproliferation," Remarks at International Workshop in Bali, Indonesia, January 20, 2005, and at US Department of State, January 25, 2005.

9. *Treaty of Moscow*, 2002.

10. Linton Brooks, keynote address at *Post–Cold War U.S. Nuclear Strategy: A Search for Technical and Policy Common Ground*, National Academies Public Symposium, Washington, DC, August 11, 2004.

11. To view the background and text of the Treaty on the Nonproliferation of Nuclear Weapons, which calls for achievement of "general and complete disarmament," visit http://www.state.gov/www/global/arms/treaties/npt1.html.

12. For an excellent review of suitcase nukes, see David Smigielski, "A Review of the Suitcase Nuclear Bomb Controversy," *RANSAC Policy Update* (September 2003). For suggestions that terrorists have acquired suitcase nukes, see Paul L. Williams, *Osama's Revenge: The Next 9/11* (Amherst, NY: Prometheus Books, 2004). For a rebuttal of these assertions by General Viktor Yesin of Russia, who claims he was directly responsible for accounting for these types of weapons, see "No Way of Nuclear Suitcases Disappearing from Russia," *RIA Novosti*, Russian News Service (July 31, 2004).

13. None of these incidents involved quantities of material that were sufficient for a single weapon. A crude nuclear weapon would probably require at least twenty kilograms of highly enriched uranium whereas the amounts reported as stolen were usually fewer than one hundred grams. *Proliferation Concerns: Assessing U.S. Efforts to Help Contain Nuclear and Other Dangerous Materials and Technologies in the Former Soviet Union*, National Research Council (Washington, DC: National Academies Press, 1997), pp. 21, 57.

14. Discussion by former UN inspectors during "Workshop on Iran's Nuclear Program," Woodrow Wilson International Center for Scholars, Washington, DC, November 9, 2004.

15. Lynn Eden, "City on Fire," *Bulletin of the Atomic Scientists* (January–February 2004): 35.

16. Ibid.

17. A summary of the problem of controlling Semtex is included in Richard A. Hess, "Czechs Try to Cap Plastic Explosive Sales," *Christian Science Monitor*, February 26, 2002.

18. *Inadequate Control of World's Radioactive Sources*, International Atomic Energy Agency (IAEA), Vienna, Austria, 2003.

19. James Glanz and Andrew C. Revkin, "Some See Panic as Main Effect of Dirty Bombs," *New York Times*, March 2, 2002.

20. *Inadequate Control of World's Radioactive Sources.*

21. Ibid.

22. Glenn E. Schweitzer, "The Nexus of International Organized Crime and Terrorism. The Case of Dirty Bombs," testimony to the Subcommittee on Prevention of Nuclear and Biological Attacks, House of Representatives Committee on Homeland Security, Washington, DC, September 22, 2005.

23. For many more examples of problems and programs related to nuclear terrorism, see Charles D. Ferguson and William C. Potter, *The Four Faces of*

Nuclear Terrorism (Monterey, CA: Monterey Institute Center for Nonproliferation Studies, 2004).

24. "El Baradei Seeks to Press Israel on Nuclear Issues," Reuters, July 6, 2004.

25. Glenn E. Schweitzer with Carole C. Dorsch, *Superterrorism: Assassins, Mobsters, and Weapons of Mass Destruction* (New York: Plenum, 1998).

26. "Israel to Acquire Two More German Submarines," Maariv International, an Israeli news and publication service, December 23, 2004.

27. Robin Wright, "A Common Desire for Nuclear Empowerment," *Washington Post*, November 15, 2004.

28. "ISIS Imagery Brief: Destruction at Iranian Site Raises New Questions about Iran's Nuclear Activities," Institute for Science and International Security, Washington, DC, June 17, 2004.

29. "Chalabi Told Iran that U.S. Broke Its Code," CNN News, June 2, 2004.

30. "Coddling the Mullahs," *Wall Street Journal*, June 14, 2004.

31. Henry Sokolski, "It's Almost Too Late to Stop Iran," *Wall Street Journal*, September 27, 2004.

32. "The Nuclear Squeeze," *Economist* (November 13, 2004): 51.

33. Kurt M. Campbell, Robert J. Einhorn, and Mitchell B. Reiss, eds., *The Nuclear Tipping Point: Why States Reconsider Their Nuclear Choices* (Washington, DC: Brookings Institution Press, July 2004).

34. See, for example, the view of the leadership of the International Atomic Energy Agency on Israel's retention of nuclear weapons reported in Walter Pincus, "Push for Nuclear-Free Zone in Middle East Resurfaces," *Washington Post*, March 16, 2005.

35. Dan DeLuce, "Accidents May Be Iran's Greatest Nuclear Threat, Special Report Iran," *Guardian* (November 10, 2004).

36. For related suggestions, see Perkovich et al., *Universal Compliance*, p. 80.

37. George Perkovich and Avner Cohen, "Devaluing Arab WMDs," *Washington Times*, January 18, 2004.

38. Sam Nunn, "Deterrence and Security," Carnegie International Nonproliferation Conference, Washington DC, June 21, 2004.

39. Linton F. Brooks, "U.S. Nuclear Weapons Policy and Programs," Carnegie International Nonproliferation Conference, Washington DC, June 21, 2004.

40. Ed Kintisch, "Bunker Buster Shot Down in Opening Volley," *Science* (May 20, 2005): 1100.

41. Brooks, "U.S. Nuclear Weapons Policy and Programs."

42. Ibid.; *Nuclear Posture Review*, US Department of Defense, submitted to Congress on January 8, 2002.

43. Rep. David Hobson (R-OH), keynote address at *Post–Cold War U.S. Nuclear Strategy: A Search for Technical and Policy Common Ground*, National Academies Public Symposium, Washington, DC, August 11, 2004.

44. A thoughtful but provocative analysis of the many dimensions of nuclear security policy is set forth in John Deutch, "Nuclear Posture for Today," *Foreign Affairs* (January–February 2005): 49–60.

45. John J. Taylor, "The Nuclear Power Bargain," *Issues in Science and Technology* (Spring 2004): 41–47.

46. Alan E. Walter, "Nuclear Technology's Numerous Uses," *Issues in Science and Technology* (Spring 2004): 48–54.

47. Dwight D. Eisenhower, *Atoms for Peace*, UN General Assembly, December 8, 1953.

CHAPTER 7

1. Karen E. Lange, "The Overwhelming Cost of Malaria," *National Geographic* (April 2004).

2. Kenneth J. Arrow, Claire B. Panosian, and Hellen Gelband, eds., *Saving Lives, Buying Time: Economics of Malaria Drugs in an Age of Resistance*, Institute of Medicine (Washington, DC: National Academies Press, 2004). For related developments, see "Malaria Drug Design on a Dime," *Chemical and Engineering News* (August 23, 2004): 4.

3. Correspondence with Professor Carol Blair, Colorado State University, September 22, 2004.

4. "Fourteen Grand Challenges in Global Health Announced in $200 Million Initiative," Bill and Melinda Gates Foundation (Seattle), press release, October 6, 2003.

5. Diego Buriot, "Communicable Diseases in the 21st Century, WHO Perspective," WHO, http://www.vector.nsc.ru/conf0904/tzO-e.htm. Also, for a scientific discussion of many emerging infectious diseases, see *International Journal of Epidemiology* (Oxford: Oxford University Press, October 2003).

6. Buriot, "Communicable Diseases in the 21st Century."

7. "The Global War for Public Health," interview with Gro Harlem Brundtland, director general of WHO, *Foreign Policy* (January–February 2002): 24–35.

8. *2004 Report on the Global AIDS Epidemic*, Joint United Nations Programme on HIV/AIDS (UNAIDS), Geneva, Switzerland, 2004, pp. 3, 5.

9. Ibid.

10. Ibid.

11. Ibid.

12. "Access to HIV Prevention, Closing the Gap," Report of Global HIV Prevention Working Group, sponsored by Bill and Melinda Gates Foundation and Henry J. Kaiser Family Foundation, released in New York City, May 2003.

13. Ibid.

14. "The End of the Beginning," *Economist* (July 27, 2004): 76–77.

15. *Engendering Bold Leadership, The President's Emergency Plan for AIDS Relief, First Annual Report to Congress*, Office of the United States Global AIDS Coordinator, US Department of State, 2005, p. 11.

16. Arrow et al., *Saving Lives, Buying Time*, p. 70.

17. World Health Organization, "Summary of Probable SARS Cases with Onset of Illness from November 2, 2002, to July 4, 2003," http//www.who.int /csr/sars/country/table2003_09_23/en/ (accessed December 17, 2003).

18. *Learning from SARS, Preparing for the Next Disease Outbreak, Workshop Summary*, National Institute of Medicine (Washington, DC: National Academies Press, 2004), p. 4.

19. Ibid., p. 43.

20. Ibid.

21. Ibid., pp. 50–56.

22. Ibid., p. 260.

23. Discussions in Moscow with the health officials responsible for handling the SARS outbreak, November 17, 2003.

24. National Institute of Medicine, *Learning from SARS*, p. 268.

25. "WHO Launches New '5 Keys' Strategy in Bangkok, Thailand," http://www.who.int/mediacentre/news/releases/2004/pr72/en/ (accessed October 13, 2004).

26. Joe Sharkey, "Aggressive Precaution in the Food You Eat," *New York Times*, October 12, 2004.

27. USDA, "Foodborne Illnesses: What Consumers Need to Know," http://www.fsis.usda.gov/fact_sheets/foodborne_illness_what_consumers_need _ to_know.

28. Hazard Analysis and Critical Control Point (HACCP) principles developed by the US Department of Agriculture are rapidly spreading internationally.

29. Jonathan B. Tucker, *Biosecurity: Limiting Terrorist Access to Deadly Pathogens* (Washington, DC: US Institute of Peace Press, November 2003), p. 11.

30. For a useful summary of bioterrorist threats, see Dana A. Shea and Frank Gottron, *Small-Scale Terrorist Attacks Using Chemical and Biological Agents:*

An Assessment Framework and Preliminary Comparisons, Congressional Research Service, June 23, 2004.

31. Tucker, *Biosecurity*, p. 12.

32. Glenn E. Schweitzer with Carole C. Dorsch, *Superterrorism: Assassins, Mobsters, and Weapons of Mass Destruction* (New York: Plenum, 1998), p. 120.

33. Ibid., p. 121.

34. Judith Miller, Stephen Engelberg, and William J. Broad, "U.S. Germ Warfare Research Pushes Treaty Limits," *New York Times*, September 4, 2001.

35. Adel Mahmoud, "The Global Vaccination Gap," *Science* (July 9, 2004): 147; Rob Stein, "New Vaccine Sharply Cuts Malaria Risk," *Washington Post*, October 15, 2004.

36. Report of Harvard University health assessment team, reported to author, May 20, 2003.

CHAPTER 8

1. For more on World Bank activities, see "What Is the World Bank?" http://web.worldbank.org (accessed December 2004).

2. Sebastian Mallaby, "Saving the World Bank," *Foreign Affairs* (May–June 2005): 76.

3. Ibid.

4. *Proposals for Change*, United Nations Secretariat, as reported by Associated Press, March 20, 2005. Also, for a broad overview of the ambitions of the secretary-general, see Kofi Annan, "In Larger Freedom: Decision Time at the U.N." *Foreign Affairs* (May–June 2005): 63–75.

5. See, for example, Ronald Spiers, "Toward a New U.S.–U.N. Rapprochement," *Foreign Service Journal* (April 2004): 52.

6. Ibid.

7. *A More Secure World: Our Shared Responsibility, Report of the Secretary General's High Level Panel on Threats, Challenges, and Change*, UN Press Office, December 2, 2004.

8. Kofi Annan, as quoted in the report of the *35th Conference on United Nation's Issues, January 13–15, 2004; The Secretary-General's High-Level Panel on Security Threats—Maximizing Prospects for Success* (Muscatine, IA: Stanley Foundation, January 2004).

9. Edward C. Luck, "U.N. Reform: A Cause in Search of a Constituency" (unpublished manuscript, New York: Columbia University, April 29, 2004).

10. Adapted from Jeffrey Laurenti, "The Geopolitical Rorschach Test: Reform at the United Nations" (unpublished paper, New York: United Nations Foundation, May 6, 2004).

11. Organization of the Islamic Conference, Rabat, Morocco, Secretary-General Ekmeleddin Ihsanoglu, June 28, 2005.

12. Pascal Teixeira, *The Security Council at the Dawn of the Twenty-first Century: To What Extent Is It Willing and Able to Maintain International Peace and Security?* (Geneva, Switzerland: United Nations Institute for Disarmament Research, 2003), pp. 43–92.

13. Michael J. Glennon, "Why the Security Council Failed," *Foreign Affairs* (May–June 2003).

14. See, for example, Edward C. Luck et al., "Stayin' Alive. The Rumors of the U.N.'s Death Have Been Exaggerated," *Foreign Affairs* (July–August 2003).

15. Kofi Annan appearing on C-SPAN 2 before the Council on Foreign Relations, December 19, 2004.

16. *Report of the Panel on United Nations Peace Operations* (New York: United Nations, August 21, 2000), pp. A/55/305–S/2000/809.

17. Ibid. pp. 10–14.

18. For an analysis of these and other aspects of the report of the UN panel, see William J. Durch et al., *The Brahimi Report and the Future of U.N. Peace Operations* (Washington, DC: Henry L. Stimson Center, 2003).

19. For more on UN peacekeeping activities, see http://www.un.org /Depts/dpko/dpko/index.asp.

20. For a discussion of peacekeeping, see Shashi Tharoor, "Why America Still Needs the United Nations," *Foreign Affairs* (September–October 2003): 67–80.

21. "Blue-Helmet Blues," *Economist* (May 15, 2004): 44.

22. *Establishing the Rule of Law in Afghanistan*, Special Report 117 (Washington, DC: US Institute of Peace Press, March 2004). For a more general discussion, see David A. Hamburg, *No More Killing Fields* (Lanham, MD: Rowman and Littlefield, 2002), p. 77.

23. Marc Lacey, "U.N. Forces Using Tougher Tactics to Keep Peace," *New York Times*, May 23, 2005.

24. *Who Rebuilds after Conflict? Report on Meeting in Loch Lomond, Scotland*, 2003, Policy Bulletin (Muscatine, IA: Stanley Foundation, 2003).

25. Laurenti, "The Geopolitical Rorschach Test."

CHAPTER 9

1. King Abdullah II ibn Hussein, "Statement at Davos World Economic Forum, January 2004," Davos Report Supplement, *Foreign Policy* (February 2004): 2.

2. Shibley Telhami, "The Ties That Bind Americans, Arabs, and Israelis after September 11," *Foreign Affairs* (March–April 2004): 120.

3. *Israel and the Occupied Territories*, Country Reports on Human Rights Practices—2004, US Department of State (February 28, 2005).

4. Walter Russell Mead, "Why They Hate Us, Really," *New York Times*, April 21, 2004.

5. Robert Art, "Ending the Israeli-Palestinian Stalemate Will Strengthen U.S. National Security," Coalition for a Realistic Foreign Policy, *Economist* (January 1, 2005): 6.

6. Wade Boese, "Israel, Iran Flex Missiles," *Arms Control Today* (September 2004): 36.

7. Art, "Ending the Israeli-Palestinian Stalemate Will Strengthen U.S. National Security," p. 8.

8. Duncan Clarke, "Israel's Unauthorized Arms Transfers," *Foreign Policy* (Summer 1995): 89.

9. "Israelis Will Use U.S. Tax Dollars on Illegal Border," *CNI Capital Update*, Council for the National Interest Foundation, June 14, 2005.

10. Madeleine K. Albright, "Bridges, Bombs, or Bluster?" *Foreign Affairs* (September–October 2003): 11.

11. *Israel and the Occupied Territories*, p. 18.

12. "Exit Arafat," *Economist* (November 13, 2004): 11.

13. *Israel and the Occupied Territories*, p. 2.

14. Saeb Erekat, "Why Did Bush Take My Job?" *Washington Post*, April 25, 2004.

15. Aaron David Miller, "Israel's Lawyer," *Washington Post*, May 23, 2005.

16. Albright, "Bridges, Bombs, or Bluster?" p. 13.

17. Juno Sylva, president of Global Mothers (Austria), in an e-mail to the publisher of *Who Will Save the Children*, London, July 24, 2002.

18. *Roadmap for Peace in the Middle East: Israeli/Palestinian Reciprocal Action, Quartet Support*, US Department of State, July 16, 2003.

19. Ronald Spiers, "The Middle East Road Map: Going Nowhere Fast," *Foreign Service Journal* (November 2003): 16–18.

20. "Israeli Cabinet State View on Road Map and 14 Reservations," http://www.jewishvirtuallibrary.org/source/road1.html (accessed May 25, 2003).

21. Richard Lugar, "A New Partnership for the Greater Middle East: Combating Terrorism, Building Peace." See http://lugar.senate.gov/pressapp/record .cfm?id=219740 (accessed March 29, 2004).

22. For a chronology of statements by bin Laden and his followers as to the linkage between the plight of the Palestinians and their targeting of American assets—a linkage that is constantly referred to by Palestine's supporters in their lobbying efforts in Washington, DC—see Curtis A. Loub, "They Hate Us for Our Policies," Center for the National Interest Foundation, http://www.rescue mideastpolicy.com/modules.php?op=modload&name=News&file (accessed January 24, 2005).

23. For behind-the-scene insights into the diplomatic dimension of the conflict, see Dennis Ross, *The Missing Peace: The Inside Story of the Fight for Middle East Peace* (New York: Farrar, Strauss and Giroux, 2004).

24. Spiers, "The Middle East Road Map: Going Nowhere Fast."

25. Brent Scowcroft, "A Middle East Opening," *Washington Post*, November 12, 2004.

26. De Hoop Scheffer, remarks at Munich International Security Conference (New York: World Security Network Newsletter, February 15, 2005), p. 2.

27. Henry A. Kissinger, "A New Opening for Mideast Peace," *Washington Post*, December 3, 2004.

28. Mike Allen and Glenn Kessler, "Bush Goal: Palestine State by 2009," *Washington Post*, November 13, 2004.

29. James A. Baker, May 22, 1991, quoted in "Israeli Settlements in the Occupied Territories," *Special Report*, Foundation for Middle East Peace, March 2002.

30. For additional discussion of the wall, see David Makovsky, "How to Build a Fence," *Foreign Affairs* (March–April 2004): 50–63; Keith B. Richburg, "U.N. Court Rejects West Bank Barrier," *Washington Post*, July 10, 2004; and Diana Buttu, "The Wall at the Court: The Case and the Hearings," *For the Record* 191 (Washington, DC: Palestine Center, February 26, 2004).

31. Mia Bloom, *Dying to Kill: the Allure of Suicide Terror* (New York: Columbia University Press, 2005), pp. 38–39.

32. James Baker, "The Future of U.S. Involvement in the Middle East" (lecture, University of Maryland, April 14, 2005).

CHAPTER 10

1. These deployments were articulated by General Richard Cody, Army Vice Chief of Staff, testimony to the House of Representatives Armed Services Committee, February 2, 2005.

2. General Michael Hagee, "Future of the U.S. Marine Corps," C-SPAN 1, August 19, 2005.

3. "Reinventing War," *Foreign Policy* (November–December 2001): 43.

4. Briefing by Colonel J. D. Johnson, chief of strategic planning for the War on Terrorism, Joint Chiefs of Staff, titled "The National Military Strategic Plan for the War on Terrorism" (Washington, DC: Woodrow Wilson Center, April 12, 2005).

5. Ibid.

6. Robert B. Kaplan, "America and the Tragic Limits of Imperialism," *Hedgehog Review* (Spring 2003): 56–57.

7. Kurt M. Campbell and Celeste Johnson Ward, "New Battle Stations?" *Foreign Affairs* (September–October 2003): 95–103. Also, for general background on overseas military deployments, see "Defense Department Background Briefing on Global Posture Review," http://www.globalsecurity.org/military /library/news/2004/08/mil-040816-dod02.htm (accessed August 16, 2004).

8. Jack Shanahan and Ben Cohen, "U.S. Best Served with Troops Back Home," *Defense News* (September 13, 2004): 77.

9. Among the worst dictators identified in one survey are Omar al-Bashir, Sudan; Kim Jung Il, North Korea; Than Shwe, Burma; Hu Jintao, China; Saparmurat Niyazov, Turkmenistan; Robert Mugabe, Zimbabwe; and Teodoro Obiang Nguema, Equatorial Guinea. "The World's Worst Dictators," *Washington Post Parade*, February 13, 2005.

10. Richard A. Haass, *Intervention: The Use of American Military Forces in the Post–Cold War World* (Washington, DC: Brookings Institution Press, 1999), pp. 29–48.

11. Ibid., p. 15.

12. Colin Powell, "A Strategy of Partnerships," *Foreign Affairs* (January –February 2004): 22–25.

13. Ibid., p. 24.

14. Haass, *Intervention*, pp. 49–65.

15. *NATO and Interventionism: Some Possible Criteria for the Future*, Research Paper 5 (Rome: NATO Defense College, May 2004).

16. See E. Wayne Merry, "Can NATO Survive Europe?" *National Interest* 76 (Summer 2004).

17. Alexei Bogaturov, "Russia in Central–Eastern Asia," Report from the Ed A. Hewett Forum (Washington, DC: Brookings Institution Press, January 2004).

18. *The South Caucasus: Promoting Values through Cooperation* (Rome: NATO Defense College, May 2004).

19. Deborah Avant, "What Are Those Contractors Doing in Iraq?" *Washington Post*, May 9, 2004.

20. Megan Scully and Gina Cavallaro, "Special Forces Brain Drain: Security Firms Snap up World's Elite Troops," *Defense News* (May 3, 2004): 1.

21. Dana Priest, "Private Guards Repel Attack on U.S. Headquarters," *Washington Post*, April 6, 2004. Also see "Dangerous Work," *Economist* (April 10, 2004): 22.

22. Barton Gellman, "Controversial Pentagon Espionage Unit Loses Its Leader," *Washington Post*, February 13, 2005.

23. For a discussion of the military's engineering capabilities for postconflict reconstruction, see Garland H. Williams, *Engineering Peace* (Washington, DC: US Institute of Peace Press, July 2004).

24. For a discussion of the likely role of the Department of Defense following hostilities, see *Transition to and from Hostilities*, Defense Science Board, 2004 Summer Study, Department of Defense (December 2004).

25. Minxin Pei and Sara Kasper, "Lessons from the Past: The American Record on Nation Building," Policy Brief 24 (Washington, DC: Carnegie Endowment for International Peace, May 2003).

26. Ibid.

27. Harold Kennedy, "The New Face of Peacekeeping," *National Defense* (May 2004): 47.

28. "Reinforcements Needed," *Economist* (June 19, 2004): 26.

29. Department of State Briefing for Nongovernmental Organizations (October 27, 2005).

30. Robert Perito, Michael Dziedic, and Beth DeGrasse, *Building Civilian Capacity for U.S. Stability Operations*, Special Report 118 (Washington, DC: US Institute of Peace Press, April 2004), p. 2.

31. Robert M. Perito, *Where Is the Lone Ranger When We Need Him? America's Search for a Postconflict Stability Force* (Washington, DC: US Institute of Peace Press, 2004).

32. Ibid., p. 30.

33. For an insightful discussion of preemption, see Andrew J. Bacevich, *The New American Militarism: How Americans Are Seduced by War* (Oxford: Oxford University Press, 2005), p. 147.

34. *Transition to and from Hostilities*, p. xii.

CHAPTER 11

1. *Changing Minds, Winning Peace*, Report of the Advisory Group on Public Diplomacy for the Arab and Muslim World, US House of Representatives (October 1, 2003), p. 36.

2. Ibid., p. 37.

3. For more on the US Department of State's recognition of Arab views, see http://usinfo.state.gov/admin/005/wwwh40218.html.

4. Walter Laqueur, "The Terrorism to Come," *Policy Review* (August–September 2004): 60–61.

5. *Changing Minds, Winning Peace*, p. 30.

6. Ibid., p. 28.

7. David S. Jackson, "The Voice of America Enters a New Era," *Foreign Service Journal* (January 2004): 25–29.

8. Thomas Dine, "Radio Free Europe/Radio Liberty: Today and Tomorrow," *Foreign Service Journal* (January 2004): 40–42.

9. Richard Richter, "Radio Free Asia: A Rare Window," *Foreign Service Journal* (January 2004): 43–45.

10. Brian Conniff, "New Directions in U.S. International Broadcasting," *Foreign Service Journal* (January 2004): 20–24.

11. Ibid.

12. Stephen C. Fairbanks, "Broadcasting to Iran," *Foreign Service Journal* (March 2004): 7–8.

13. Terrence Smith, moderator, "A New Voice," *Online Newsletter*, Public Broadcasting System, April 15, 2004.

14. Ibid.

15. Ibid.

16. Marc Lynch, "Taking Arabs Seriously," *Foreign Affairs* (September–October 2003): 94.

17. Gabriel Weismann. "How Modern Terrorists Use the Internet," Special Report 116 (Washington, DC: US Institute of Peace Press, March 2004), pp. 5–9.

18. Mollie M. King, "Going on Line at VOAnews.com," *Foreign Service Journal* (January 2004): 38–39.

19. Glenn Harlan Reynolds, "The Blogs of War," *National Interest* (Spring 2004): 59–64.

20. "King Backs Jordan Internet Centers," *Frontlines*, USAID (March 2004): 6.

21. Lynch, "Taking Arabs Seriously," p. 83.

22. Ibid., pp. 85–86.

23. Ibid., pp. 81–87.

24. *Changing Minds, Winning Peace*, p. 35.

25. Ibid.

26. *State Department Response to the Report of the Advisory Group on Public Diplomacy for the Arab and Muslim Worlds*, US Department of State, 2004.

27. Lynch, "Taking Arabs Seriously," p. 82.

28. *Changing Minds, Winning Peace*, p. 36.

29. Remarks by National Security Advisor Condoleezza Rice, August 19, 2004, White House, Office of the Press Secretary.

CHAPTER 12

1. To review similar concerns over US policies, see Senator Chuck Hagel (R-NE), speech to the National Conference of the World Affairs Council of America, Washington, DC, http://hagel.senate.gov (accessed January 28, 2005).

2. For one projection of future trends, see *Mapping the Global Future*, Report of the National Intelligence Council's 2020 Project, NIC 2004–13 (Washington, DC: US Government Printing Office, December 2004).

3. Ibid., pp. 9–18, 80.

4. Bernard Lewis, "Islam and the Middle East" (lecture, George Washington University, Washington, DC, April 29, 2004).

5. Ibid.

6. Henry A. Kissinger, "Intervention with a Vision," *Washington Post*, April 11, 2004.

7. Lewis, "Islam and the Middle East."

8. James Baker and Warren Christopher, "More Ways to Stay Safe," *Washington Post*, December 17, 2004.

9. King Abdullah II ibn Hussein, "Statement at the Davos World Economic Forum, January 2004," Davos Report Supplement, *Foreign Policy* (February 2004). For a more complete commentary on the impact of US policy toward Israel, see Michael Scheuer, *Imperial Hubris: Why the West Is Losing the War on Terror* (London: Brassey's, 2004).

10. For an extensive discussion of soft power, see Joseph S. Nye, *Soft Power: The Means to Success in World Politics* (New York: Public Affairs Books, 2004).

11. John L. Esposito, *Unholy War: Terrorism in the Name of Islam* (Oxford: Oxford University Press, 2002), p. 160.

INDEX